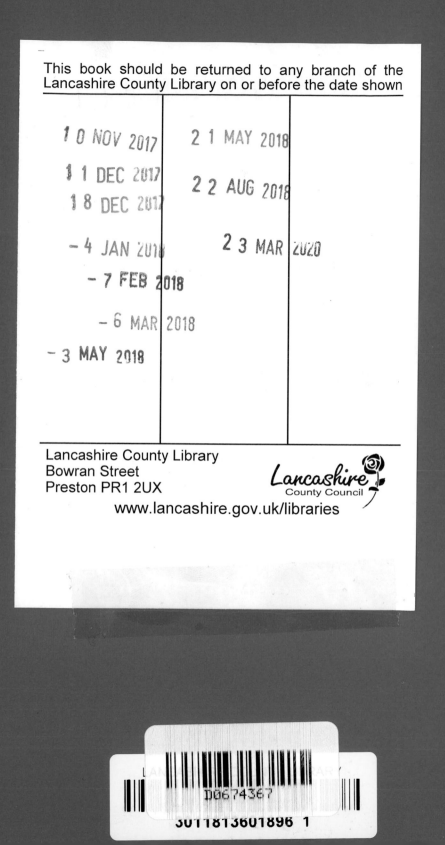

This book should be returned to any branch of the
Lancashire County Library on or before the date shown

Lancashire County Library
Bowran Street
Preston PR1 2UX
www.lancashire.gov.uk/libraries

Lancashire
County Council

RED GLORY

MANCHESTER UNITED AND ME

RED GLORY

MANCHESTER UNITED AND ME

MARTIN EDWARDS

First published in Great Britain in 2017 by
Michael O'Mara Books Limited
9 Lion Yard
Tremadoc Road
London SW4 7NQ

A CIP catalogue record for this book is available from the British Library.

Papers used by Michael O'Mara Books Limited are natural, recyclable products made
from wood grown in sustainable forests. The manufacturing processes conform to the
environmental regulations of the country of origin.

ISBN: 978-1-78243-812-0 in hardback print format
ISBN: 978-1-78243-813-7 in trade paperback format
ISBN: 978-1-78243-811-3 in ebook format

1 3 5 7 9 10 8 6 4 2

Designed and typeset by www.glensaville.com, using Adobe Text Pro & Vollkorn by
Friedrich Althausen, vollkorn-typeface.com, and ITC Mixage

Cover design by Envy Design Ltd

Printed and bound by CPI Group (UK) Ltd, Croydon, CR0 4YY

www.mombooks.com

To my dad Louis, who led the way and made it all possible for me

CONTENTS

FOREWORD
by Peter Schmeichel

I moved back to Denmark many years ago, but whenever I am back in Alderley Edge in Cheshire, I go to a place called The Bubbleroom for breakfast and a read-through of the day's papers. I prefer to sit by myself and ooze in the village that I used to live in when I played for Manchester United from my usual armchair by the window.

At these random visits to The Bubbleroom, I see Martin Edwards going into a coffee shop across the street at approximately the same time in the day, every time I am there, without fail.

He goes in for a coffee and he sits with the same group of people every time. On nice days, when the sun is up, they sit outside and I can see them from where I am sat. They talk about football – I don't need to listen in to know that – and more often than not, I know their talk is about Manchester United.

It is a very passionate conversation: I can see it in their body language, so I can also see how important the club is to them.

For Martin Edwards, Manchester United has always been the most important thing in his life.

When I was seven years old, I dreamt of playing for Manchester

United. To this day I still don't have any idea of how or why that dream came to me – I didn't live in England, never mind Manchester. Football matches shown on television in Denmark were few and far between – not weeks but months went by without one being shown live, and it was like winning the National Lottery if the Red Devils were on. And my parents were busy, hard-working people with four kids, and therefore had very little time for football.

But even so, there I was, in the suburbs of Copenhagen dreaming, night after night, of being at Wembley Stadium, winning the FA Cup Final and being the hero for Manchester United.

My dream came true thanks to the chairman, Martin Edwards, and Sir Alex Ferguson.

I would never have set foot inside Old Trafford, and had the career I had, without the chairman.

Football is a rough, tough and at times dishonest business, where money is the law and language. Pride and honesty is a rarity these days. But when it comes to Martin, I think of those two words: pride and honesty.

I don't think he was ever a poker player; when dealing with him that never occurred to me. He would speak his mind, but also the truth.

Negotiating team bonuses, he would never lie to save the club money; he would lay it out there from the club's perspective, and you would never go away feeling played or cheated on. Disappointed, yes, but never let down.

Our negotiations for bonuses for the Champions League in the 1998–99 season serves as a good example of Martin's straightforward approach to running the club. That year we had to qualify in order to reach the group phase of the Champions League but, because we did this successfully, we ended up with a bonus much larger that the bonus we got for winning the final! For the club, getting into the group stage would turn over more money than actually playing in the final would, and the chairman thought it was only fair that the players got their share of that, too.

Sat there in his office at Old Trafford, overlooking the pitch, Martin would have a notepad and a big calculator on the table, and where others would use their pokerface and twist the truth, some even lie to you, he would listen to what you had to say, treat you with respect, and tap on the calculator to come up with a number that was fair, if that was what you were there for.

If he or the club had made a clear mistake, he would play fair and honour it, even if it wasn't what he had agreed to in the first place.

Pride, honesty and, more than anything, integrity.

Back in 1991, Manchester United wanted me as their new goalkeeper. They had asked me to come over to Manchester and I arrived at Old Trafford full of hope, wanting my agent to go straight to work on the contract, get it agreed and signed, but the chairman had other ideas.

Martin took me to the museum; he wanted to make absolutely sure that I knew the basics of the club's history and the key figures in it – Bobby Charlton, Denis Law, George Best, and his favourite, Duncan Edwards.

He gave me a lesson in the Manchester United way, making sure that I knew that signing for the club was not only about football, it was about much more than that. United was a way people lived their lives, he told me, and being a player carried an enormous responsibility to all of these people.

Looking at me, as he toured me around the museum, he weighed me up, he assessed me, he judged me and was making a decision on my suitability as a future Manchester United player. He didn't take the decision to sign new players – players that would ultimately determine the future success of United – lightly. He always weighed up what was best for his beloved club.

I liked him! Instantly. He was my kind of person; the passion he held for the club was shared by me.

Martin never disappointed me. Many have disliked him, even hated him, over the years. They've looked at him and seen a fat cat just there to make money out of the club.

But I saw him behind the scenes, knew him and spoke to him on a regular basis. I saw his passion for Manchester United first-hand, and I understood the direction he knew he needed to steer the club in order to be competitive as English football eventually made the changes it so badly needed and moved into a new era.

He knew where he wanted the club to go, but didn't feel he had the money to take United to the next level. And therefore he made sure the club was in the best possible condition before he floated it on the stock market. With that move, he put the club well ahead of all competitors and United's dominance of the Premier League is a direct consequence of that move.

He prepared the club for the future, and what a spectacular future it turned out to be. With the introduction of the Premier League, the new era had dawned and he wanted United to be the first to stake their claim to it.

Martin always had an eye to the future and had brought Alex Ferguson to the club with that in mind, and as history shows, it was the best thing that ever happened to United.

Ferguson had a difficult beginning: the first three and a half years were lean and fruitless, and not much was going his way. In spite of the lack of success, Martin was never in any doubt about the choice he had made with the manager. Even when it came down to the FA Cup Final in 1990 against Crystal Palace, a match billed in the media as the end of Alex Ferguson if he did not win, he knew he had the right guy.

Martin has said time and again that Ferguson's job never was in question, a statement that has been backed up by a few of the board members from that time. And I believe him.

What he wanted was a manager who could build a team for the future, who could produce his own players, someone who could repeat some of the great deeds achieved by Sir Matt Busby and his assistant Jimmy Murphy; someone who could write the next great chapter in Manchester United's history book.

Alex Ferguson was the one. He knew that, he saw the work that was being done behind the scenes at the club, and he liked what he saw.

Ferguson was working with a new breed of players, young hungry-for-success lads willing to go the whole nine yards for him and the club. The chairman was there on the touchline, watching it and protecting a manager he knew was the right guy for the job, but that the fans, the media and the general public wanted gone.

Martin's ambitions for the club were quite simple. All he really wanted was for Manchester United to become the best club in the world. And, thankfully, at a time when he was still the chairman of the club, Manchester United became the biggest and the best club on the planet, in large part because of Martin's careful management and how he put the pieces in place for United to achieve the feats it did.

I am happy for him that he managed to get there; I am happy and proud that I was there to help him achieve that.

Sometimes I go across to the coffee shop for a chat and a catch-up, and it was on one of those occasions that Martin asked me if I would write the foreword to his book. For him to ask me to do so, considering all of the talented people and big names he has met through his many years of great service to Manchester United, is a source of great pride for me, and a challenge I was only too willing to take on, considering all he did for me. I only hope my words can do justice to the man that has done so much for our beloved Manchester United.

INTRODUCTION

Not long after stepping down from my role as chairman of Manchester United in 2003, I was approached to write about my experiences running the world's most famous football club. I resisted such overtures. I didn't think the time was right. The events and emotions were still too raw for me. I needed distance to lend them more perspective.

In 2015 I turned seventy, a good age to begin to look back on what you have made of your life and to weigh up your achievements. This is what I've attempted to do in this book.

It is not an autobiography in the strictest sense, as it deals with just one aspect of my life, albeit a significant one: my long association with Manchester United, both as a fan growing up and then as chairman and chief executive. In some ways you could call Manchester United a family business since, between us, my father and I were in charge of the club for just short of four decades.

I am very proud of what I managed to achieve at Manchester United, building upon the stewardship of my father, and leading a club that hadn't won a league title or a European trophy for years into the most successful era of its history. It was a journey of highs and lows, with its share of controversy, from which I sometimes emerged bruised and battered. But those bruises were worth it, because those years were the happiest of my life. Every decision made, every choice, was for the wellbeing of the institution I both cherished and revered: Manchester United. This is the story of my time there.

1 CHAMPAGNE LOUIS

I was twelve when I was told the news about the Munich air disaster of 1958 and of how close my father Louis came to being on that fateful trip. I was away at boarding school at the time. The matron, who knew of my father's friendship with Matt Busby and his connection with Manchester United, came into the dormitory to tell me that the plane carrying the team back from a match had crashed and a lot of them had been killed and that Busby was very seriously ill. I've never forgotten it.

Father had booked his seat to go out with the team but changed his mind at the last minute. It was a decision that probably saved his life. Father had cause to be grateful to a man called George Whittaker, though it didn't seem so at the time. Busby wanted my father to join the board of directors at United and in the last week of January 1958, a couple of days before the team were due in London to play Arsenal, my father was put up for election. Whittaker, a local businessman, was the only board member to oppose it. At the end of the meeting the club chairman, Harold Hardman, who also wanted Father on the board, made the position clear: 'I don't want to bring Louis on unless it's totally unanimous.' Then, speaking directly to Whittaker, Hardman said, 'I'm going to put Louis up for election again at the next board meeting, but in the meantime I want you to think about it.'

A few days later Whittaker was found dead in a London hotel room. He'd passed away in his sleep on the eve of the Arsenal away match. As a mark of respect both teams wore black armbands, and a minute's silence was observed prior to kick-off. The game turned out to be an absolute thriller, with United edging out the Gunners 5–4. What nobody could possibly have known at the time was that this would be the last occasion this remarkable Manchester United team, the Busby Babes, would grace a British football pitch.

They next faced a daunting European Cup quarter-final second-leg trip to meet Red Star Belgrade. And because of that one vote cast against my father at the board meeting, and with a few pressing matters at work, he decided to stay at home. So, if Whittaker had agreed to my father going on the board he would almost certainly have been caught up in the terrible events at Munich.

What happened on that fateful day is now well known. The team were flying back from Belgrade when the plane stopped in Munich to refuel. The weather was atrocious, it had started to snow heavily, and the first two attempts to take off were aborted. On the third attempt the plane overshot the runway, hit a house and burst into flames. Twenty-three people, including eight players and three members of the club's staff, were killed. It remains the darkest day in the history of Manchester United.

With everyone still reeling from the tragedy, Harold Hardman called an emergency meeting of the club directors and brought my father on to the board. With George Whittaker now gone there was no opposition left and the vote was unanimous. So my father officially became a board member at Manchester United on 7 February 1958, the day after the Munich air crash.

⚽

To me Matt Busby was 'Uncle Matt'. I used to see quite a lot of him because every Saturday night he and his wife Jean, along with my parents, would go out for a meal at The Bridge restaurant in Prestbury and Matt and Jean would call at the house first for a drink. I'll always remember the Christmas before the Munich disaster. My father held a cocktail party at our house in Alderley Edge and Matt came up to my sister Catherine and me and gave us half a crown each. What a treasure that Christmas present seemed. I don't think I ever spent it. I felt as though I owned the crown jewels.

My father and Matt were very close friends. They first met around 1950 through a mutual acquaintance called Tommy Appleby who ran the Opera House in Manchester. In those days the Opera House played host to an array of top productions starring the likes of Howard Keel and Maurice Chevalier. I remember once when Vivien Leigh and Laurence Olivier arrived to perform Shakespeare there. My parents were always invited to see these shows and through Tommy Appleby came into contact with a lot of the celebrities of the day. Matt and Jean were also regular attendees and that's where Father and Matt were first introduced. I heard that sometimes if Matt became bored with a show he and Father would leave halfway through and go to a nearby pub to talk business and football.

From very early on in their friendship I think Matt saw in Father someone who could be an ally in the boardroom at United, someone who could support his ambitions for the club. For the past few years Matt had been on the lookout for fresh blood and fresh thinking at board level and Father's business acumen looked like it might be just the thing to provide the perfect initiative and leadership.

Father had been a hard grafter all his life. He was born on 15 June 1914 in Salford, Greater Manchester, not too far away from Old Trafford. He loved playing football as a kid and played at right back for the school team. When he left school at the age of fourteen he went into the family business, Louis C. Edwards & Sons, a meat company owned by my grandfather. That was my grandfather's name, Louis Charles Edwards, and my father was named after him, Louis Charles Edwards junior. Father worked long hours and one of his escapes from the daily grind was going to watch Manchester United. And it was there watching United that his passion for the club began – one that was never to leave him.

Father must have been quite independently minded growing up because he could drive a car by the time he was fourteen, even though he wasn't actually allowed to at that age. When war broke out in 1939 Father was called up and joined the 14th/20th Hussars, which was seconded to the Eighth Army under Montgomery. He spent most of the war as a desert rat in Egypt in a tank regiment. Then, when my grandfather died in 1944, he got called back home to take over the company because of its importance to the war effort. There was nothing much of him when he returned to Manchester that summer, just skin and bone because of the privations he'd endured in the desert. Later in life, when he'd made his fortune, he ate well and enjoyed the high life, earning the nickname of 'Champagne Louis'. He was determined that he was never going to starve again. Perhaps that was a part of his drive.

Settling back into civilian life, Father rekindled a romance he'd started a few years before the outbreak of war. The girl in question, Muriel, was best friends with his younger sister, and they'd begun dating and fallen in love. Now he was back home they quickly married in June 1944, the day after D-Day. For them it seemed the old saying that opposites attract was true: my father was jovial and had a great sense of humour, whereas my mother was quiet and more serious. They were well matched nonetheless. She'd originally moved to Manchester from the North-East, where her father had been an engineer. After leaving school she worked for a time as a model, mainly in department stores. As with so many others, the war demanded more from her, and she aided the war effort by driving an ambulance.

On 24 July 1945 I came along and some of my earliest memories are of my parents going to the matches on a Saturday afternoon at Old Trafford. I always knew when they'd been to a game because they brought a programme back for me and talked enthusiastically about what they'd seen. I went to my first game at Old Trafford in 1952 and I'll never forget it: it was against Wolves and I've still got the programme after all these years.

When I was almost eight I was sent to a boy's boarding school, Terra Nova, in Cheshire, where cricket and rugby were the two main sports, and not football, to my disappointment. But I took to rugby and cricket in a big way. I was the youngest player at prep school ever to play for the first eleven at cricket. I was put into the team for one match at the age of ten, playing with boys up to thirteen years old. Later on I made the team proper and opened the batting.

As a schoolboy I idolized Denis Compton, one of the most dashing of all the England batsmen. The other big cricket personality of the time was Len Hutton, but I thought Compton was the more cavalier of the two. He was the original Brylcreem boy, with almost film-star good looks. When he wasn't scoring runs for Middlesex and England, Compton played on the wing for Arsenal and was also capped by the England football team. He really was a magnificent all-round sportsman.

When Sir Matt Busby celebrated his eightieth birthday in 1989 we held a special dinner for him at Old Trafford and one of the guests was none other than Denis Compton. I'd never met him before, and towards the end of the evening Danny McGregor, the club's commercial manager, approached me to ask if I wouldn't mind running Denis back to his hotel, as I passed it on my way home. To say I was delighted was an understatement.

We got in the car and Denis started off the conversation by saying, 'Oh dear boy, I never thought for one minute that I would be driven home by the chairman of Manchester United when I came to this dinner tonight.'

'Mr Compton,' I said. 'You've no idea what a thrill this is for me to be able to spend a few moments with you, because you were one of my schoolboy heroes.'

'Don't be ridiculous,' he said. 'You're far too young for that.'

'No, I remember you batting for England. I also remember that your very last game for Arsenal was the 1950 Cup final.'

Compton smiled at the memory. 'Well, you're nearly right.'

'I thought that was your last game.'

'No, no, we won the Cup and as a result of that the Cup winners play the league winners at the start of every season. And because I played in the Cup final they invited me back to play as a sort of guest appearance.'

'Did you win, Mr Compton?' I asked.

'We did, 4–2.'

'Did you score?' I enquired.

'I managed a couple,' he said, with a twinkle in his eye.

⊗

At school I also played for the rugby fifteen, and I enjoyed my time there. Terra Nova was a typical boarding school of the 1950s, very much like that in *Tom Brown's Schooldays*: it was cold, no central heating in the dormitories, early morning swims and regular beatings. And as we didn't know anything different we all just got on with it and didn't complain.

When my father joined the board at United, I was able to attend matches at Old Trafford on a regular basis, sitting up in the directors' box, and I became quite a fanatical supporter. My father also began to take me with him on away games and we used to travel on the team coach. One memory is of the time we played Norwich in the third round of the FA Cup in 1959. I remember it was absolutely freezing; the match should never have gone ahead as it was literally played on ice. We lost 3–0 and, coming back, the windscreen of the coach smashed and we all nearly froze to death. Can you imagine a seven-hour trip back to Manchester with an icy wind blasting through the coach? I can still remember sitting on the back seat of that bloody coach freezing and feeling miserable about our loss.

⊗

As I was away at boarding school I never saw the Busby Babes. In the aftermath of Munich, however, you couldn't help but get emotionally involved with the team. I remember my father going to all the funerals of the players. It's impossible to underestimate the effect Munich had on United. To lose eight players, and two who never played again, plus the secretary and coach, was absolutely devastating. Matt knew that we had to rebuild Manchester United quickly and my father became a highly influential figure, as both men worked in close partnership in this huge undertaking.

It was a massive challenge and took a long time. It was five years before we won a trophy again, the FA Cup in 1963, which all things considered was a remarkable achievement after what was still a relatively short space of time. With our side decimated, a lot of the reserve-team players and youth players had to be drafted into the first team, people like Mark Pearson, Alex Dawson and Shay Brennan. And new players had to be bought. I remember Albert Quixall joining us from Sheffield Wednesday in September 1958 for a then British record fee of £45,000. I was there that afternoon at Old Trafford when he came running down the tunnel and on to the pitch to a huge ovation; there was such a great sense of excitement from the crowd. I got to know that post-Munich team very well. In fact, when United set up the Old Boys Association thirty years ago they made me its president, a role I still fulfil today, and I still get to see a lot of those old players that I knew growing up.

Father's involvement at United was important to Matt because at the time Harold Hardman was the chairman and he was quite a conservative man. He was also getting on in years – he was in his seventies around the time of Munich – and perhaps his outlook was to an extent characterized by the way football used to be run. In his youth Harold had played professional football for Manchester United and Everton and appeared in two Cup finals for the Toffees, and was also twice an Olympian with the Great Britain soccer team. To be fair he had been a successful chairman at United, winning the league with Busby in 1952, 1956 and 1957. Possibly because of his old-fashioned view of the sport he didn't necessarily believe in spending big money in the transfer market. I don't think he was happy paying £30,000 for Tommy Taylor back in 1953. I'm sure Matt felt that Father was more ambitious in terms of buying players. Indeed, when we bought Quixall, Hardman had advocated caution, saying that the club couldn't afford to buy him. It was Father who Matt turned to for support and encouragement, and it was Father who accompanied him to Sheffield to finalize the deal.

Another example was the signing of Denis Law in July 1962. Law was playing in Italy for Torino and not enjoying his football. Father, Matt and Harold flew out to persuade him to come to United. He eventually signed for us for a new British record fee of £115,000. It was a huge sum for a player at the time and Father was instrumental in getting that deal done. If he hadn't been there supporting Matt, I doubt that Harold Hardman would have gone ahead with such a purchase.

Denis went on to become one of our most important players. I loved watching him play. Normally when you win a league there's one or maybe two players that stand out. Robin van Persie is the obvious one in the 2012–13 season. And before that, Eric Cantona's goals were instrumental in us winning the league in 1995–96. Nineteen sixty-five was the first time we had won the league since the Munich air disaster and Denis Law was the most influential player that season; he was outstanding. Denis could play midfield or up front, and he was equally happy doing either, though Matt preferred him in the striker position. But the trouble with Denis was the knee injuries he suffered quite early in his career; he was dogged by them, so we sometimes missed out on his best. But a fully fit Denis Law was a fantastic player. He'd definitely be in my top ten United players of all time.

Besides backing Matt in the transfer market, another important thing my father did was to bring a man called Bill Burke to the club. In the early 1960s the cost of improvements and refurbishments to Old Trafford was quite restrictive. Despite the team's relative success on the pitch, money wasn't exactly flowing into the club's coffers.

Bill Burke ran a successful and highly profitable Football Pools competition at Warwickshire County Cricket Club. In 1961, Father managed to persuade Bill to come over to United to set up a similar operation. It turned out to be a real innovation and raised a substantial amount of money that over the years helped greatly towards the much-needed redevelopment of Old Trafford. Don't forget, during the war the ground was bombed and for years the team had to play their 'home games' at Manchester City's Maine Road. They moved back in 1949 but it was a bit of a patchwork Old Trafford; they didn't even have floodlights until 1957. Then we had the Munich disaster, after which things remained difficult from a financial point of view, so my father's business expertise was very much needed.

The Pools idea was an immediate success, helping to fund the installation of 700 wooden seats at the back of the Stretford End terrace. Then in 1964 father lent his support to a massive £300,000 scheme to construct a new cantilever stand that would run along the United Road side of the ground and be the longest and most advanced stand in the country (later named the North Stand, and in 2011 renamed the Sir Alex Ferguson Stand). Also included were thirty-four private boxes, the first of their kind in British football. It really was a magnificent piece of construction and one of the reasons why Old Trafford was selected as a venue for several fixtures during the 1966 World Cup.

When Father became chairman in 1965 he never shied away from pumping more money into the continued expansion of the stadium. He even came up with a bizarre, futuristic idea in 1969 of installing some kind of retractable roof that could slide across the top of the ground when the Mancunian weather got a bit too miserable. This project was actually discussed at board level but the estimated price tag of £700,000 soon put an end to that dream.

By the early 1970s Old Trafford had seating on all four sides and was without question the best club ground in the country, the 'Wembley of the North', as some called it. In 1975 there was the rebuilding of the South Stand incorporating an executive suite and two restaurants, facilities that were also available during non-match days and could be hired for banquets, conferences and private functions. All this provided the club with extra sources of income, and in future years, whenever we extended the stadium, even in my time as chairman, it was never a case of just adding more seats or putting extra boxes in; the question of what's behind it, what extra revenue can you earn from those facilities, was always considered. And that all started with my father. I think we set the tone that other football clubs followed. It did, however, lead to things like Roy Keane's famous 'prawn sandwiches' quote. A lot of the more old-fashioned or nostalgic supporters do feel that football has become too commercialized, and that it's not necessarily about die-hard football fans any more, just another branch of the entertainment industry. They feel that they've been paying higher prices for their facilities and that they've been marginalized. But, like it or not, that's progress.

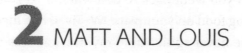2 MATT AND LOUIS

In April 1964, when I was eighteen, I went into the family business, where I worked for the next sixteen years. I'll always remember my first day. I got up, walked to the bus stop and caught the bus down to Alderley Edge. Getting the train through to Manchester Piccadilly station I walked to the bottom of Oldham Road to catch another bus, which took me to the factory. I was supposed to be there at eight o'clock but when I arrived and put my card in the machine it was one minute past. 'I'm sorry, Mr Edwards,' said the foreman, almost apologetically. 'I've strict instructions to send you home if you're late.' The actual instruction from my father to the foreman was: 'If the f***er's one minute late, send him home.' So it was back on the bus and back on the train and when I walked through the front door my mother asked what I was doing home so early. I had to admit I'd been sent back for being late. It was a salutary lesson and it made sure I was never late again.

Looking back, I can see that my father was quite strict with me; less so with my sister, and by the time my brother Roger arrived eight years later Father had mellowed considerably. So as the oldest I bore the brunt of it. But it's not something I complain about, and actually it probably did me good.

Father had a terrific work ethic and I think he tried to instil that into me at an early age. He hated it if you laid in bed in the morning; you had to get up, even if you went back to bed when he'd gone. And he hated waste, like leaving food on your plate. We lived in a nice house in a very good area but he never spoilt me – my first car was my mother's old Zephyr; nothing fancy.

When I joined the company it had expanded massively from when my father and uncle first took it over after the war, when there were just four butcher's shops managed by six employees simply serving their regular customers. My father and his brother Douglas, who was joint chairman, had added significantly more shops and retail concessions over the years, but also both realized that the future of the company lay not just in the retail side but in the acquisition of contracts to supply schools, offices and the catering industry in general. Over the years these contracts were steadily built up to the point they were supplying local authorities, holiday camps, hotels and even the army. They also got into the canned and convenience food act, making many of the large supermarkets' own brands.

I started off working in the central butchery, cutting up sides of meat. That's all you did all day: cut up the huge carcasses that came in. I can't say I enjoyed the job; I had to do it. The idea was for me to work in all the different departments so I would learn and understand every element of the business. It was six months here, six months there, on the factory floor, in the shops, on the road, in the office.

Since leaving school I had continued as much as possible to play sport. I had joined Alderley Edge Cricket Club in my last year, for whom I would play for the next twelve seasons, and played for the first eleven while I was still at school. The first-team captain, Pat Kelly, who was a county player for Cheshire, used to put me in when I came home for the school holidays. I could run around and field a bit and hold my own as a batsman if the team was struggling.

I was also playing a bit of football in the amateur Manchester Wednesday League. I even managed to get a winners' medal playing at centre forward. We had a guy called Billy Myerscough as our captain.

He had played in the FA cup final for Aston Villa against Manchester United in 1957, the match where our goalie Ray Wood got injured early on and had to be carried off and we ended up playing with ten men and lost. I also used to play on a Sunday morning for the work team. But I was always a better rugby player than I was a footballer and when I was twenty I joined Wilmslow Rugby Club. It was really in an effort to keep fit; I didn't necessarily think I was going to play. I went down for the pre-season trials and got selected for the second fifteen as a centre. Occasionally when players were away on county duty I'd be drafted into the first team, eventually becoming a fully fledged first-team player in my own right. I was very keen and trained three times a week. When Matt Busby came up to the house on a Saturday night after United had played we'd often joke with each other about who had won that day.

In 1962 my father and uncle had floated something like 20 per cent of the family business on the London Stock Exchange. The sum raised was not insignificant and with it my father began to buy Manchester United shares. When he was first made a director at United the board sold him ten shares. Back then all directors had to have a nominal percentage of shares in order to comply with FA regulations. In a bid to acquire a much greater number, Father contacted as many shareholders as he could, including then current board members, and offered them a premium price for their shares. It was up to each individual whether they accepted or not. At the time there were 142 shareholders in the club but not one of them owned a majority share. All these transactions were approved by the board and by 1964 Father had become the club's largest shareholder, owning over 50 per cent of the club. Whether this had been his intention right from the start, to build a power base at United, I don't know because I never asked him. It was not, however, to make a financial killing. Remember that in those days Manchester United was a private company and shares were looked upon as being of more of sentimental than monetary value. I suspect that at the beginning Father just wanted to be part of the board;

then he must have realized how much he liked it but also that, to have a significant influence, he needed to get a substantial holding. Don't forget, my father was a businessman and in business if you see an opportunity you go for it. That's exactly what he did. I'm sure Matt was happy with the situation because this was an ally on the board who was becoming the dominant shareholder.

Father had also been undertaking much of the running of the club due to the fact that over the previous year or so Harold Hardman had been quite ill, and in 1964 he was made vice chairman. When Harold died in June 1965 nobody objected or was really surprised when Father took the chairmanship over. By then he was seen very much as Hardman's natural successor.

Over the years Father had become a well-respected figure within the football fraternity and he went on to become a popular chairman. The players all liked him. Some chairmen in the league were quite austere and aloof. Father was very down to earth and loved the football side of his role at the club, the whole atmosphere of match days. He'd go into the dressing room to mix with the players and later sometimes have a drink with them. He embraced all that. Many remember him as a cheerful man, a good storyteller. People would describe him as a character: he used to smoke but never inhaled, and his love of champagne was well known. Keith Kent, the groundsman at United, once told me a story about Father. Keith had been the groundsman at Leicester before he came to Old Trafford and whenever United arrived in town to play a match, one of his duties was to go to the local supermarket to buy some champagne because Louis Edwards only drank champagne. That happened at quite a few clubs we played at.

There were other luxuries: a villa in Majorca and a Rolls Royce, which he bought in the late 1950s. I recall the chauffeur used to drive me back to school in it and when we arrived through the gates all the boys would crowd round. But he did not set too much store on the trappings of wealth even though he was willing to spend money and was always very generous to my mother. He was a generous host and very sociable with the people he knew. As chairman, though, Father tended to avoid the media spotlight. You either like publicity or you don't and my father wasn't one for it. He was quite a shy man, and in some ways I take after him in that respect. I was never one for shouting the odds, and during my time at United I wasn't interested in public relations or having PR people around me extolling my virtues. Indeed, it wasn't until Peter Kenyon took over from me as chief executive in 2000 that United employed a full-time PR person. Perhaps I could have done myself a favour if I had concentrated a bit more on PR, but all I wanted to do was run a successful business. I am wary of personal publicity because if you put yourself up there you also ready yourself to be shot down.

Father had a slight stammer, one of the reasons why he didn't like public speaking. If he could get somebody else to speak in his place he would. My mother was always there when he was required to speak in public, sitting next to him, and when she saw a stammer coming on she'd give him a slight knock and he'd get through it.

Something else that I think people appreciated was that, as chairman, my father only ever focused on the business side of the club, and never interfered with the team – he left all that to the manager. It was the same when I became chairman. Of course I was interested in the squad because I was a supporter, and all supporters are interested in who you're going to buy and who you're going to sell, the shape of the team and all the rest of it. But while you can make suggestions – would you like this player if I can get him? – I was never going to tell a manager you've got to buy someone or you must sell this player; that has to be their decision.

In those days chairmen didn't really get involved with any of the negotiations for players, either. A fee would be agreed by the board but then the manager and the club secretary would do all the negotiations and terms. It must have worked because Father and Matt made a great team, working in perfect harmony together: Matt the football man and Father the savvy businessman. It's been said that Father's control of United was the foundation of Matt's power. It's true that Matt was quite powerful anyway because of what he had achieved on the field, but his relationship with Father certainly enhanced that. I believe it gave Matt confidence as well, knowing his chairman backed him 100 per cent. Father was a great supporter of Matt in every way and saw it as one of his duties as chairman to provide a stadium to match the team Matt was building.

And what a team we had. They were a joy to watch, not least the famous trio of Law, Best and Charlton. Any United fan from the 1960s will rave about all three of them. But backing them up you had marvellous players like Tony Dunne, a fantastic full back, Pat Crerand, who was very important to the team, and Nobby Stiles. It was an iconic team. But Law, Best and Charlton were outstanding, all voted European Footballer of the Year in their own right. Denis won it in 1964, Bobby in 1966 and George in 1968. That just shows you how good they were. It was a dream come true to go to Old Trafford every Saturday and see the three of them in action on the same pitch. The only disappointing thing was that that team should have won a lot more than they did. We lost four FA Cup semi-finals in five years, though we did win the FA Cup in 1963 and the league in 1965 and again in 1967, before finally winning the European Cup in 1968, at Wembley. I'm not saying United had any divine right to win everything, because there was a lot of quality opposition about back then, but that team was good enough to win more trophies.

Commentators over the years have spoken a lot about George Best. I knew him when he was just a skinny teenager who had come over from Belfast with dreams of playing for Manchester United. Before he even made the first team there were stories from training about how good he was and how he was making fools out of established stars. In those days the team used to train at the back of the stadium and on one occasion George kept nutmegging Harry Gregg, and Harry threatened to let him have it if he did it again. There were lots of reports about how good George was going to be. It's a bit like Ryan Giggs, who people talked about before he even kicked a ball for United because, at fifteen, they knew they were seeing the future. That's how it was with George; people knew he was a star in the making.

George made his debut against West Bromwich Albion in September

1963 at the age of seventeen, plucked from the junior ranks by Matt. He came up against the Welsh full back Graham Williams, quite a tough lad, and again George nutmegged him and generally had a very good game. Matt waited until Christmas to play him again, this time against Burnley, and he had a stormer, snatching his first goal. After that he was pretty much undroppable. This was when I got to know George. I used to pick him up in my car after evening matches and drop him off at the bowling alley in Stretford, where he spent a lot of time. He hadn't learnt to drive yet so always asked me to give him a lift. And of course I used to watch him play regularly at Old Trafford, and you were always off your feet when George got the ball. He really was a magical player. There was nothing of him, he was skin and bone, but he could walk round players, beat players, then go back and beat them again. He was an entertainer.

People always ask: who was the best out of Law, Charlton or Best? I find it very difficult to come up with an answer because they were all so different. Denis was an outstanding goal scorer, but could also play midfield, and as well as being particularly good in the air he was dynamite in the box, pouncing on the slightest error. The supporters loved him, nicknaming him 'The King'. In the dressing room he was a bit of a joker, and great pals with Paddy Crerand. The two of them were inseparable. One thing I remember about Denis was that whenever he was injured he never watched the team play. He hated watching football if he wasn't involved. He'd rather stay at home.

Bobby could score great goals and had a fantastic pair of feet; it didn't matter what side he took the ball on. He was one of the Busby Babes, having earned himself a regular place in the team as a striker. After Munich he was on the left wing for a while before becoming a permanent midfielder. He could play in any forward position for both United and England. Bobby wasn't as lively a personality as someone like Denis. He was a fairly quiet figure. I didn't know him before the Munich tragedy but believe he had been a much more lively character. Losing all those friends, many of them his contemporaries, I think that changed Bobby.

George was a magical dribbler, but a great tackler as well; he would work back for the team. He was just a super all-round footballer. There are stories of him being targeted by defenders and hacked down, but he rarely got hurt. He was tough, considering the size of him.

What really put George on the map was Benfica away in 1966. He destroyed them that night, absolutely destroyed them. It was the start of his fame. They used to call George the fifth Beatle. I don't think Matt, or football for that matter, had ever experienced a star player of that nature before. George was the first modern football superstar.

It did turn sour later on. George started to mess about and go missing. Most of the players loved him because of his sheer ability, but his antics did rankle a bit with some of the senior players towards the end, especially Bobby, who got fed up with it. The relationship between George and Matt was always special but even Matt became frustrated by him. He did his absolute upmost to defend George in front of various FA commissions. There was the famous time when George didn't turn up and Matt went on his own; George had done one of his disappearing acts with an actress in London. Matt must have been at the end of his tether at that. George would go into Matt's office and agree with everything he said, then come out and just do his own thing. He had so much respect for Matt but simply couldn't control himself.

By the time I became chairman in 1980 George was an iconic symbol of the club. If he rang up for tickets to see a game he was always welcome. And there were invites to some of the functions we held at Old Trafford, although he wasn't totally reliable. You were always on edge if George was supposed to appear at a function because you never quite knew if he was going to turn up or not.

The only thing that I recall George not being happy about was when the board refused to grant him a testimonial at Old Trafford. This was in the early 1980s when he approached the club after he'd fallen on hard times, but I think the feeling was that he hadn't done the full qualifying period and that he had on occasions let the club down, so he wasn't the best example for granting a testimonial. George was very disappointed about that. But, despite everything, the thing about George was that he loved the club; even though he caused problems from time to time, his first love was always United.

The pinnacle of Father and Matt's time together was undoubtedly the 1968 European Cup triumph, which has gone down in the history of United as one of our most famous nights. We'd beaten Real Madrid in the semi-final, a match that I wasn't allowed to go to because I had to work. Despite being the boss's son I had no privileges whatsoever. The final was at Wembley against Benfica and this time I was able to attend; there was no way I was going to miss it. It was an unbelievable evening. I was with the official party, which was something of a family affair. I went with my wife to be, my brother and sister were there, and of course, my mother and father. We all had good seats near the halfway line, while Father was sat next to Prime Minister Harold Wilson in the Royal Box.

In the days leading up to the final I wouldn't say the mood at the club was one of overconfidence but there was a strong feeling that with it being ten years since Munich this was our destiny. There was also a sense of fear, because it was probably Matt's last chance to win the top prize in club football. He was getting tired by this stage and thinking about retirement, so he was running out of years to win it. He should have won the European Cup in 1966. We lost to Partizan Belgrade in the semi-final – a tie we should never, ever have lost. We'd beaten Benfica in the quarter-finals, slaughtered them 5–1 in their own stadium and beaten them 3–2 at home, and we really felt that should have been our year. Yet here we were in the final, with perhaps one of the last opportunities Matt would have. So there was a lot of tension because of the belief we should win.

Our opponents, Benfica, were a hell of a side, though. The final they played against us was their fifth final in ten years; they'd won it twice and lost it twice. A measure of how good they were was that most of that side had represented Portugal against England in the 1966 World Cup semi-final. They had fantastic players like José Torres, António Simões, José Augusto, Mário Coluna and of course Eusébio. But we had a great side, too.

Watching the game was incredibly tense. We took the lead eight minutes into the second half when Bobby Charlton scored with a fine header. Benfica equalized twenty-two minutes later and had a chance to win the match near the end when Eusébio went through and was one-on-one with our goalie, but Stepney denied him heroically. So the game went into extra time and I remember thinking, *Oh, bloody hell, we had the lead but this is anybody's now.* But in extra time we came out stronger. George Best scored pretty quickly and then we got another and that was it – we destroyed them in extra time and finally won the match 4–1.

And I'll never forget this: on his way up to collect the trophy, the first thing Bobby Charlton did was to give my father a hug and a kiss. It really was a special night: the nerves everybody had endured throughout the game, the excitement of extra time, mixed with all the emotions about Munich, especially for Bill Foulkes and Bobby Charlton, who had both been in the crash and were there on the night to win the Cup; they were both very emotional. Matt was emotional too. Understandably so because he was the first English club manager to take a team into European competition back in 1956, against the wishes of the Football League, only two years before the tragedy of Munich, so he must have carried that guilt with him. Winning the European Cup in 1968 was a vindication of a kind. You could never bring back those who were lost, but it brought glory to the club and to the supporters. It was certainly one of my great nights as a United fan and I've been lucky enough to see us win that trophy three times; they have all been magical in their own way.

It was a special night for my father, too. That was his crowning achievement, no question. To be a United supporter all his life, to work hard for the club for ten years, and then to be champions of Europe, the first English club to win the European Cup, that was his proudest moment. And to do it with his mate Matt made it extra special.

After the match the team went back to their hotel in the West End for a celebratory dinner. I remember Joe Loss and his Orchestra played 'Congratulations' when the team walked in. The atmosphere in that room was euphoric. Funnily enough, Bobby Charlton never came down for the celebrations. He was fast asleep in his room. I think the emotion of the whole thing had got to him.

The following day everyone caught the train back up to Manchester for the victory parade. The reports I read said there were something like 300,000 people lining the route but there may have been more; it was an incredible sight. I was with the wives and guests in a coach behind the open-top bus the players were on but we still got the atmosphere. It was a memorable day. And a memorable year for Manchester United.

3 ON THE BOARD

The year 1969 began with a bombshell: Matt Busby announced his intention to resign as manager at the end of the season. In a statement to the press he gave his reasons: 'Manchester United is no longer just a football club. It is an institution, and I feel that the demands are beyond one human being.' By this time Matt was approaching his sixtieth birthday, a good age for a manager back then, and when you think of what he'd been through – recovering from Munich after having the last rites read over him in hospital, then putting in so much effort over the next ten years to rebuild a team – he was understandably tired, so I felt his decision to retire was the right one. He'd given everything to the club and had been rewarded with a much-deserved knighthood following our European Cup victory. Father had been very keen that Matt be recognized with a knighthood and I'm sure he took every opportunity to lobby the prime minister, Harold Wilson, whom he often met at sporting events, about recognition for Matt.

Matt had so many qualities as a manager; he'd done it all. He'd been a successful player – cultured, a great passer of the ball in his day – ironically for our two greatest rivals, Liverpool and Manchester City, and he brought that experience to the club – Manchester United always played in a certain style when Matt was manager. When you speak to the players of Matt's era they all say the same thing: that Matt was the boss, they all respected him, and they all trusted him. He was like a headmaster to them all – some of them were perhaps a little bit intimidated by him, but he was fair, if tough. I never heard about any confrontations when he had to drop a star player. He would call them into his office and get them to volunteer the information that they weren't playing very well. 'I think you're right, son,' he'd chip in. 'Maybe it would be good for you to have a wee rest.' And that player would leave the office almost thanking Matt for dropping them from the team.

As a thank you for all he had done for United, Matt was invited to join the board. He also came into possession of the Red Devil Souvenir Shop, which had been open less than two years. It was located on the Old Trafford forecourt, at the front underneath the offices, and sold simple items like badges, photographs and key rings. The decision to give Matt a twenty-one-year lease on the shop came after a directors' meeting on 23 July 1968, which suggests that this was a way for Father and the rest of the board to reward Matt for winning the European Cup, just two months before. The price Matt paid for the shop was £2,000 and permission was granted for the business to continue trading from the Old Trafford ground with a nominal rent of £5 a week. The deal was not made public.

This wasn't the first time Father had rewarded Matt. Back in 1965, to recognize Matt's twentieth anniversary as manager, Father gave him the option to buy 500 ordinary shares in the club at the par value of £1 each. Since only 4,000 of the club's 15,000 ordinary shares had previously been issued, this meant that Matt now owned over 11 per cent of Manchester United, becoming the third largest shareholder. However, it wasn't until 1973 that Matt decided to take up his share option and put them in trust for his family. Over the years the Busby family sold off their shares in United, but it is interesting to note that the value of those shares in 1998, within twenty-five years of Matt taking them up, had a market value of over £100 million.

Matt's number two was Jimmy Murphy, who often gets overlooked when people talk about the Busby years. I knew Jimmy from when I was a young boy going to the matches and seeing him sometimes in the dressing room. He was a football man through and through and what he did around the time of Munich was nothing short of remarkable. Because he was manager of Wales at the time and attending one of their matches, Jimmy wasn't on that fatal plane trip. When he arrived back at Old Trafford he went into the office and Alma George, Matt's secretary, informed him of the crash. Jimmy was devastated because he'd helped nurture and bring through nearly all of the Busby Babes. Those players were like his boys. But he idolized Duncan Edwards. There's a story that Bobby Charlton tells of when he joined United in 1953. Jimmy Murphy picked him up at the station and talked about Duncan Edwards all the way back to Old Trafford: I've got this player, Bobby, and he's this and he's that, he's the best header of a ball in the world, he's got two feet, he's absolutely fantastic, and when I knock the rough edges off him …

With Matt taking months to recover in hospital it was Jimmy who had to pick the team up after Munich and get them going again, bringing in youth- and reserve-team players. He even got them to the Cup final that year, an unbelievable achievement.

He was a real character, Jimmy. His language could be quite choice at times and his team talks were legendary. There's a story of when Wales were playing Germany, he opened the dressing-room door so that the players could hear the roar of the German crowd outside and then slammed it shut again and said, 'Those are the bastards that bombed our houses!'

In his later years Jimmy fell on hard times and the club helped him out financially by giving him a job as a scout. He was still working for us when he died in 1989. I believe Jimmy felt that he was never fully recognized for his achievements, that he'd been at Old Trafford all those years but lived very much in Matt's shadow. But when you spoke to the old players who played under Jimmy, they all thought the world of him. And Matt valued him, too, no question about that. When Matt took over at United in 1945, Murphy was his first appointment and Jimmy was to be a huge part of the success United enjoyed from the end of the war up to the Munich air crash.

To my knowledge there was only one name in the frame to take over the managerial reins at Manchester United: Matt wanted Wilf McGuinness. Wilf was already in-house as reserve-team coach and had a bit of experience as a member of the backroom staff with Alf Ramsey's England team at the 1966 World Cup, but he had never managed a club, let alone a club as big as United. He was also quite young at the time, just thirty-one, having been with United since he was a schoolboy, playing in the same youth teams as Bobby Charlton and Duncan Edwards. Sadly his career was cut short at the premature age of twenty-two when he broke his leg in a reserves game against Stoke. But Matt felt that Wilf was a reasonable managerial prospect and should be given the opportunity. The board accepted his recommendation and Wilf took charge in June. He was given a three-year contract and inherited a team that some said was in decline, although when you look at the age of the players who were supposedly over the hill – people like Denis Law and Pat Crerand – they'd only just turned thirty, which by modern standards isn't old at all. In fact, in 1969, when Matt retired, the team almost got to a second European Cup final in a row. AC Milan beat us in the semis, thanks in part to a perfectly good goal from Denis Law being adjudged not to have crossed the line.

Some players like Bill Foulkes, however, were coming to the end of their careers and the talent coming through probably wasn't of the standard it had been in the past. It wasn't like the 1950s when United won the youth cup five years on the bounce. But given Matt's age and what he'd been through, it was perhaps asking too much for him to continue to build successful teams.

In March 1970 Father put me on the board at United. His stated aim was that I should start to learn the business, but there was an ulterior motive. I was still playing rugby for Wilmslow and I'd had a couple of bad concussions that put me in hospital for a week on both occasions. My father had always intended that when I stopped playing rugby I'd go on the board. There was a sense of trying to persuade me to quit the sport because of the injuries, as he was getting a bit worried. I was just a few months shy of twenty-five and became one of football's youngest directors.

By the end of that summer I'd had time to recover from my concussion and still wanted to have one more go at the rugby. I played the whole of the next season with no injuries. Then the third game of the following season, in September 1971, we were playing away at Waterloo and I got another knock; back to hospital again, and that was it. Father organized for me to see Dr Richard Johnson, who was the top neurosurgeon in the country, and I was told that if I didn't stop playing rugby I could end up like a punch-drunk boxer with head injuries for the rest of my life. So I had to give it up and it broke my heart not to be playing any more, not least because we had a very good team that year. The last full season I played we were second in the north of England, the Sunday Telegraph League as it was known in those days. And then in the following season, when I got injured early on, the team got to the semi-final of the newly formed national knock-out cup having beaten Harlequins away at Twickenham in the quarter-final. The following season Wilmslow were crowned North of England champions. So it was a very successful period for the club and I was proud to have been part of it. I missed my rugby, but at least I could now devote more of my time to watching football. Of course that didn't stop a lot of journalists using my rugby past against me, saying things like he's not really interested in football, he's a rugby man. I had to put up with all that rubbish for years.

When I was appointed I was by far the youngest member of the United board, which then consisted of Father; Alan Gibson, the vice chairman; Bill Young, a farmer and close friend of Gibson's; Matt; and my uncle Denzil Haroun, who worked in the textiles business and had married my father's sister. Denzil was a real character and remained on the board until he died in 1985. There's one particularly amusing story about Denzil. Not long after I became chairman, the team went on tour to Vancouver at the end of the 1981–82 season. One afternoon we were all sunbathing. I was with one or two of the staff and the tour operator. Denzil, who was in his early seventies at the time, was sunbathing some distance away in his Bermuda shorts and monocle, reading a book. Turning to me the tour operator asked, 'Who is that gentleman over there?'

'That's my uncle,' I replied.

'He looks quite a distinguished gentleman,' the tour operator said. 'What did he do during the war?' I think this question came from the fact the Falklands War was going on then.

'I don't know actually,' I answered. 'We can ask him later on.'

Well, the sun went in around five or six o'clock and Denzil packed up his things, took his monocle out and was walking back to the hotel. Nudging the tour operator I said, 'Now's your opportunity.' So he went over to Denzil, 'Excuse me, Mr Haroun,' he said. 'I hope you don't mind me asking you but were you a naval man?' And Denzil replied, 'I've always preferred tits myself', and carried on walking into the hotel.

I was to spend ten years as a board member, deliberately keeping a low profile, observing how everything worked, watching how my father and people like Matt operated. I couldn't help but soak it all up. I learnt about the full workings of a football club – things like approving transfers, the selling of players, listening to the manager's report, the reading and interpretation of Football League rules and regulations, dealing with complaints from supporters, building plans, setting seating prices, appointment of staff and wages – the full gamut of running a football club.

Board meetings used to be held once a month on a Tuesday evening, followed by a dinner where we would carry on our discussions. Before all the executive facilities were built at the stadium these dinners took place over at the Lancashire County Cricket Club because they had a grill room down there. It was all quite laid back and most of the meetings were of a cordial nature. There were other duties, too, such as entertaining guests on a match day and going to away fixtures. As a board member you were also expected to attend one or two functions a year such as the annual ground committee dinner, which was put on for the people who worked for the club on match days as stewards.

My first couple of years on the United board were characterized by the club's struggle to replace Matt. In Wilf's first season as manager he'd steered United to an FA Cup semi-final only to finish a disappointing eighth in the league. I liked Wilf – he had a lot of enthusiasm for what he did and was very popular within the club – but in the end it was all too much for him, a case of too much too early. Don't forget, he was asked to manage players who he'd been in the same team with just a few years earlier. Some, like Bobby Charlton, were about the same age. In fact Wilf was just two weeks older than Bobby; they played together at schoolboy level and signed their first contracts at Manchester United on the same day. A lot of the other lads had been Wilf's teammates, too, so to be thrown into the dressing room and given all this authority, it was like asking a boy in class suddenly to become the teacher. It was very difficult for him. And Wilf had to make some tough decisions, like dropping Bobby and Denis from the team, players who were starting to come to the end of their careers.

It was a loss in the League Cup to Aston Villa, then in the Third Division, that sealed Wilf's fate. Just after Christmas 1970 he was asked to step down. I don't think the board wanted to get rid of Wilf completely, because he hadn't done a lot wrong. They'd given him the opportunity but it hadn't worked out. They must have felt a bit guilty, for they tried their best to retain his services by offering him his old job back as reserve-team coach. He stuck it out for a couple of weeks but I guess his pride must have been too hurt to carry on and he accepted an offer to manage a club in Greece. Sadly Wilf wasn't to make a success out of football management and I know it broke his heart when he left United, but he was never bitter or held a grudge; he's always been a Manchester United man through and through.

With Wilf gone it seemed only common sense for Matt to take over full-time responsibilities for the team until the end of the season; that way the board had plenty of time to look for the best replacement. The thinking this time was that we needed a manager with a lot of experience and

Matt's preferred choice was Jock Stein, who had successfully managed Celtic for years. Stein was initially quite interested but his wife killed the deal stone dead when she declared she had no intention of going down south to live. So that was that.

Back in those days the choice of manager rested much more with Matt than it did with my father, who always bowed to Matt on the footballing side of things. That's why when Matt suggested Wilf as manager Father would have thought, *Well, Matt knows what he's talking about.* And it was the same with Wilf's replacement: Frank O'Farrell was again Matt's choice. Frank was manager of Leicester City and had done well there, getting to the FA Cup final, where they lost narrowly to Manchester City, and winning them promotion to the top tier of English football. So he looked a good bet at the time. Another plus was his West Ham heritage. The general assumption was that anybody coming from West Ham had a certain managerial nous, because a lot of their ex-players had made the grade as managers – Malcolm Allison, Dave Sexton, John Bond and others. So Matt made the approach and a week later a clandestine meeting was arranged with Frank, Matt and Father in the back of Dad's Rolls Royce parked in a lay-by just off the M1. This was June 1971 and Frank was hired.

Things got off to a good start and we were top of the league at Christmas. Frank's first signing was excellent, too, bringing in Martin Buchan, a cultured central defender from Aberdeen who became a stalwart at the club for years. He also gave youth prospect Sammy McIlroy his first-team debut. It all went spectacularly wrong in the second half of the season, however, when we lost seven on the bounce and could only manage an eighth-place finish.

Frank was a very smart and debonair individual, and very Irish; a gentleman, decent and honourable. But the players found him a bit aloof. They said he spent more time in the office than on the training ground. Someone was quoted as saying he came into Manchester United as a stranger and left as a stranger. Things weren't quite right. I heard that Bobby went to see Father on behalf of the players to say that the team weren't happy and that they didn't think it was going to happen under

Frank. Following a disastrous 5–0 mauling by Crystal Palace at Selhurst Park on 16 December 1972, the decision was made to sack Frank eighteen months into his five-year contract. I was there at the meeting and when he was told Frank wasn't at all happy with the decision. All he said afterwards was that with the sun shining it was a nice day for an execution.

With Frank's departure the club had overseen two failures in three years. But what can you do? You appoint those who you think are the best option available at the time. And both were not crazy appointments: Wilf knew the club and the players inside out and Frank had done great things at Leicester. Two reasonable bets on paper that just didn't work out, which was very worrying for the board. Some have put this down to Matt casting a long shadow over his successors by still being at the club. When Matt stepped down he became General Manager, Wilf's title was chief coach, so Matt still had an office at Old Trafford and came in every day. I believe that was a natural thing to do with it being Wilf's first managerial appointment, so that if he had any problems or needed advice Matt was around.

Frank has been the most critical about what he claims was an impossible situation, saying how he felt the presence of Matt everywhere at Manchester United. Matt probably didn't get involved or try to interfere, but that doesn't stop other people going to him, and I'm sure a lot of the senior players spoke to Matt behind Frank's back, which must have made him feel undermined at times. I feel it was ultimately down to the individual manager in question, though, because I know Tommy Docherty didn't have a problem with Matt, and when Alex Ferguson arrived he never questioned why Matt was still at Old Trafford; indeed, he welcomed it. It's very easy after the event to say that Matt should have left the club completely, but that's easier said than done: he'd been there for years, it was his life. He was a special case.

4 TOMMY DOC

Within days of Frank walking out of the door, his replacement arrived in the form of Tommy Docherty. Whereas both Wilf and Frank had been Matt's appointments, Tommy was a mutually agreed one with my father. I don't think anybody else came into consideration. Tommy had started his managerial career at Chelsea in the early 1960s, putting together an exciting team of youngsters that included Terry Venables, Peter Bonetti, Ron 'Chopper' Harris and Peter Osgood, before going on to boss Aston Villa and Porto. With it being mid-season, any deal had to be done quickly and efficiently, so it helped that Tommy wasn't in club management at the time, although he had to leave his post as Scotland's national coach.

It's been claimed that Tommy's brief when he arrived at Manchester United was to clear out the old stalwarts. Really his main priority was to get success for the club in the right style, by playing attacking and attractive football, and if he thought the best way to do that was by getting rid of some of the older players then that was his decision to make. By 1973 both Bobby Charlton and Denis Law had left. They were soon to be followed by George Best in January 1974. Best's behaviour was now pretty much out of control; he regularly missed training and there were accusations of him turning up for matches having had a few drinks. Tommy eventually had had enough and wanted him gone. Naturally these matters came up before the board and we decided to support Tommy and terminated George's contract. Nobody wants to lose a player like George Best but if he's genuinely disruptive you have no choice but to support your manager.

So within the space of just six months the three players most associated with the glory and glamour of Manchester United in the 1960s had gone, never to put on the red shirt again. Best and Law went to play for other clubs, with Law moving across the city to Maine Road on a free, while Bobby retired from the game, which surprised a lot of his fellow players because they said he was still very fit in training. Bobby went to manage Preston North End, who were in League Division Two. For a time he even put his football boots back on and made several appearances for them.

It was clear that a new era was beginning, and in his early days Tommy was very active in the transfer market, bringing in a host of new players, many of them Scottish: Alex Forsyth, Jim Holton, George Graham, Stewart Houston and forward Lou Macari, who arrived from Celtic for a £200,000 fee. Macari went on to become something of a United legend, playing over 400 games for us. I remember he scored on his debut against West Ham, slipping past Bobby Moore to get the equalizing goal in a 2–2 draw.

Tommy was quite a strong and ebullient character, and could be a bit wild sometimes. He got on very well with Father; he made Dad laugh. And he did well with the team, taking over from Frank O'Farrell when we were near the bottom of the league and saving us from relegation.

The 1973–74 season, however, was a disaster. This time we were relegated, in the cruellest way possible. Our penultimate game of the season was the Manchester derby, a game we simply had to win, but it was Denis Law's infamous back-heel goal that put an almost Greek tragedy spin on to the club's demise. Our thirty-six-year unbroken run in the top flight of English football was at an end.

There was never any thought of getting rid of Tommy. Everybody agreed that he'd done his best and that we'd get back to the top flight.

And that's exactly what happened. We stuck with Tommy and we came storming back with an exciting team playing attractive football and using wingers.

The football wasn't nearly as exciting when Tommy first arrived; it was all a bit desperate to be truthful, a real struggle. Going down actually did Manchester United a favour. It gave the team the confidence to come back the way they did and they never really looked back after that. And I honestly don't think any of the fans in the long term regretted the fact that we went down. Certainly that season in the Second Division they had a field day. We averaged 48,000 that season at home and broke numerous attendance records on the road. Tommy also had time to stamp his own personality on the team and bring in some new young talent like centre forward Stuart Pearson, brought in from Hull City, Steve Coppell from Tranmere, Gordon Hill, a left-winger purchased from Millwall, and Jimmy Nicholl, who was promoted from the youth team, all talented and exciting players.

Sadly, while we were in the Second Division we had a group of hooligans travelling to all of our matches that season. By and large Old Trafford was a safe environment to watch football, very well policed. I can't remember too many really bad incidents. One was the European tie in 1969 against AC Milan, when someone from the Stretford End threw a piece of brick at the Milan goalkeeper, Fabio Cudicini, hitting him on the back of the head and knocking him to the ground. Play was suspended for five minutes while the player received treatment. Unfortunately, that violent element of our fans in the Stretford End were known for their foul and abusive behaviour, which included throwing projectiles on to the pitch. This got so bad that in 1971 the club was forced to erect special barriers behind the goal at that end of the ground. A few years later the decision was taken to extend the fencing right round the ground to prevent any crowd invasions. But generally Old Trafford was safe and well policed; it was mainly a minority of our supporters behaving poorly when we were visiting opposition grounds who gave us a bad name.

As United slipped to the second tier of English football my own professional prospects were on the rise. In 1974 I was made general manager of the retail side of the meat business. I was twenty-eight. The retail side consisted of some sixty of our own shops dotted around Cheshire and Lancashire. We also ran the meat department in about sixty other cash and carry stores up and down the country and the hundred or so Woolworths stores that sold meat. This also included Scotland and Wales. So it was a big operation and I used to travel all over the country to see the area managers and visit the various shops and meat departments within the stores or cash and carries. At one point I was controlling a turnover of £10 million and a staff of a thousand. It was a big responsibility and I really enjoyed it. Most importantly, though, it was a great training ground for what was to come down the line.

Things were quickly looking up at Old Trafford. We were promoted to the First Division as champions in 1975 and fought our way to the FA Cup final in our first season back. We played Southampton, were overwhelming favourites and should have won. To this day you won't convince me that their winning goal by Stokes wasn't at least a yard offside. It was a disappointing day to say the least. But we made up for it the following year when we got to the final again and beat Liverpool 2–1. We had a little bit of luck that day. We scored first, a good goal, and then they equalized almost immediately. Our second goal came about from a Macari shot that was going wide when it hit Jimmy Greenhoff on the chest and went in. Liverpool put us under great pressure after our second goal but we managed to hang on for a memorable victory.

The Cup final is always a great day. I love going to Wembley. The excitement comes from the cumulative effect of the whole occasion: the journey down, the anticipation and then the game itself. Sadly I'm not sure the FA Cup final has the same cachet as it once did. Nowadays it's all about Champions League football and the Premier League because of all the money swilling about in it and the huge stars that attracts. If you're one of the top teams you want to be in the Champions League, if you're in the middle you're fighting for places and TV money, and if you're near the bottom you're desperate not to get relegated. Managers don't always field their top sides in the FA Cup nowadays; the league is just too important. I don't see that changing.

Some of the new rules haven't helped, although I appreciate that some changes needed to be made. Back in the old days, if it took several replays to finish the tie, then that's what happened. Now, during the latter stages of the competition, games are decided on the day. I feel that's taken some of the glamour away from the competition. I do understand the reasoning behind it, though, with the bigger teams unable to give the FA Cup as much attention as they might wish, particularly if they're involved in the Champions League or going for the league title as well.

In the past, if the final itself went to a draw, you'd all come back again on Thursday night for the replay. United won two finals that way, against Brighton and Crystal Palace. Nowadays that can't happen. You go to Wembley and get the result on the day. That's fine, but it's a shame that any final has to be decided on penalties.

For me, the biggest mistake was the move to hold the semi-finals at Wembley. This was a purely commercial decision rather than a football one. Supporters used to look forward to going to different grounds around the country depending who they drew in the semi-final. Now, after the semi-final, they're at Wembley again just a few weeks later for the final. Part of the mystique, uniqueness and excitement of going to the nation's premier ground for that big showpiece day has been taken away. It's a shame because at one time the FA Cup was almost as important as winning the league and for many people the highlight of the season. I don't see those days coming back.

From the enormous high of winning the FA Cup, a telephone call the following Saturday evening brought me crashing back down to earth. It was Tommy Doc and what he told me came as a complete surprise. He was having an affair with the wife of Laurie Brown, the team's physiotherapist, and the story was about to break in the newspapers. My first question was, 'Who have you told?' He said he hadn't told anybody yet. I said, 'Well, don't tell anybody until I speak to Father and see what we can do.' I put the phone down and immediately called Father, who was shocked by the news. I don't think any of the board knew anything about Tommy's affair with Mary Brown.

After the initial surprise Father's first thought was: *We don't want to lose Tommy; how are we going to deal with this?* When we discussed the revelation with Matt, he had a different view on it, because he'd heard other rumours about Tommy. There were stories going around that Tommy was involved in selling Cup final tickets on the black market, and was asking for money from supporters to have their photograph taken with him and the FA Cup. Matt had heard these rumours, along with other things that were reputed to be going on behind the scenes, and he felt this was the final straw. Father was more protective, still wanting to save Tommy.

Over the next few days I remember Tommy Doc and others coming up to the house for various meetings and discussions, and it came out that Tommy had been visiting Mary Brown during the day while Laurie was working, even keeping him at the training ground for longer hours so he could see Mary. That made it very difficult for the board, because physios are always very close to the players. They work with them every day – they're almost like an extension of them – and no player would like it if one of their wives was involved. They'd support each other, so we felt that they would support the physio in this case more than the manager. Matt wasn't happy about the situation and Father felt he couldn't defend the indefensible, though he was sad to have to let Doc go because he felt Tommy was on the verge of bigger things with us. We'd just won the Cup and were playing exciting football, but it was the sensible decision to make under the circumstances. Talk, though, to most United supporters about Tommy Doc's era and they will remember it with fondness. They loved the style of football we played.

5 SHARE DEALINGS

When Father rang up Dave Sexton to offer him the post of Manchester United manager, the then boss of QPR admitted later to taking all of twenty seconds to say yes. On 14 July 1977, barely a fortnight after Tommy Doc was shown the door, Dave Sexton was unveiled to the press. There was no one else in the frame. Dave Sexton was our first choice, and for a couple of reasons. First, and this would have been partly Matt's influence, because of all the things that had gone on with Tommy Doc we wanted somebody who was a totally different personality and Dave Sexton fitted that bill. And then there was his excellent track record as a manager, winning both the FA Cup in 1970 and the European Cup Winners' Cup the following season with Chelsea. He was also doing a fantastic job over at QPR, having just secured them their highest ever league position as runners-up to Bob Paisley's Liverpool.

Personally I liked Dave Sexton very much; he was a nice man, a gentleman. He had good manners and was very well read. I don't think he had a lot of time for the press. He could also be very set in his ways. He had his own ideas on coaching and approach to the game. In some respects, when you look at his past record and the reasons why we chose him for the job, you might have expected things to have gone a bit better than they did. The signs were there quite early on, such as when he decided to get rid of fan favourite Gordon Hill and brought in Mickey Thomas. Gordon was a very exciting left-winger who scored at probably a ratio of once every three games; very useful. Mickey Thomas was never going to be as prolific as that. He would run all day for you, but he wasn't Gordon Hill in front of goal. It was things like that which showed you how Dave Sexton viewed the game. His style of football wasn't as exciting as Tommy Doc's, that's for sure.

Another fan favourite to go was Stuart Pearson, though in fairness to Dave the player had been picking up some bad knee injuries. We did manage something of a coup by signing Joe Jordan and Gordon McQueen from rivals Leeds, however. That was a big statement, but they didn't come cheap: £350,000 for Joe Jordan and £500,000 for McQueen, whose combative, battling styles the fans loved.

In Dave's first season as manager we finished in a disappointing tenth place and faced an uneasy passage in the European Cup Winners' Cup. In September we travelled to St Etienne, a tie marred by crowd violence. The trouble began forty-five minutes before kick-off, with fistfights and bottles being thrown. Riot police moved in and several United fans ended up in hospital. I remember everyone at United was shocked a few days later when UEFA banned the club from the rest of the competition, and St Etienne were given a bye into the next round. This was the first time United had faced such a sanction in its history. Father was furious. Over the years he had been extremely vocal in his criticism of the hooligan element among our supporters, but this time he was quick to point out that we had been victims of heavy-handed policing and intimidation by opposition fans. It did seem we were paying the price for our bad record in the past and not just for what had happened at St Etienne.

Feeling hard done by we immediately appealed and UEFA reinstated us, but we had to play the home tie 200 miles away from Old Trafford. It was an odd ruling. In the end the venue we chose, or perhaps they volunteered it themselves, was Home Park, Plymouth. Thirty-five thousand United fans showed up and we won 2–0. I didn't go because I was on holiday in Malta but I remember continually ringing through to keep up with the score.

In the next round we performed terribly in Porto and were beaten 4–0. There seemed no way back, but the return leg almost became one of the greatest nights at Old Trafford. The atmosphere inside the packed stadium was truly electric and there were periods during the game when I thought we were going to pull off a miracle escape. But it seemed like whenever we scored and looked like pulling away the Porto team came back at us with those all-important away goals, and even though the score on the night ended up a breathless 5–2, we were out.

By early 1978 I had been on the United board for eight years and decided it was time to secure and strengthen my position, even though the previous year my father had given my brother Roger and me a large fraction of his shares, amounting to 16 per cent of the club each, reducing his own personal stake in the club to 18 per cent. I approached Alan Gibson, our vice chairman and the largest individual shareholder in the club, with an offer to buy 1,138 of his shares. I went into the red to do it, borrowing £200,000 from the bank and putting my house in hock as security. I told my dad what I was going to do and he didn't try to put me off; he thought it was a good idea. 'If that's what you want to do,' he said, 'do it.' My plan was that one day I hoped to run Manchester United and having the biggest shareholding would help to secure that.

Gibson seemed happy to sell all but 100 of his shares to me. By this time he was getting on in years, and although he had received a very lucrative settlement from his father when he died back in 1951, it was now 1978 and Alan had enjoyed a very comfortable life. I think £200,000 at that stage of his life was very welcome. Alan's father, of course, was the great James Gibson and something of a legend at Manchester United. A wealthy businessman, James saved the club from financial ruin during the Christmas of 1931 by donating a substantial amount of money at a time when the club couldn't even afford to pay the wages of its players.

Installed as chairman, James Gibson remained in the post until his death and also brought Alan on to the board.

While I thought buying Gibson's shares was a good investment, obviously there were risks attached to it, especially borrowing so much money. I was rather sticking my neck out, especially since at the time the club were paying out minimal dividends. For example, in both 1977 and 1978 the total dividend payment was just £323. Back in those days the value of owning football club shares was in their prestige, and the fact that you had voting rights and control, rather than as a source of income. Of course you hope that the shares go up in value the more successful the club becomes, but I never visualized Manchester United becoming quite the financial success it turned out to be when I first bought them.

Following the purchase of Alan Gibson's shares, not only did my personal stake in the club rise significantly, but I was now the largest single shareholder with 1,904 shares. As for the family's total shareholding, that went up to 74 per cent. It was a situation that led to my father renewing his interest in an earlier plan to raise capital for the club by means of a rights issue, which is an issue of shares by a company to its existing shareholders in proportion to their holding of old shares, offered at a favourable price. Back in October 1976, Father and Matt met with representatives of the London merchant bank Kleinwort Benson, purely as an exploratory exercise to see what they needed to do if they wanted to raise money. The introduction had been made by Roland Smith, who was professor of marketing at Manchester University and had very good City contacts. He was also on the board of Louis C. Edwards & Sons, which is how Father got to know him. Much later, Smith became chairman of British Aerospace and would also play an important role at Manchester United after we went public in 1991.

There had been a degree of opposition to the idea of a rights issue when it was first explored, and things had gone quiet for a while, but I have a feeling that my buying those shares from Gibson led Father to want to have another look at it. What followed turned into one of the most controversial episodes during my time at United.

After making healthy profits in the previous couple of years (in 1977 the club turned in a record profit of half a million pounds), we knew from our internal accounts that we were on course for a bad year in 1978. Indeed, we went on to make a £290,000 loss, largely due to the expensive acquisition of Joe Jordan and Gordon McQueen, whose combined transfer fees cost us £850,000. That was a big chunk of money, and at a time of greatly increasing costs in all our activities Father identified the need for United to raise more capital in order to compete and buy more players. The idea was to raise approximately £1 million by issuing a million new shares at £1 each, but to do it on a rights issue basis in order to protect the interest of current shareholders. Each of those would have the option to buy 208 new shares at £1 for every one share they currently held. Of course, as holders of 74 per cent of United shares, this meant that the Edwards family would have to pay £740,000 to preserve its existing shareholding.

At first there was opposition to the scheme, most notably from Matt, who argued that the club didn't need to raise money this way. But what was the alternative? To raise that kind of figure you either sell shares or you get a loan facility from the bank, Matt's preferred option, or you go into overdraft. And would a bank be happy to lend you a million pounds? Probably not for the purchase of players. Also, this was a time of double-digit inflation and high interest rates. We calculated, at those rates, that such a loan would involve interest charges of around £100,000 a year without reducing the capital originally borrowed. Besides, the fact that our family was going to take up its rights more or less assured that the scheme was going to be a success. The family had also agreed to underwrite the issue, taking up any shares not bought by other shareholders. So in the end the thinking was that a straight rights issue was the most equitable, simple and efficient method of raising the finance.

There were other dissenting voices, however. One local businessman and lifelong supporter of the club, John Fletcher, started an action group that launched an injunction to stop us going ahead with the rights issue. We had no option but to defend ourselves in the high court. In the end the judge heard full arguments on both sides of the case and was quite clear in his judgement that the rights issue should be allowed to proceed.

Unfortunately, by then the matter had gone public, with stories appearing in the newspapers triggering a lot of unpleasant and prejudiced accusations. In some quarters it became a focal point of criticism of the way United was being run. I know Father was upset at the way the controversy was presented as an Edwards versus Busby situation, with newspaper headlines appearing like 'dis-united'. He felt such a situation was harmful to the image of the club. But we stayed on course, steadfast in our belief that this was the right thing to do, and in September 1978 the board unanimously approved the proposal. The Football Association also studied the scheme and put up no objections. We were not oblivious to all the controversy and opposition. Indeed, we called an extraordinary general meeting on 18 December for shareholders to question the board in person. After just half an hour the scheme was approved by an overwhelming vote of thirty-seven for and only three against.

One of the arguments levelled against the rights issue was that it was a huge sell-off in order for the Edwards family to make a personal fortune and obtain more power. But of the million pounds that the club eventually raised, the Edwards family put up three-quarters of a million pounds themselves. How many people would have put up that sort of money in 1978 for their local football club? You hear all the time of fans wanting investors to come in and throw money at their club. We were prepared to do it; we put our money where our mouths were, and at a time when the club was losing money.

I also had to borrow another £400,000 in order to take up my rights. Together with what I'd previously borrowed to buy the Gibson shares that took my personal debts to over £600,000. So it's easy in hindsight to look back and say, it was the Edwards' way of making a lot of money. It was a huge gamble. I can remember at the time my wife being very unhappy about it. And I don't think my mother was pleased about my father putting more money into the club either. These were decisions we made because we thought that in the long term they were the right things to do. No one could have foreseen the way football was going to go, the advent of the Premier League, television money and all the rest of it. And far from making a quick profit I went more heavily into debt. By the early 1990s, because the interest charges kept building up and up, my loan had grown to something like £950,000. I must admit it was quite a burden at the time to have such a huge debt hanging over me, and I became quite a heavy smoker during that period to help cope with the stress. It was tough because if at any time the bank called in the debt I would have been in real trouble. But I never regretted my decision, certainly not in the end. There were times, though, along the way when I thought, *Have I done the right thing?* It was only when we floated the club in 1991 that I was finally able to pay off my debts and get my house released from the bank.

The rights issue went ahead in January 1979 and was an unqualified success. Looking back, it was quite revolutionary for a football club to raise so much money in this way at the time. Unfortunately, by the end of it all, Father and Matt had grown apart. The rights issue wasn't solely to blame, because in the end Matt had not gone against the scheme, preferring not to split the board by voting against it. Indeed, the issue probably magnified lingering ill feeling. Matt had always resented the fact that his son Sandy had never been invited to join the board as, some years before, a deal had been put in place where Father and Matt had agreed to support the election to the board of each other's son. I had been elected to the board back in 1970, yet Sandy had still not been offered a place and Matt always put the blame for this on Father. I don't know why Sandy wasn't elected; all I know is that the decision impacted on their friendship, which was a real shame because for almost thirty years they'd been such close friends and allies, and it would never quite be the same again.

6 TAKING OVER AT THE TOP

Dave's second season in charge, 1978–79, was not much better than the first, as we finished ninth. During some of the matches you could hear the beginnings of discontentment emanating from the stands. You could tell the fans weren't happy with the brand of football being played: it was too cautious and a world away from the excitement they'd enjoyed under Tommy Doc. It was disheartening to hear the players booed off the pitch.

In contrast to our poor league form the team enjoyed a successful run in the FA Cup, making our third final in four years. Our opponents were Arsenal and the game itself was a real kick in the teeth, even worse than the Southampton defeat. With four minutes to go we were two nil down and out of the game completely, when suddenly we came to life and scored two goals in a minute. Then Arsenal immediately went up the other end and Alan Sunderland put the ball in the net. It was unbelievable. I was so happy to be going into extra time and then bang, it was all over. That was one of the cruellest moments during my time in football, but that's the nature of the sport: it's unpredictable and you can never take anything for granted.

As the team geared up for another tough season in 1979, Dave Sexton entered the transfer market with a vengeance, paying a club record fee of £825,000 for midfielder Ray Wilkins, a player he'd once signed as a fifteen-year-old when he was Chelsea manager. It was a big price tag but Ray was Chelsea's captain and an England international. There was a perception that he played the ball sideways all the time, rather than forwards, and was not attacking enough, and I don't think our next manager Ron Atkinson helped much when he nicknamed Ray 'the crab' for his propensity to move the ball sideways. But Ray stayed with us for five years and was a valuable part of the team.

The new season was filled with the usual highs and lows. Hitting the top of the league table with a 5–0 win over Norwich in November 1979 was particularly satisfying, but for the most part the football under Dave Sexton's management wasn't particularly entertaining and crowds had started to dwindle. We also had a terrible run in the FA Cup, unceremoniously dumped out in the third round at home to Tottenham. Entertaining football has always been important to our supporters: they have been used to the best and now expected it. Of course, it's difficult to play open attacking football with flair all the time, but that was always our aim.

Behind the scenes Father was now devoting all of his time to United, having earlier in the year sold part of the family meat company to entrepreneur James Gulliver. Father was now into his sixties and not really putting as much effort into the business as he had in the earlier years. He'd started to have a few health problems as well. He weighed over eighteen stone and his doctor had prescribed him tablets for his heart. In truth, the business had started losing money. There were two sides to Louis C. Edwards & Sons: the retail side, which I looked after, and the wholesale side. The retail side was profitable, the wholesale side was losing money. Profits had begun to dip from around the early 1970s, and by 1978 the company made an overall loss of £172,000. I suspect that because of his commitments at United, Father took his eye off the ball a little with the meat business; his first love was always United. His brother Douglas also perhaps devoted too much time to his civic career; he had been both Lord Mayor of Manchester and High Sheriff of Greater Manchester. So Gulliver approached them both at just the right time. As a member of the board I was consulted about the plan to sell and was broadly supportive, although ultimately as joint chairmen it was my father and uncle who made the final decision. They retained a large number of shares in the company after the buyout, but their day-to-day involvement was now at an end.

Father also thought it made sense for Gulliver to take a seat on the United board; that he would be a useful addition due to his business experience. Gulliver remained on the board until the mid-1980s, and although he was based in London he attended most of the board meetings and went to as many of the home matches as he could.

As for me, I remained head of retail for another year. When I became chairman at Old Trafford I no longer wanted to work at the meat company full time so went to see Gulliver. He agreed to my becoming a non-executive director, a post I kept for several years.

Having attended to the family business, Father now faced a new battle of an altogether darker nature. Because of the media spotlight brought to bear on the club due to the controversial rights issue, investigative journalists from Granada Television's current affairs programme *World in Action* had begun digging around Father's dealings as chairman of Manchester United. When the programme aired in January 1980 I remember it being pretty hard hitting. There were accusations of slush funds and backhanders given to the parents of young players as an inducement to bring them to Old Trafford. I honestly don't know if that happened; certainly I wasn't party to any of it or aware it was going on. The only thing I would say is that whatever Father did was always for the benefit of the club. Probably such practices were fairly endemic in football at the time.

There were also serious allegations concerning Father's meat company; suggestions that bribes had been given to council officials in order to win lucrative contracts. Many people were shocked by the programme, which arguably was the first instance of 'trial by television'. There's no question that my father felt victimized, and understandably it was a very traumatic time for my whole family.

While my father had been advised not to make any public comment about the programme, I do know that he hired a firm of lawyers to go through his business transactions and private papers in order to build up a defence against all the charges levelled against him. Sadly, my father never had the opportunity to clear his name. Four weeks after the *World in Action* programme was broadcast he died of a massive heart attack at home. He was getting ready for bed when my mother heard a loud thud. She ran upstairs only to find him dead on the bathroom floor. It was a huge shock to all of us. He was only sixty-five.

I've always firmly believed that the strain of that programme contributed to my father's death – the tension and the build-up to it going on air. He knew for a long time it was coming, because people on the inside in television were telling him. Although he remained confident that he would be vindicated, his fear was that, by the end of it, his name and reputation would be sullied anyway. And I saw the physical deterioration in him over the weeks leading up to the programme.

At the time I was very bitter because my father had done a lot for Manchester United and I'm sure had he lived longer he would have carried on doing good things. Just prior to his death he gave the go-ahead for work to begin on a new £1 million building to complement the existing executive suite in the middle of the South Stand. It would feature more private boxes, but also the provision of two large rooms that could be used for social activities by ordinary fans and supporters' clubs. Father lived and breathed Manchester United and some of my fondest memories of childhood are of him taking me to Old Trafford on match day, where I'd sit in the directors' box.

Father's memorial service took place at the Church of the Holy Name in Manchester. It was heart-warming to see so many of his friends and colleagues turn out to say their final goodbyes. Matt read the valediction, the full typescript of which is presented here for the first time.

My Lord Mayor, Your Worships, My Lords, Ladies and Gentlemen, we meet today in this very beautiful church to pay tribute to one of Manchester's renowned sons, Mr. Louis Charles Edwards, and it is my privilege to address you.

Louis, or Lou as he was so affectionately known to us all, was born almost 66 years ago in a Catholic home to loving and caring parents and was one of five children.

Louis was educated at De La Salle College under the stern but effective control of the Christian Brothers. He later became apprenticed to the family business, which his father had developed in the wholesale, retail and manufacturing fields of the meat industry.

As happened to so many of us the War plucked Louis out of civilian life and it was always a source of great pride to Louis to have served with that very famous regiment 'The 14th/20th Kings Hussars' with which he spent most of his war service in the Middle East.

Despite the many difficulties of the post-war years, coupled with those of having returned to a very depleted business, Louis, by sheer hard work, outstanding ability and business acumen, became the joint chairman and Managing Director of one of the largest meat companies in the country and certainly the largest in the North of England.

He was, however, above all else, a great family man who loved his family dearly and who was in turn greatly loved by a most devoted wife and their family.

He was a happy man, a warm and generous person who was always ready to provide for, or help, others less fortunate than himself. He was renowned for his substantial gifts to charities involving literally thousands of pounds. Only weeks ago he gave at no small expense, Christmas parcels to 250 people he humorously referred to as 'fellow old age pensioners'. There are many other instances, too numerous to mention, in which he has given quietly and without any publicity or fuss substantial sums of money to worthy charities.

He was, however, best known both nationally and internationally through his association with football and more particularly because of his highly successful chairmanship and stewardship of his beloved Manchester United Football Club.

His jolly and genial personality together with the warmth and sincerity he showed to victor or vanquished endeared him to all he met wherever he travelled with the team in whichever part of the world they were playing.

He was not just a chairman but more of a father figure not only to all the members of the team but also to every employee in the club.

It is a source of great sadness to us all that Louis suffered such unhappiness in the last weeks of his life being hounded and harassed by the media after a recent television programme which, according to expert medical opinion, undoubtedly hastened his death. A programme in which Louis, a person of such admirable qualities, was vilified so viciously, whose good character was attacked with such concentrated venom, a programme which, in the opinion of so many, appeared to deliberately contrive to assassinate Louis' good character, choosing to ignore with equal deliberation all the good their enquiries must have discovered about Louis.

These opinions were expressed with great indignation and disgust in the many letters received by members of the family all of which thoroughly condemned the programme as being grossly unjust and unfair and the irresponsible action of third-rate reporting. They also condemned with equal force the television authority concerned, accusing them of displaying an appalling lack of decency and good taste and an equal degree of irresponsibility.

The very presence of so many of us in this beautiful church, here to pay tribute to our very dear friend, is proof, if proof be needed, of the love, admiration and respect which we all had for Louis.

His passing is a great and irreplaceable loss to his family, his friends, the club and the world of football.

Father's death made many of the front and back pages of the newspapers, with one headline referring to him as 'Mr United'. Without doubt the stadium and financial stability of Manchester United stands as a lasting and living testimony to my father's efforts. Father was really responsible for putting United into the big league of its day commercially. Combined with Matt's footballing know-how, Father built a thriving financial empire, basing it all on sound profit-making principles. Just a few weeks before he died he told Manchester journalist David Meek that his biggest ambition was for the club to earn just as much income from off-field activities as it did through the turnstiles on a match day. In that way his beloved Manchester United would be able to weather any storm while at the same time maintaining income to continue expanding facilities for the fans and buying top players. This was certainly something that I was determined to continue and substantially build on.

⚽

With my father's death being so sudden, no plan had been put in place for his successor. Over the years he and I never really discussed what his ambitions were for me. I think he hoped that one day I would take over – that was sort of implied – but there was no clear pathway for me to succeed him as chairman. Interestingly, since my father had retired from the meat business he had become reliant on me as a source of information, as I was still there as retail managing director. He also started to consult me a lot more about footballing matters, such as asking what I thought about us signing Ray Wilkins, and he increasingly wanted to know my opinion at board meetings. By this time, I'd been there for ten years and, having recently bought those shares, which gave me a sizeable holding, Father must have realized how ambitious I was. I'll always remember David Meek telling me after Father died, 'Louis would not make a decision until he had discussed it with you. Towards the end it was Martin this, Martin that.' So I do think he was grooming me to take over and I always had it at the back of my mind that one day I would like the job. I don't think he was ready to retire though; he could have carried on for many years and maybe brought me more gradually into the picture, but when he died he left a power vacuum at the top of Manchester United and everything was now up for grabs.

A few weeks after my father's death the club secretary Les Olive came to see me on behalf of the board. There had been a secret meeting in which it was decided that maybe I wasn't quite ready yet to assume the position of chairman. They recognized that one day I would be ready to take over, but in the short term they felt Matt should assume those responsibilities with me learning alongside him. I told Les that I disagreed with this decision; that I felt I was ready now. After all, I'd been on the board for ten years and observed the way things were done. I also had a lot of confidence in myself from running the retail side of the meat business and going on the Harvard marketing business course at Cambridge University. And at thirty-four years old, if you're not ready, you're never going to be ready. I was ready to run Manchester United. I was young, enthusiastic, and I had decided that this was my destiny.

Les took this news back to the board and on the morning of 22 March 1980, a few hours before the one hundredth derby match against Manchester City, a board meeting was held at Old Trafford. The board decided that I would be made chairman and Matt would take the honorary role of Club President. It had been a tough decision because the board had genuinely anticipated that Matt would take over and I would wait my turn, and when that didn't happen I suppose they felt they needed to appease Matt. Giving him the title of Club President was a way of honouring him for all the work and services he'd given the club throughout the years. It was a nice gesture by the board, one I fully endorsed. So that was the compromise; it meant that Matt would still be around and if I needed any help I could consult with him.

Inevitably this new position entailed a loss of potential influence and power for Matt, but I don't think he felt marginalized. Nor did I ever get the impression that he wasn't always 100 per cent supportive of me. If Matt did harbour any grudges he certainly never showed them. He was a true gentleman, someone I came to admire even more over the years, if that was possible. He had this great presence. In life you don't meet many people whom you feel a little in awe of. Matt definitely had that special quality; most of the players who played under him will tell you the same thing. He had a calm authority about him. I just liked Matt as a man and had huge respect for him, and the more I got to know him, and realize his achievements, the more my respect grew.

Matt still retained an office at the club and remained a highly visible presence around Old Trafford. I used to enjoy him being there; you always knew when he was around because you could smell his pipe. I'd often see him at lunch when he ate in the grill room. 'Hi, Sir Matt,' I'd say. I always called him Sir Matt, not Uncle Matt any more. Gradually, of course, as the years passed, his appearances became less frequent.

I think the supporters have always felt I was lucky to take over from my father; that the position was gifted to me. But don't forget, I had taken a huge gamble buying up all those shares to become the club's major shareholder. I wanted it and pushed for it. My view would always be: judge me on what I did, not on what I got. Of course, if you'd given the supporters an actual ballot with two names on it, mine and Matt's, it would have been pretty unanimous. I was an unknown, Matt was a hero, the man who had built the club, from a football point of view, from nothing in 1945 to an institution. Matt was a great manager, there's no question about that, but I don't really subscribe to the theory that football managers necessarily will be able to run football clubs successfully. And Matt was seventy years old at the time, so there was the age factor to consider. In fact, shortly after I took over he did have an illness. With Matt's age, then, and my youth and solid business background, I just felt, for the club's sake as well as mine, that it was the right time for me to become chairman. So, at the age of thirty-four, I was the second-youngest chairman, after Watford's Elton John, in the Football League. And the youngest in the First Division.

Becoming chairman of Manchester United was a very special and proud moment for me because above everything else I was a fan; United were the only team I had ever supported. Since 1958, when my father was invited on to the board, they had been a huge part of my life. I knew the whole history of the club; at the drop of a hat I could name the team that won the 1908 championship or the 1909 FA Cup-winning side. And I had my heroes: Law, Best, Charlton. United were my team, and how many supporters haven't sometimes wished they could run their own football club?

I was under no illusion of the challenges ahead of me at Manchester United, but for years I had been running the retail side of the family business, controlling a turnover of £10 million and a staff of a thousand butchers all over the country. So for me to step from running a large division of a busy public company to taking over at United was actually a much easier job than you'd expect. Not in terms of PR or profile, but in terms of the size of the operation; turnover at United then was just over £2 million and the staff numbered 152. It didn't daunt me at all. Manchester United was a huge football club back in 1980, but it wasn't the global brand that it was to become. And the football landscape was very different, too. This was pre-Sky and pre-today's media world. Now everything you do is absolutely magnified; it's all over the front pages of newspapers and on television, radio and social media. The world's gone media mad.

Because I took over halfway through the season I didn't want to get involved with the playing side of things. I didn't think I needed to because obviously Dave Sexton was committed to trying to win the league. If Dave came to me wanting a player, that would be a different matter. I can, however, remember a couple of board meetings where we talked about the style of football that was being played, which was a touchy issue with Dave, because he was quite a sensitive character. As it was, we finished the 1979–80 season well, coming second behind Liverpool and qualifying for the UEFA Cup.

As chairman your target was always to win the league; failing that, you want to win the FA Cup. The League Cup was always secondary. There was no Champions League in those days; it was the European Cup, and the only way you could be in the European Cup was to win your domestic league. We hadn't done that for thirteen years, and it was to be another thirteen years before we did so again. We'd been reasonably successful in the FA Cup, getting to a few finals. We just couldn't win the league. When I took over, my ambition was for the club to be successful on the field – as a fan that's what I probably thought about more than anything else – and to seize back domestic dominance from our old foes Liverpool. I knew that regaining our old position as the number-one club in the country would take time, but I was confident we could do it in the long run.

Another aim was to turn United into a much more business-like operation. When I took over as chairman the club was in a solid financial state but I felt we could do better. You won't believe this but they didn't even do a budget. The argument was: how could you budget when you didn't know how many games you were going to be playing; how many additional cup matches you would play; whether they would be home or away; what numbers of supporters would turn up? I felt we needed to start somewhere; even if we took the worst-case scenario we needed to know roughly what to expect in terms of profits that year. That, then, was my first aim, and getting it done was difficult enough. Later, going for a three-year plan, and then a five-year plan, was even more challenging. But we did it. It was all about getting a financial structure in place to run the business and make the club as financially successful as possible to keep developing the ground and buying the best players.

It, of course, meant keeping an eye on expenditure as closely as possible. For example, the team used to spend the Friday night before a home game at a luxury Cheshire hotel at a cost of £700. I didn't see that as a particularly useful way to spend money so I quickly got rid of it. But I didn't come into Old Trafford with the intention of taking an axe to everything. I wasn't saying, right we're cutting this out and we're cutting that out, or we're cutting back on staff, but over time I simply made sure that things like player wages and negotiations didn't get out of hand, that the players didn't just get what they wanted or what their agent was pushing for. My financial control was more about making sure that where we spent money it was spent wisely.

Back when I took over there weren't the same opportunities for creating income as there are now. We got money from the turnstiles on match day but not a lot else. There was some ground advertising and we did have the odd match-day sponsor, but it was done in a very low-key way and you had limited rooms in which to entertain any corporate guests. All that came later with the expansion of the ground. There was no shirt sponsorship either; that didn't come in until 1982. And there was no television income to speak of. We got £25,000 a year for TV highlights, the same as all the other ninety-one clubs in the Football League. We didn't even own the souvenir shop.

I also discovered that it was the manager who always negotiated the deal with the shirt manufacturer, which at the time was Admiral, and that the money went straight into a pool for the players to share out; the club didn't get a penny. Not long after I came in I remember renegotiating a new shirt deal with Admiral – it was something like £15,000 per year – and Dave Sexton was furious, absolutely livid that I had taken over the negotiation. I also put a stop to the money going to the players' pool; it was actually club money. Can you imagine if that practice had continued to this day, especially in light of the recent £750 million, ten-year Adidas shirt deal? All that would have gone to the players. That's the way it went in those days.

The manager and the club secretary always handled transfers and player negotiations back then, although even in Matt's day they needed the approval of the board first before going out to buy a player. The secretary had a lot of power; he pretty much ran the club. Managers were also very influential behind the scenes. Our secretary Les Olive, for example, very much deferred to Matt. That all really started to change when paid chief executives came in and the emphasis of control moved away from the manager and the secretary to them. When Ron Atkinson became United's manager in 1981, for instance, he never handled player negotiations or wages; it was established by then that this was very much my job.

Such a big change was always going to be a sensitive issue for Les because that meant a change of role for him, although he did still have a very important part to play in the day-to-day running of the club. I got along very well with Les and had a lot of respect for him. He was as straight as a die, totally trustworthy and very thorough in his work. He was quite a religious man and a lay preacher at his local church. He loved everything to do with Manchester United. When he retired in 1988, rather than lose all that accumulated knowledge and experience I asked Les to join the board of directors, as part of which he made a valuable contribution for many years until his death in 2006.

The funny thing was that everybody was so friendly and familiar with Les that they all called him by his first name. I could never do that; I always called him Mr Olive because I'd known him since I was twelve years old. I was on good terms with all the staff at Old Trafford because many of them had worked there for years. Les Olive had been a player with us before getting a job in the office; Jim Barker was catering manager under Father for several years; and Ken Merrett, who subsequently took over from Les as club secretary, had been at the club for most of his working life. Then there was Arthur in the ticket office and Cath on the switchboard, who had both been at Old Trafford since the 1960s, along with Pauline Temple, my PA, and Ken Ramsden, who went from office junior to ticket office manager, programme editor, press officer, assistant secretary and through the ranks to club secretary. We had a lot of people who had been there a long time. Indeed, some of them even saw me out! We were a family club in that respect; there was a real family atmosphere around the place.

Taking over as chairman, I wanted to retain that family atmosphere. That was always my style anyway; I'm pretty laid back as a person. As a chairman my father was quite jovial and pally with the staff; he liked to have a drink with them, that kind of thing. Ken Merrett told me about an overseas trip with the team during which Father would always be at the bar of an evening. 'Come on, Ken, have a drink with me,' he'd say, and he'd spend hours drinking and chatting. They sounded like great nights. I was probably a little bit more distant, but still involved the staff in the major decisions. So I didn't come in stamping my feet – I didn't need to, because Manchester United meant something to the staff. We were all in it together, we all had the same ambition and the same goals: to make Manchester United the most successful club in the country.

7 BIG RON

Very quickly I settled into my new role as chairman. Really my responsibility was to make everything click: the team was vital, of course; so too the stadium, the fans, pricing, catering. You've got to manage and balance the whole business. From the outside, though, the only thing anyone really sees is what happens on the pitch, and that's how you get judged. We'd finished the season well, so I was delighted, and promised Dave Sexton that he would have my backing for any player he felt could come in and strengthen the squad for the next campaign.

One player we did try to buy was Arsenal's Liam Brady. The Irish international was highly gifted and Dave had heard that he wanted to leave the London side. Brady had an agent in Leeds and I remember spending an evening with them both talking about the possibility of Liam coming to United. After the meeting I was told they would let me know Liam's decision. In the end he went to Juventus, which was a huge disappointment. Liam did say, at least, that if he had stayed in England the only team he would have considered joining was United.

Instead we signed centre forward Garry Birtles from Nottingham Forest for a record British fee of £1.25 million. Birtles had been terrific for Forest, winning two European Cups with them, but he had a nightmare time at United; it never worked out for him. He took almost an entire year to score his first goal for us, and that was indicative of the level of our football at that time.

As the 1980–81 season went on, work was progressing on several building projects around Old Trafford, including an extension to the executive suite. In December 1980 the £1.5 million development, which my father had instigated, was opened. Old Trafford now had five specialist function rooms: the Grill Room, Stretford Suite, Trafford Suite, Europa Suite and Jubilee Room. All of them were different. Both the Grill Room and the Trafford Suite were open to the public for dining during the week as well as on match days. The Trafford Suite had the added distinction of including an impressive showcase of club trophies and memorabilia. The other rooms were likewise used for entertaining during match days but could also be hired out for private functions. The idea was to make Manchester United a seven-days-a-week venue, not just somewhere you turn up to watch a game of football on a Saturday afternoon. That's one of the reasons why in my first year as chairman we started behind-the-scenes tours of the stadium. A tour guide could be booked and would walk you round for a small fee. At first these tours were limited to just walking round the ground. Later on we built them up to include access to areas supporters wouldn't normally be allowed to visit, like the dressing rooms and the players' lounge, and a look at the honours board.

In my first year the pitch was also in dire need of repair; it really had become worn down. We'd had quite a few complaints about its poor quality and there had been some press criticism, too. So at the end of the season the pitch was ripped up and re-laid for the first time in twenty years. I remember watching from the office window as car loads of supporters turned up to help themselves to bits of turf piled up outside the ground. This was the start of quite a few pitch restorations. We seemed to go through a period of time when we just couldn't get the surface completely right. Various consultants were brought in, including John Souter from Scotland, a kind of Red Adair of the playing fields who had worked on football pitches from Hampden Park to Anfield, until we eventually got it right.

You always know when things are going wrong by the atmosphere in the ground, and you could just feel that the crowds weren't happy with what they were watching. It wasn't necessarily that results were bad; it was still the style of football. The plight of Birtles in front of goal seemed to sum up our whole season. Back in Europe we were knocked out of the UEFA Cup in the first round by the unfancied Polish side, Widzew Łódź. We also had a bad run in the FA Cup. Never once, though, did I hear the players criticize Dave Sexton. Whether that was because they liked him or felt they'd let him down on the pitch I'm not sure.

What was of deeper concern was that the fans were continuing to vote with their feet and were staying away. The empty seats at Old Trafford told their own story. That's why I, with the support of the board, who were happy to be led by me on most matters, made the decision at the end of the 1980–81 season, after we failed to make the top five, to make a change. It wasn't an easy decision because I got on well with Dave. I liked him as a man; he had good morals and good principles. I just felt that after four years, and even though those included a Cup final appearance and a second-place finish in the league, it wasn't going to happen for him. We'd lost a bit of our excitement on the pitch and he hadn't improved the team.

I think it came as a big shock to Dave when I called him in and said it was the end of the road. He wasn't expecting it, particularly as we'd just finished the season with seven successive wins. Though he took it well, Dave was clearly upset by the decision, understandably so given his commitment to the job. But as a manager, getting the sack is an occupational hazard. Not many managers reach the position Busby or Ferguson got to, where they have a long tenure and retire at the end of it as heroes. Naturally all Dave's staff had to go with him as well, because when you have a new manager they'll always want to bring in their own personnel.

This was the first time as chairman that I'd had to sack a manager, and it was a very unpleasant experience. But I've been luckier than most; with

Ferguson lasting as long as he did I only ever had to sack two managers during my twenty-three years in charge.

I had a very clear idea of who I wanted to replace Dave Sexton. The manager who was particularly successful at the time was Lawrie McMenemy. What he did with Southampton was quite extraordinary and I liked Lawrie personally: he was a real football man and very well respected within the game. I approached Lawrie and he said he was interested; in fact he said more than that: he said he'd do it. He later changed his mind, saying that his wife Anne didn't want to move from Southampton because the children were in the middle of their education and would have to move schools. That was the reason given for Lawrie not coming. Funnily enough, a bit later on, after we'd finally settled on Ron Atkinson, I saw Lawrie at some football function and he came up to me and personally apologized. 'I'm sorry I let you down,' he said.

My second choice was Bobby Robson, who had achieved terrific results at Ipswich Town for many years and won the FA Cup with them in 1978. They had also just won the UEFA Cup. For a relatively small club to be challenging the top teams here and in Europe really was some achievement. I called Bobby and we had a chat. While he appreciated my offer Bobby explained that it was difficult timing and he felt he would be letting Ipswich down if he left. So I was back to square one.

The next name on my list was Ron Saunders, who had just guided Aston Villa to the First Division title, their first for seventy-one years. Again I was turned down. I must admit things were getting a bit fraught by this stage. The team had just gone on tour to the Far East but I'd stayed behind, feeling that it was more important to secure a new manager. Towards the end of May 1981, I was contacted by a journalist called John Maddox, who worked on the *Sunday People* newspaper. John had been approached by Ron Atkinson to pass on a message to me, saying that he very much wanted the job. Ron was manager of West Bromwich Albion and a rising star. What he'd done with that team was quite phenomenal: in a very short space of time he'd made them challengers for the league, and they were an exciting, vibrant team that scored lots of goals. I remember when they beat us 5–3 at Old Trafford in a memorable match in 1978.

Ron was next on my list anyway, but more importantly he wanted the job and that sealed it for me. John Maddox organized a meeting at his home in Sale with Ron, who I found to be extremely enthusiastic, so we agreed a deal. I then had to phone the West Brom chairman, Bert Millichip, to tell him that it was my intention to approach Ron, even though I'd already met with him. Bert suggested we discuss the matter in person, and since he lived in the Midlands and I was coming down from the north we decided to meet at the Forte hotel just off the M6. This was on 31 May. I think Bert quickly realized that he wasn't going to be able to keep Ron, so it became a question of compensation. We eventually agreed on £65,000 and that was it, Ron arrived that June.

Even before he joined Manchester United, Ron had an image with the media, who referred to him as Mr Bojangles. He played up to all that; it was part of Ron's showbiz persona. He liked to say things like he loved to drink champagne, but in reality when Ron had a glass of champagne he'd sip it rather than gulp it down. In fact he'd probably leave the glass half empty. There was, however, an undeniable twinkle of showbiz about Ron. At the same time he loved putting himself about with the players. Ron had been a reasonable midfield player himself with Oxford United, where he was nicknamed 'the tank'. He was a bit of a bruiser and loved joining in with the players in training.

When a new manager comes in, he's always got his own ideas of the players he wants and the players he wants to sell, and there's normally quite a bit of activity at the start of his tenure. I always worked on the premise that the chairman's role in relation to the manager is to support them. You appoint them to do the job, so you've got to support them until you realize that it's not happening and that they may not be there much longer; that somebody else might be coming in who wants a different set of players. I can't recall ever blocking a transfer that one of my managers wanted. There might have been a situation where the player's wages made it impossible for the transfer to go ahead, though. If you feel that through buying a player you're putting the club at financial risk, either because of the size of the payment or because other players will want the same personal terms, then you can't go ahead with the deal. So you've got to be sensible. In that respect I always had the final say on transfers, but generally if a manager wanted a player it was very rarely that he didn't get what he wanted.

Somebody Ron was very keen to buy was Mark Lawrenson, who was at Brighton at the time. I offered them a very large fee, plus one of our players, Ashley Grimes; we valued the offer at £900,000, which for a central defender was a lot of money back then. Brighton turned it down. The next thing we heard Lawrenson had gone to Liverpool. We had better luck with Frank Stapleton. Frank had been quite a prolific goal scorer for Arsenal but his contract was up and he was keen to come to United. Agreeing personal terms with Frank was quite a convoluted affair and the first really complicated contract that I was involved with. We met with his representatives at the start of August and were still in discussions four days later. Normally it would have taken no longer than a day to finalize matters but this was for me an early indication of the way contracts were changing, with new issues like image rights starting to appear.

Having finally agreed personal terms with Frank I contacted Arsenal. They wanted £1.5 million for him, a figure I was not prepared to pay. When my offer of £900,000 was rejected it went to a tribunal. The tribunal came into effect when two clubs couldn't agree a fee and the player had agreed to the move; you each made your case and then the tribunal fixed the fee. The date of the tribunal was set for 20 August and took place at The Midland Hotel in Manchester. By the end of the afternoon they had reached a decision and what pleased me was that they arrived at exactly the fee I'd originally offered Arsenal. The following day we announced the signing at a press conference.

Frank became a very useful player for us. He was a bit of an all-round centre forward who both led the line well and laid things on for other players – he was more than just a striker. And he was what we needed at the time because Ron felt that the squad he had inherited from Dave Sexton needed freshening up.

With that in mind, Ron went back and raided his old club West Brom, taking two of their best players, Remi Moses and Bryan Robson. We paid £500,000 for Remi but getting Robson was not easy because they didn't want to sell him. Robson was probably the best prospect in English football at the time and in the end we had to pay a British record fee of £1.5 million to prise him away. Ron said to me, 'You'll never regret whatever you pay for Robson because you'll have years out of him; he'll play in midfield for you and when he gets older he'll be able to play centre back, he's so good.' Bryan was prone to the odd injury. Actually, he'd broken his leg three times before we bought him, so there was an element of risk in signing him. But that was the way he played. And I never regretted buying him: we got thirteen years' service out of Bryan and he became one of the legends of the club, captaining us to three FA Cup triumphs and the European Cup Winners' Cup. He also won a couple of league titles with us at the end of his career. He was tremendously influential, especially in the early years of Alex Ferguson's reign. He was a captain in every sense of the word, not only by instruction but also in effort and leadership.

One unfortunate consequence of the Robson transfer was that Matt Busby resigned from the board over it, though he stayed on as president. Matt was not happy paying that kind of money for a player, but transfer fees were beginning to rise substantially. The first million-pound player had been Trevor Francis in 1979, and everybody thought that was crazy, yet here we were just two years later at £1.5 million. Matt felt that fees for players had gone too far, or at least past what he was comfortable paying. But it was my duty to support Ron and we needed that lift for the coming 1981–82 season. Ron was ambitious to win the league. I was a new chairman and I was also ambitious to win the league, so we went for it.

8 MY FIRST TROPHY

When I took over at Manchester United my role as chairman went unpaid due to strict FA rules disallowing paid directors. In those days, football clubs didn't have paid chief executives, even though I was pretty much doing both jobs. As chairman I took charge of board meetings and represented the club at all other football-related meetings. I was also carrying out the full-time duties of a chief executive: supporting the manager, dealing with all player negotiations, transfers, contracts, staff wages and the day-to-day running of the club. It was the same for my father, who as chairman spent a great deal of time at the club but did not receive a salary. To be salaried I would have had to give up my board directorship. And so in order to earn an income I took up non-executive appointments outside football. One was for an office cleaning business; another was a printing firm in Manchester; and also a labour recruitment company.

Many had long felt that not being allowed to appoint a paid employee to the board was an archaic, nonsensical rule and that it was only a matter of time before paid directors would be allowed. I know Liverpool wanted to make their club secretary, Peter Robinson, chief executive and bring him on to the board. So in the end it was pressure from the clubs that forced the FA to reconsider, and in November 1981 I and many others voted for the FA's proposal that professional football clubs could have one paid executive on the board, the proviso being that these must genuinely be working full time for their clubs. It was a natural and correct change to make. On 4 December, at the very next United board meeting, I was appointed one of the first full-time paid chief executives in British football, in addition to my role as chairman. As a consequence I resigned from my other jobs, since I did not want them to interfere with the running of United.

My initial salary was £30,000 per annum, which the following year went up to £41,000. These are the official figures from United's statement of accounts and they make interesting reading as an indicator of how the game has evolved. For example, in the whole of 1982 only two employees were earning over £50,000 a year; that includes both staff and players. And not many of them earned over £20,000 either. What a change from today.

Almost from the word go Ron had the team playing exciting football and we finished third in his first year, the 1981–82 season. He was also planning for the future and performed a masterstroke when he brought in Eric Harrison to take control of the youth system, which has always been important to Manchester United. The pair were old friends, having played football together for the RAF during National Service, and Harrison was looking for a new challenge after spending nine years at Everton. Of course, Eric's greatest achievement was to be the pivotal role he played in producing that group of players known as 'The Class of 92', including David Beckham, Ryan Giggs, Nicky Butt, Gary and Phil Neville and Paul Scholes. But more about them later. When Eric arrived at Old Trafford towards the end of 1981, our youth team set-up was already in pretty good shape, with some terrific prospects in Norman Whiteside, Clayton Blackmore and Mark Hughes.

It was Norman Whiteside who made the fastest impact when he broke into the first team as a sixteen-year-old in April 1982, becoming the youngest United player since Duncan Edwards. Norman was a year younger than Mark Hughes but had matured much quicker. Norman was already a man at sixteen. He gained even more publicity when he broke Pelé's record as the youngest player to appear in a World Cup, debuting for Northern Ireland aged seventeen years and forty-one days at the 1982 World Cup in Spain.

Unfortunately, Norman suffered knee problems at quite an early age and as a consequence his career at United was relatively short. His demise was also linked to a drinking culture that existed at that time within the club, of which Norman and Paul McGrath were among the main culprits. Robson also liked to drink but it didn't seem to affect his football as much as the others.

At the same time as youth players were breaking through into the first team I had made the decision to change things at board level. I wanted to make it younger and more forward thinking, with an eye to the future, by bringing new people on. When I first took over as chairman, the rest of the board had a slightly veteran look to it, with most of my fellow directors now retired from business life and all over the age of sixty. Matt had since left as a director, followed by Bill Young and Alan Gibson. I don't think Bill and Alan necessarily wanted to leave. I made them vice presidents so they would still have their perks. I just felt we needed a new, younger set of directors. One of these was Michael Edelson, who had been a friend of mine since the early 1970s and was an absolute United fanatic. He was a local businessman and I felt he was young, enthusiastic and could make a contribution. I still had a few old experienced hands around like Les Olive and my uncle, Denzil Haroun, but I was looking for younger recruits.

I continued with this policy when I brought Maurice Watkins on to the board. Maurice was a Manchester United fan and still played local amateur football for Old Mancunians and cricket for Hale Barnes. He was a partner in the Manchester law firm James Chapman & Co, which United used as its solicitors. He first appeared on the scene in 1977, advising the club on the termination of Tommy Docherty's contract.

We had a very good relationship; I worked very closely with Maurice on things like players' contracts and transfers. So the value to me was having Maurice coming to board meetings and being briefed there rather than me having to brief him all the time on what the board had agreed. I felt that he was a useful addition, which he proved to be over many years. Contracts are so important to United, not just players' but also commercial contracts, and there's a lot of legal work connected with the Premier League; Maurice brought all that expertise. He was in a way a bit like a right-hand man.

I also decided to make Bobby Charlton a director. The thinking behind this was that Bobby had been a great footballer for the club and was very well thought of by the public. Over the years he became extremely useful as an ambassador for the club because wherever Bobby went around the world he was – and still is – recognized, and he provides a great function for the board in that important role. I believed Bobby would be another good addition and that this would keep him in the United family. In some ways he filled the gap that Matt left, although, of course, Matt was still around as president and still travelled with us when we went on tours and away games. Everybody always made a great fuss of Matt, and to have both of them around was a real bonus.

Another significant development in the spring of 1982 was our shirt sponsorship deal with the electronic company Sharp. There was a time when the league didn't allow you to put any form of name or advertising on club shirts. That all changed in 1979 when Liverpool agreed a deal with Hitachi to become the first professional English football club to have a sponsor's logo emblazoned on their shirt.

For some time we had made it known that we were looking for a sponsor ourselves and had sent out a few feelers in the business world. Of course we didn't enter into this lightly, being fully aware of the importance and symbolism of United's famous red shirt, but at the same time the club always had to look to as many sources as possible for income and this was an untapped area. In the end the deal came about because Sharp put aside a sum of money every year allocated for spending on advertising. And the argument put forward by their finance director

Alan White to the company's managing director was that if by the end of the year they hadn't used that advertising surplus, it might be better used sponsoring Manchester United than going back into the head office coffers. White's argument won the day and when Sharp approached us to say they were interested it simply became a question of negotiation, which I conducted myself with White.

The deal eventually reached was worth £500,000 over two years, which when you think about what those contracts are worth today isn't very much, but at the time it was a British club record. Of course, there were strict rules as to where you could put the sponsor's name on your shirt and the size of the lettering, which had to be approved by the league.

Sharp remained our shirt sponsor for a very long time, until the end of the 1999–2000 season. Indeed, I think that deal helped put Sharp on the map. It was an extremely complementary partnership because even though the company was Japanese its UK head office was in Manchester. To be more precise, the firm was based in Newton Heath, the very place where Manchester United Football Club was born. Of course, part of the package involved promoting the company through advertising sites around Old Trafford and hospitality. I also remember that when we went on tour to Japan we organized for the team to visit the Sharp factory. There were benefits for the players, too; they were allowed to pick a range of products from Sharp's showroom in return for photo shoots and specified public appearances.

Always on the lookout for additional ways of raising revenue, in the summer of 1982 we explored the idea of holding a rock concert featuring Queen at Old Trafford. For any live event of this nature you need to apply for a licence, so Les Olive, the club secretary, Danny McGregor, our commercial manager, and I went down to Trafford council to make a presentation. At the meeting there was a solicitor called John Hugill, who was actually a neighbour of mine in Siddington, where I lived at the time. He was the council's specialist on licensing and he grilled us very hard. Because we had applied for the licence in the company secretary's name, even though it was Danny McGregor who was putting the concert together, it was Les who had to answer all the questions, and he didn't know much about the event.

'Now, Mr Olive,' said Hugill, who at six-foot-six was quite an imposing figure. 'Do you know what time this concert is due to finish?'

'I don't know,' said Les.

'You don't know, Mr Olive? You're running a pop concert and you don't know what time it's due to finish.' Hugill looked disapprovingly at us and carried on. 'Mr Olive, what is the decibel level of this concert?'

'I don't know.'

'You don't know, Mr Olive? You don't know! You applied for a licence in front of this council and you don't know what the sound level is. I can't believe it!'

This went on for several minutes and every question received the same miserable answer from Les. 'Mr Olive, how many outside toilets will you have for this concert?'

'I don't know, Mr Hugill.'

'You don't know?! Do you know anything at all about this concert, Mr Olive?'

Hugill absolutely slaughtered us. We never did get the licence to hold the concert. We didn't get anywhere near it. It wasn't until 1991 that we finally got permission to hold a pop concert. Rod Stewart was the first one and that was followed by the likes of Simply Red and M People. They were always very popular, which was great for us, because making the best use of Old Trafford in order to put the money back into the club was always something we were keen on.

With Ron Atkinson comfortably secure in the managerial hot seat we began to compete for silverware. We lost 2–1 to Liverpool in the League Cup final in March 1983 but made amends two months later in the FA Cup final against Brighton. Everyone expected us to win and it looked that way when we went 2–1 up with a wonderful goal from Ray Wilkins. With just four minutes to go they equalized and forced extra time. Both teams looked out on their feet when, right at the death, Brighton had a two on one but, with glory beckoning for them and our defeat seemingly inevitable, Gary Bailey made a great save. I was watching it all unfold from the Royal Box and there was a real feeling that we'd got out of jail; they'd had that great chance to win it. So we lived to fight another day and when we came back to Wembley the following Thursday evening for the replay we won easily, 4–0, with Bryan Robson having an absolute stormer, scoring two.

That was a very special and significant win for me personally because it was my first trophy as chairman. I'd been in the role for three years now and had been a director at the club for thirteen, so emotions were high. What made that victory extra special was the fact it fell on Matt's birthday and he was able to celebrate it in style with us that night. The next day we all returned to Manchester with the cup to attend a town hall reception. Wonderful memories. And most of that team went on to win the Cup again two years later, so it clearly showed them what it took to win, too.

I've always thought that Gary Bailey, our saviour in that initial Cup final match, was one of the best goalkeepers United ever had. He established himself as our keeper in the late 1970s following the retirement of Alex Stepney and made almost 300 appearances. Peter Schmeichel revealed a few years ago that he idolized Gary as a youngster growing up in Denmark.

I remember one story about Gary. In the early 1980s he was dating the daughter of David Plowright, who was head of Granada Television. David was also the brother of the famous actress Joan Plowright, who herself was married to Laurence Olivier. A couple of days before we were due to play Chelsea at Stamford Bridge, Gary asked if I might do him a favour. 'Could you look after Laurence Olivier for me, because he's my guest at the Chelsea game and I'd like to give him more than a seat in the stand. Is there any chance you can take him in the directors' box and look after him for me?' I said that I would be absolutely delighted to. What Gary didn't know was that I'd always been a huge fan of Olivier

– he was by far my favourite actor. Sure enough, on the Saturday Sir Laurence arrived and it was a great thrill for me to look after him for the afternoon. Celebrities often come to see United games, but I've never been particularly star-struck. Olivier was different. He was by then in his late seventies and quite frail; even so, there was an unmistakable aura surrounding him and lots of people wanted to say hello. I took him into the dressing room, where he met all the players, and sat with him during the game. I doubt he was a fervent fan of football; this was more of a day out for him, but he thoroughly enjoyed the occasion, and he was absolutely charming.

That summer United went on tour to Swaziland to play a couple of exhibition matches against Tottenham. At the time South Africa was still under the apartheid regime and British clubs were not allowed to go there, but because Swaziland was on the border a lot of South Africans were able to make the journey across to see us play.

While we were there someone organized a staff match between the two clubs. The directors played, as did the respective managers, Ron Atkinson and Keith Burkinshaw. Tottenham came out on to the field resplendent in their kit, while our lot arrived wearing T-shirts. I was quite annoyed and insisted that the first-team kit be brought out and everyone change into it. I played as centre forward and managed to grab a couple of goals. The Spurs chairman Irving Scholar got a hat-trick. The final score was 8–4 to Tottenham but there were mitigating circumstances for our poor showing. We had Gary Bailey's father Roy in goal, who had been a very good goalkeeper in his day and was part of the 1961–62 Ipswich team that won the league, but he had just had an operation on his shoulder and couldn't dive, so every time Tottenham took a shot at goal they scored. Tottenham had a chap called John Barr in between the sticks. John was one of the tour operators but also played in the Southern League as a goalkeeper, and he was young and fit, so every time we had a good shot Barr tipped it round the bloody post.

During the match I did a flying tackle on Keith Burkinshaw and he ended up limping all night. I was sat next to him at the dinner table later in the evening and he was muttering, 'If I find out that bastard who kicked me . . .' Irving and I were sitting near each other, killing ourselves laughing, because Irving knew it was me who got him.

That trip was the first time I met Irving and we became friends. We were of a very similar age and had become chairmen of our clubs at roughly the same time. Irving had been a Tottenham supporter all his life, holding fond memories of the 1961 Double-winning side. He knew the club backwards in terms of players and its history, much as I did with Manchester United.

During my years in charge at United I was also friendly with Arsenal's vice chairman David Dein. David likewise knew the history of Arsenal backwards and was of a similar age to Irving and me. Most of the other chairmen in the league were much older. It helped that the three of us were all coming up to the age of forty and shared similar ambitions for our clubs. I don't think it was a coincidence that Irving, David and I made up three of the main people involved in the eventual formation of the Premier League.

In spite of the intense rivalry between Tottenham and Arsenal, Irving and David were very good friends. Neither of them shared the hatred of each other's clubs that Spurs' and Arsenal's fans did. I guess it wasn't ingrained in them when they were growing up. When I was young I supported Manchester United and followed the players, but I was also interested in players from other teams. They were all footballers to be admired; the game was less tribal then. I always remember David Dein telling me how devastated he was when he heard about the Munich air crash because he'd been to that very last game before Munich when United played Arsenal; he was there, he'd seen the Busby Babes. He kept a scrapbook with pictures of Duncan Edwards and all the United players from that game – I think he's still got it. David was also a keen follower of the England team, and although Roger Byrne, Tommy Taylor and Duncan Edwards were all United players they played for England, too, so he was devastated after the Munich air crash; he said he cried his eyes out. I remember myself as a kid going to see Matthews and Finney and being in awe of them. I remember also going to Everton and seeing Alex Young. Okay, so he wasn't a United player, but he was still so exciting to watch. I recall likewise going to see Liverpool and raving about Ian St John. You don't get that respect for opposition players' ability today, sadly.

My relationship with other chief executives was also good. In fact there was a group of about three or four of us, including Peter Robinson of Liverpool, Jim Greenwood of Everton and Ken Fryer at Arsenal, who used to ring each other up to chat and discuss things. We'd keep each other informed about transfers, players' wages and bonuses, a whole host of different things. We all wanted to keep up to date and keep control of these matters – not let them get out of hand – so I used to talk to them regularly.

As chairman I was always looking to upgrade the ground and make improvements when I could. And thanks to our successful Cup run we were able to plough something like £800,000 into ground improvements. Some of the terracing got a bit of a facelift and, following a rearrangement of the restaurant, executive suite members now had a perfect view of the pitch from the bar and dining room. We also earmarked £500,000 to renovate the private boxes.

Without being mercenary, you're always looking to make improvements for the supporter but you're also looking to enhance the income as well. It isn't just the seating that's important but the facilities behind it: the bar, the restaurant and everything else. That's why we also put aside £150,000 to spend over the next two years improving the overall standard of catering. Twenty sites around the stadium were to get a facelift, and a bigger and better variety of food and refreshments would be available on match days.

Our victory in the FA Cup also got us back in Europe and we had a great run in the Cup Winners' Cup in the following 1983–84 season, including a memorable tie against Barcelona, whose star player was

Maradona. We'd lost the away leg 2–0 and most people thought it was asking a bit too much to come back and beat them by three clear goals. But what happened on 21 March 1984 has gone down in Manchester United folklore as one of our greatest nights of European football. Ron Atkinson remembers me telling him on the day of the game, 'You will hear a noise inside Old Trafford tonight like you have never heard in your career.' And I was right. The atmosphere inside the ground that night was unbelievable. The noise levels didn't drop for the full ninety minutes. Again Robson was fantastic, scoring twice – the Barcelona players just couldn't handle him. And then Stapleton got the winner. It was an absolutely unbelievable night, 3–0 the final score to give us a 3–2 aggregate win and defy all expectations; a great comeback – one that, for anybody who was there, will never be forgotten. There had been one nervous moment late on in the game, when Maradona broke away and Mark Hughes tripped him; it looked an absolute stonewall penalty but the referee didn't give it. We hung on and at the final whistle the supporters invaded the pitch and carried Robson off shoulder-high. Those are the types of moments that stick with you as a fan.

Unfortunately, after our heroics against Barcelona we got knocked out in the semi-final by Juventus, unluckily as it happens. We drew the first leg at home and they were leading the second leg 1–0 when we brought Whiteside on as sub; it just seemed to turn the game and we got back to 1–1. Coming up to the final whistle we quite fancied ourselves in extra time because the momentum was with us, but Paolo Rossi scored right at the death. That was hugely disappointing after our heroics against Barcelona, but that's the fickle nature of football. In our defence, we'd had a lot of injuries going into that match. We'd had a makeshift side in the first leg and still weren't at full strength going out to Italy. It had been quite an adventure, though, and our league form had been reasonably good: we ended up fourth and six points off the eventual champions . . . yes, Liverpool again.

Not long after losing to Juventus in Europe the Italians put in a world-record bid of £3 million for Bryan Robson. We rejected the offer; there was no way I would have countenanced losing such an important player.

We did tell Bryan about the approach and – even though we had the right to refuse it as he still had time to go on his existing contract – it must have seemed like an attractive proposal; Juventus had Michel Platini among its star players. In the end what we did was sit down with Bryan and his agent and say to them that we wanted to make it worthwhile him staying. That's exactly what happened: we offered Bryan the security of a new long-term contract with vastly improved terms and I don't think he ever regretted his decision to stay.

That summer, however, we did sell Ray Wilkins. We had been approached by AC Milan with an offer of £1.4 million. I put it to Ron and he thought it was a good deal. So it was purely a commercial decision. Usually with a transfer like that, once the manager and the chairman have made the decision you have to put it to the player, and then the player has to decide. Players don't have to move, they can stay, but most players if they know that the manager is prepared to sell them think, well, what future have I got here? Am I going to be playing next year or not? Also, let's not forget that AC Milan were a big club in Europe and Ray probably would have seen it as a career move, offering better personal terms. In other words, the deal was beneficial to both parties.

A lot of transfers do tend to be straightforward commercial transactions, although there can be an emotional element as well. I remember seeing former Stoke captain Jimmy Greenhoff on a television programme, and he was talking about when he was at the Potters and manager Tony Waddington told him that Manchester United had put an offer in. Jimmy loved Stoke, he was the hero there and the crowd loved him, so he was really shocked that Tony Waddington was prepared to sell him and asked why. It was quite simple: the top of a stand at the old Victoria Ground had blown off in a storm and they weren't insured. Waddington was quite open with Jimmy, saying, 'You're the most valuable player we've got and we need the money to build a new stand.' Jimmy's first reaction was to storm off – he wasn't happy at all – but when he calmed down a bit he thought, *It is Manchester United, the biggest club, and Tony is prepared to let me go*, so common sense prevailed.

When I bought Bryan Robson, West Brom's Bert Millichip told me they were going to use the £1.5 million to build a new stand. I playfully suggested, 'I hope you're going to name that stand after me.' I was told later that for a while in the boardroom at the Hawthorns they did refer to the new stand as the Martin Edwards stand.

Thanks to the Wilkins sale we were able to freshen up the team a bit by bringing in Jesper Olsen from Ajax and Gordon Strachan from Aberdeen. I remember flying up to Edinburgh with Maurice Watkins in mid-April to meet Gordon and his family to discuss his potential move to United. It was only later that we discovered Gordon had already signed a pre-contract agreement to go to Cologne, which caused enormous complications. This necessitated another trip for Maurice and me to Edinburgh, in early May, to see what we could do about the situation. It was at this meeting with Gordon and his agent that we came into contact with Aberdeen's manager, a Scot named Alex Ferguson. Alex was keen for Gordon to come to United because we'd offered £525,000, considerably more than he was going to get from Cologne. In the end the whole affair was settled when we made an agreement with Cologne that Manchester United would play a match with them and they could keep the gate receipts; it was a sweetener to release Gordon from the contract. Funnily enough, we didn't actually play that match because Cologne never contacted us for a date.

Had Gordon's contract been straightforward then the history of Manchester United may have looked somewhat different: we may never have had that face-to-face encounter with Alex, and it was during those discussions that I got to know him quite well and saw how he operated. I left impressed, and stored the experience away, thinking that perhaps one day it might prove useful.

9 FROM MAXWELL TO HEYSEL

I never did quite find out if media proprietor Robert Maxwell was serious in his ambition to buy Manchester United or if it was all one big publicity stunt. He approached us early in February 1984 through Roland Smith, again using his City contacts, and to be honest I was always sceptical about it. But because of who and what he was, we decided to meet him.

Once the approach had been made I knew it had to be kept secret. The last thing we wanted was for the press getting hold of it. Oh yes, Maxwell said on the phone, let's keep it quiet. The very next day it was all over the newspapers; someone had leaked it and we had reams of ridiculous speculation that continued to run for the next ten days on both the back and front pages of the tabloids. It put me under intolerable pressure because the whole thing had been blown out of all proportion. I mean, I hadn't even sat down and talked with Maxwell yet, and some reports were saying the deal was already as good as wrapped up. It reached the point that I couldn't wait to get the meeting over with one way or the other, just to put an end to all the nonsense that was going on in the press.

Finally, we fixed a time to come down and see Maxwell. We were playing Luton away on 12 February, so Maurice Watkins and I stayed overnight at London's Royal Lancaster hotel with a view to meeting Maxwell the following afternoon. We were nothing if not prepared. On the morning of the 13th we met with board member James Gulliver to discuss the situation and then had a meeting with Kleinwort, Benson, who were our financial advisers.

Our meeting with Maxwell at his London office, situated behind Liverpool Street Station, was a strange one because the Soviet leader Yuri Andropov had died a day or so before and news people were constantly streaming in through the door. 'I've got to deal with this,' Maxwell would say. 'Andropov has died; he was a great friend of mine.' So all this crap was going on.

Over the previous few days the asking price for taking control of Manchester United had never been mentioned, either by ourselves or Maxwell. It was only after our discussions with Gulliver and Kleinwort, Benson that we decided that if Maxwell wasn't prepared to pay £15 million for both my shareholdings and those of my brother Roger, then he could forget it. In the end Maxwell never made us an offer. At one point during our meeting he asked what we wanted and when we explained there was no response from him at all.

So that was it: the meeting lasted maybe two hours, and although nothing had been agreed we decided that it made sense to release a joint statement. Maurice Watkins told Maxwell, 'Give me a chance to get back to the office and I'll draft something. We'll send you a copy for approval and then announce a joint statement together.' We were driving back to Manchester in the car and the next thing we heard was Robert Maxwell on the radio saying negotiations had broken down and blaming us.

I don't know if Maxwell ever had the money or not. Whether he thought he could get Manchester United on the cheap or just did it for publicity purposes, who knows. I had no real desire to sell anyway. I hadn't been in the United hot seat for very long. And I was only thirty-eight with my whole future still ahead of me. So it didn't bother me at all that the Maxwell deal fell through. Although if you read the press at the time I was the one trying desperately to sell the club. That just wasn't the case. Maxwell approached me.

Of course, with what we've learnt subsequently about Maxwell, the pension fund scandal and all the rest of it, I realize it was a lucky escape. Had Maxwell taken over it could have been the ruination of United. I must admit that, going into that meeting, Maurice and I were suitably wary, and my impressions of Maxwell did not improve during the course of the afternoon. He was too bombastic and spent half the meeting on the phone. 'Get me the Kremlin,' he'd bark at his minions in a bid to impress us. It was 'Do this' and 'Do that' and 'What do you want?' He was very forceful, and at lunch his table manners were appalling. I didn't take to him at all.

Around this time a new ruling from the league allowed home sides to keep all the money they took through the turnstiles in league games. Previously gate receipts were always shared between the home and away club. This had been the case ever since the foundation of the Football League. For years many of my fellow chairmen and I had argued for change. In our view the ruling didn't make much sense because during the season every club played each other both home and away, so why didn't we just keep our own gate receipts when we played at home and they keep their gate receipts when we played at their ground? Of course this new ruling was of substantial benefit to clubs like Manchester United that had the bigger stadiums. Having said that, a club like Tottenham could be taking just as much money as United on home matches because they charged more for tickets. Although attendances in the North-West were bigger, the pricing of tickets was much cheaper. In any case, the new rule change proved highly significant and brought in much-needed extra revenue.

The team began the 1984–85 season in good shape. Mark Hughes, who had now established himself in the first team, and Frank Stapleton were a formidable front line and we had a nice blend of youth and experience. But still the league eluded us and with each year that passed without winning it the burden became heavier. To add salt to the wound, our old adversaries Liverpool were continuing to dominate English football. The irony was that we always seemed to perform reasonably well against them, but over a long season Liverpool invariably seemed to come out on top, and if they didn't they weren't far behind. And they were winning European Cups, as well. It was daunting. We wanted to be number one, yet thirty-odd miles down the road Liverpool were the main force for a long period, and winning with flair, to boot.

At least we made it back to Wembley for the 1985 FA Cup final. Our opponents Everton had just secured the league title, keeping it in the city, while we finished fourth again, and just a few days earlier they had won the Cup Winners' Cup, so they were going for a treble. Not surprisingly they were the favourites. It was a very close game and could have gone either way until our centre back, Kevin Moran, unluckily became the first player ever to be sent off in a Cup final. It was for a late tackle on Peter Reid and I remember the referee, Peter Willis, a great big tall chap who towered above all the players, six-foot-five, pointing to the dressing room. In fairness to Peter Reid he didn't think it was a red card and pleaded with the referee not to send Moran off; I've always admired him for that.

After Moran's dismissal the game seemed to open up a bit and it was Norman Whiteside who provided a moment of magic to win it when he let fly this incredible left-footed shot from something like twenty yards that went right in the corner to beat Neville Southall, which took some doing. It was an extraordinary victory considering we were down to ten men. And that was Whiteside's greatest moment in a United shirt, the winning goal in the Cup final.

Delight at winning the Cup quickly turned sour just over a week later when the tragedy at the Heysel Stadium in Brussels unfolded. Thirty-nine Italian fans died and hundreds were injured when a stadium wall collapsed before the start of the European Cup final between Liverpool and Juventus, after crowd trouble culminated in a surge by Liverpool supporters towards the Italian spectators. United were on tour in Australia when the awful news came through. Within days the FA announced that all English teams would be withdrawn from European competition. This was later followed by UEFA placing its own ban on English clubs playing in Europe 'for an indefinite period'.

I've always been of the opinion that the FA sacrificed the clubs in

The family business: running a football club was hard, but not as tough as carving up fresh meat every day! It was at Louis C. Edwards & Sons (above) that I started to learn about managing a business, skills that proved vital when I took over as chairman of Manchester United from my father (below).

My father Louis was great friends with Sir Matt Busby, and my parents, Matt and his wife used to socialise regularly (above). He was 'uncle Matt' to me but, by the time I joined the board in 1970, I'd rather outgrown using that name, so he became simply 'Sir Matt' (below).

(Above) Standing with the board members after winning the FA Cup and Charity Shield in 1977 (*l–r* me, Matt Busby, Louis Edwards, Alan Gibson, my uncle Denzil Haroun and Bill Young).
(Below) With Peter Swales, the Manchester City chairman, on the Old Trafford pitch.

Having taken over as chairman following my father's death in 1980, I quickly got to grips with all aspects of running the club.

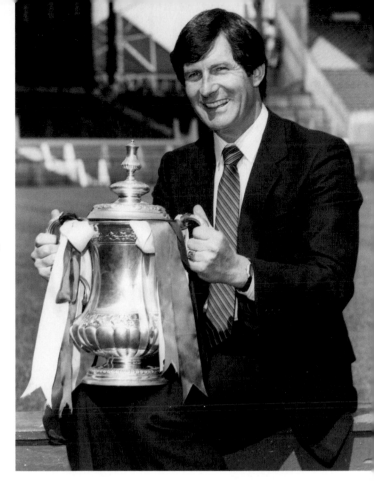

(Right) Posing with my first major trophy as chairman: the 1983 FA Cup. We'd beaten Brighton and Hove Albion 4–0 in a replay and the delight on my face is clear to see. (Below) A slightly more formal display of the trophy with manager Ron Atkinson (left) and captain Bryan Robson (centre), along with the Charity shield, which we won the same year.

As chairman I was lucky enough to meet the great and the good – whether at functions or as they came to watch United. Here I am with (top to bottom) the then prime minister, John Major, Prince Charles, Nelson Mandela and Pelé.

Manchester United was the subject of several takeover attempts. Arguably Michael Knighton's in 1989 was the most controversial. Before the deal was signed off he decided to go out on to the Old Trafford pitch to do tricks as a way of announcing himself as the new owner (right). His bid subsequently failed. BSkyB also made a bid, in 1998, which was accepted but later scuppered by a report from the Monopolies and Mergers Commission. Here I am with Sky's then chief executive Mark Booth (below).

I had to let Ron Atkinson go in November 1986, but this paved the way for the appointment of United's greatest ever manager, Alex Ferguson, and I introduced him to United fans later that month (above). We quickly formed a strong working relationship (below).

order to continue to benefit themselves financially by carrying on playing internationals, because if you're pulling the clubs out why don't you pull the national side out as well. It's the same fans that support clubs that support England. In fact very often it's the noisy element of clubs' supporters who travel with the England team. So how can you justify pulling the clubs out and not pulling the national team out? I found that a very odd decision, hence my suspicion that the FA did it to save their own skin. The decision was also taken without consulting the clubs. The first any of us knew about it was when the ban was announced.

Of course, the ban only affected those teams that qualified for European competition. It's not like the Champions League now, where the best footballing countries are represented each year by three or four teams; it was just Everton going into the European Cup, Manchester United going into the Cup Winners' Cup, and Liverpool, Southampton and Tottenham having qualified for the UEFA Cup. If such a ban happened today it would certainly impact on more clubs. But it was a huge blow, especially since in the years leading up to Heysel English clubs had been consistently winning the European Cup. We ended up being out of Europe for five years, which would have a hugely detrimental effect on the level English teams played at. When United were the first club allowed back into Europe for the 1990–91 Cup Winners' Cup we managed to beat Barcelona in the final, but after that it took English clubs a long time to catch up and regain their competitive status among the European elite.

I remember we did try to appeal against the decision. Our argument was: how can you ban all clubs because of one incident that has happened abroad, that was out of all the other clubs' control, and that occurred in a stadium that was probably not fit to hold a final anyway? I appreciate some action had to be taken, but our feeling was that UEFA had tarred all English clubs with the same brush due to the actions of a minority of supporters. Our appeal fell on deaf ears.

Faced with the prospect of not playing any European football, along with the financial implications, it was decided to launch our own knockout cup competition. It was called the Football League Super Cup, and consisted of two groups of three teams: ourselves, Everton, who would have been in the European Cup, Liverpool, Southampton and Tottenham, who had qualified for the UEFA Cup via the league, and Norwich as League Cup winners. On paper it may have looked a good idea but in reality it failed to grab the interest of supporters and lasted just one year.

Another repercussion of the Heysel tragedy was the introduction of a complete ban by the government on the serving of alcohol at football stadiums in England and Wales. We appealed against this decision and, while we were successful in winning our alcohol licence back, supporters were still not allowed to consume alcohol 'in view of the pitch'. These rulings also applied to executive areas, restaurants, window tables and private boxes in the half hour before a match. I think the argument was that those supporters looking into the boxes would be able to see others drinking alcohol while they themselves were banned from having a drink on the terraces, which could understandably cause some irritation. Even in today's era of safe all-seated areas, where it is easier to eject drunken fans than it was on the terraces, this rule still applies. Which I find very odd. After all, it's only those seats directly by a window that are affected; people sat just behind are allowed to drink until kick-off. I can understand not taking alcohol on to the terraces, since it's much more difficult to eject someone drunk and disorderly from among a sea of supporters than it is in a private box or in a restaurant – or you simply refuse to serve them anymore. I do think it's a bit of a nonsense.

10 THE TEN-POINT PLAN

I've always believed that television needs football as much as football needs television. No other sport in the world commands the kind of viewing figures football does. Highlights packages of games had been a staple part of our TV diet since the mid-1960s with the BBC's seminal *Match of the Day* and then ITV's *The Big Match*. The transmission of live games had been sporadic over the years, but a deal was struck for the start of the 1983–84 season to show them on a more regular basis. Tottenham Hotspur versus Nottingham Forest kicked things off on ITV at the start of October, and Manchester United featured in the BBC's first live league match two months later.

It's strange to think that, back in the 1980s, and in view of the fortunes football makes from television now, clubs were extremely nervous about live matches being shown because of what it might mean for attendances. Would the fans still turn up on a wet and windy afternoon if they could watch the game on telly in the comfort of their own home? This concern led to a compensation plan: if you appeared on live television at your own ground you could be compensated for any loss of revenue, and this was calculated depending on your average home gate. In time, however, people realized that being on TV was actually an advert and didn't affect attendances. Pretty soon afterwards clubs realized they couldn't live without live matches; even if it did affect the gate, the money pouring in from television was so huge it dwarfed any compensation anyway. So the compensation plan was eventually abandoned.

The original deal was for two years and for ten live matches to be shared equally between the BBC and ITV, but pretty quickly the broadcasters realized what a ratings winner they had in live football and wanted to show more. So, early in 1985, the clubs were approached about a new contract. However, many of my fellow chairmen, like me, had a major problem with this, since it was our belief that the BBC and ITV, who were rivals to screen matches, were in fact conspiring to keep the value of the rights down. Their negotiators would sometimes turn up at meetings in the same cab, and they'd send us almost identically worded letters. There was absolutely no competition when it came to bidding for the rights to football; the BBC and ITV effectively acted as a cartel.

Several meetings took place over the next few months between the clubs and representatives of the BBC and ITV. These were generally heated affairs. The new proposal on the table was a four-year deal worth an initial £3.8 million, a figure that would rise by 6 per cent in both the second and third year and by 8 per cent in the final year. This was for sixteen live league matches per season, plus the semi-finals of the League Cup and the final itself. There was also an option to show an unspecified number of live regional matches on their regional television stations. The clubs were not at all happy with this. I remember the most vociferous among us being Robert Maxwell, chairman of Oxford United. He thought the whole thing was absolute nonsense and that the clubs were grossly underselling football. In his view the figure should be closer to £10 million a year, a fantastical sum of money we all thought, although in light of recent TV deals it sounds pretty paltry now. However unpleasant my recent dealings with Maxwell had been, one can't fault his tough business stance on this issue and also his foresight into how much football was worth to the TV companies. Indeed, so formidable was his presence that at one stage the TV negotiators refused to attend meetings if Maxwell was in the same room.

Maxwell's figure of £10 million may have been plucked out of the sky for all we knew, but what had been made plain to us during these discussions was that none of us had any idea what televised football was worth. Irving Scholar sought out independent advice and brought in Saatchi & Saatchi to do a study. The report, which took into consideration the extra advertising revenue grossed through the transmission of football matches, was hugely important because for the first time we had some idea what the value of football was. All we'd known before was whatever BBC or ITV were prepared to pay us and that they were obviously trying to keep the figure low. But what they were offering and what we were increasingly coming to realize were our true worth were two different things. We still had to break the grip of the BBC and ITV and make them bid separately.

Any hope that the TV companies would come back to us with a bigger offer was soon scuppered. Instead they played hardball. So it was a stalemate and the 1985–86 season began with no football at all on the nation's television screens for the first time since *Match of the Day* started back in 1964.

The standoff with the TV companies had caused serious implications for many clubs. Not only had the television revenue dried up but clubs weren't getting ground advertising revenue either. Sponsors want television. If somebody's sponsoring a game they want their boards to appear on television. To be frank, all of this left something of a bad taste in the mouth. Back in those days all ninety-two clubs in the Football League got paid the same for their television rights, £25,000, whether they were Manchester United or Stockport, Liverpool or Tranmere. This made no sense whatsoever because it was always the high-profile games involving the top clubs that the vast majority of viewers wanted to watch. We brought in the audiences, we brought in the revenue, and so not unreasonably we felt we had the right to a better share.

The top clubs had other complaints, too. We felt that we had little control over how the league was run, that the voting system was unbalanced and that it favoured the lower divisions. It was very difficult to introduce rules favoured by the top tier because the other divisions would gang up and block it. A good example of this was when we wanted to put the players' names on the back of our shirts. It seems such an obvious idea now but there was resistance to it and it was voted out. Probably the resistance was due to the fact that the lower-division clubs didn't want to spend money putting names on shirts. They weren't looking at the commercial value of it, as we were; they were looking at the extra expense involved. And you can understand why. But there was a very definite sense here that the tail was wagging the dog.

This was by no means a new feeling. While the summer of 1985 had been a traumatic period in the English game – with the Heysel disaster and its loss of thirty-nine lives, the Bradford City stadium fire that claimed the lives of fifty-six people, hooliganism and falling gate receipts – discontent had been festering since 1983 when the Football League commissioned Sir Norman Chester to look into the structure of football. The report came up with certain recommendations and talked about revamping the divisions. It wasn't a call for a complete breakaway, but it talked about change in the game.

Taking our cue from the Chester Report, Irving Scholar of Tottenham, David Dein of Arsenal, Everton's Philip Carter, Peter Robinson of Liverpool and I met on 29 September 1985 to discuss the very real possibility of forming a breakaway super league. Put simply, we wanted to control our own destiny. The Football League was too cumbersome. It had been in existence for almost a hundred years and in that time had hardly changed, and change was needed. We had to make a start somewhere, and the only way we could do so was by exercising our muscle and challenging things. But we always knew we had to bring other top teams on board. To that end, representatives of Newcastle, Manchester City and Southampton were also invited to our discussion.

It wasn't a question of us necessarily wanting to break away. We wanted to get control within the existing league. Certainly that was my view. I was all for keeping the league, provided we had our autonomy and were happy with our fair share of the income and voting – that's all I wanted at that stage. So Philip Carter, Irving and I were nominated by the First Division to negotiate with the rest of the league to see if a solution could be found.

The negotiations, which were held in secret, were heated at times and usually ended with everyone at loggerheads. Finally, on 18 December at the Post House Hotel, Heathrow, a deal was thrashed out. Sitting round the table, as well as Philip Carter, Irving and me representing the First Division, were Ron Noades of Crystal Palace, Lawrie McMenemy of Sunderland and Bill Fox of Blackburn on behalf of the Second Division, while the other divisions were represented by Aldershot's Reg Driver, Martin Lange of Brentford and Ian Jones from Doncaster Rovers. Gordon Taylor of the Professional Footballers' Association was also brought in, largely to act as mediator.

After six long hours of discussion we all reached what became known as the Heathrow Agreement, or the Ten-Point Plan as it was also called. Realizing the importance of keeping the league together, the lower divisions were prepared to accede to most of our demands. Importantly, the agreement created a new sharing formula for television and sponsorship money: 50 per cent to the First Division, 25 per cent to the Second, 25 per cent to the Third and Fourth. The voting system was also changed in our favour. We may have still needed some support from the Second Division, but basically it made it a lot more favourable. There was a chance now that we could get things altered if we wanted to.

Significantly, the First Division was to be cut from twenty-two clubs to twenty, while the Second Division would be increased to twenty-four, along with the introduction of play-offs to determine promotion places. This change would be phased in over a two-year period. Another thing we hadn't been happy about for years was the 4 per cent league levy. On every league game 4 per cent of the gate receipts went into a league pool, which was shared out at the end of the season to every club. Obviously this affected the bigger clubs more because we had the bigger attendances. Thanks to the Ten-Point Plan we managed to reduce the levy to 3 per cent. There was also an improvement in the amount retained by each competing club in FA and League Cup matches from 33 per cent to 45 per cent.

In many ways the Ten-Point Plan was a compromise. We didn't get everything we wanted but we got enough to keep the league together. The breakaway league was the nuclear option. If you don't give us these changes we'll press the button, that was the rationale behind our position. Had the First Division clubs not got most of what they wanted we might have been prepared to go down that route. Whenever negotiations got tricky the threat was always there: are you going to force us to go? So perhaps the breakaway that eventually happened in 1992 with the creation of the Premier League could have happened six years earlier if the Ten-Point Plan had not been agreed.

To confuse matters, the two biggest clubs in Scotland, Rangers and Celtic, expressed a desire to come down and join our league if we decided to break away. But there was no way that clubs towards the bottom end of the First Division would allow these two teams in at their own expense. In my opinion that idea was always a non-starter, from a safety point of view, if nothing else. I don't think the police would have been very happy due to the potential for crowd trouble.

The Ten-Point Plan was put into effect from the 1986–87 season and was a success for many years. I don't think the smaller clubs suffered as a consequence of the larger clubs exercising more power. They still got a proportion of TV monies, still received some of the league levy, still earned money from the Pools companies for the use of their league fixtures, and still got to play against bigger clubs in cup competitions.

Two days after the Heathrow Agreement, our impasse with the TV companies was finally broken when we accepted what turned out to be a dismal £1.5 million for the privilege of BBC and ITV covering the rest of the season. It was a cobbled-together agreement, although something was better than nothing. But you could see the control the TV companies had over us. We were still determined to break it.

⚽

The lack of televised football at the start of the 1985–86 season was a shame because United had enjoyed an unbelievable start, winning our first ten games. I think everybody began to get carried away: ten wins on the bounce had only been done once before, and everybody thought we were on course for our first league title since 1967.

Amazingly, we had spurned the chance in pre-season to get our hands on one of the hottest strikers in the country. I had received a call from Jon Holmes, who was Gary Lineker's agent, and Gary had been scoring goals for fun at Leicester, in quite a poor side really. He was a highly coveted player. Holmes told me that he and Gary were travelling up to Liverpool. 'Gary is about to sign for Everton,' said Holmes. 'He would prefer to come to you, but we need a quick decision, if not he's going to sign for Everton this evening.' Whatever I was working on at that moment I immediately put aside and told Jon to leave it with me. Unfortunately, Ron had already left home and we had to track him down; remember there were no mobile phones back then. Eventually I got hold of him and said, 'Ron, Jon Holmes has been on the phone. Lineker is on his way to sign for Everton tonight. He'll come to us if we want him. Do you want him?' And I'll always remember Ron's reply. 'Well, I've got Whiteside, Davenport, Stapleton and Hughes,' he said. 'No, I don't really need him.' And that was that. I rang Jon Holmes back and told him that I appreciated the opportunity but we already had four strikers. So we turned down Lineker and he went off to the then-champions Everton, where he was a huge success; he nearly helped them win the league again that season, before they sold him on to Barcelona.

In hindsight it was obviously the wrong decision not to go for Lineker, but I don't think a chairman of a football club can ever say to a manager who he's got to have and who he can't have. It's always the decision of the manager, even if you think it's wrong. You can offer your opinion. I would say to a manager: the offer is there, do you want the player or not? It's up to him. I think it would be totally irresponsible to force a player on a manager that he doesn't want. If you end up bringing a player into the club that the manager doesn't like and ends up not playing, then you've wasted your money. Besides, I don't think any manager worth his salt would accept the chairman telling him what player he has to play.

After fifteen matches we were still unbeaten and sitting top of the table. Then we started picking up injuries and our form slumped badly. Robson was the first to go in mid-October, and when he eventually fought his way back into the team in January he dislocated his shoulder and was out until pretty much the last few games. Robson's absence had a detrimental impact on our midfield because his natural replacement, Remi Moses, was also out injured, along with other key players Strachan and Olsen.

Another problem was the loss of form of Mark Hughes, who had been prolific at the start of the campaign. What the fans and media didn't know was that since the beginning of 1986 his agent had been in discussions with Barcelona about a possible transfer, and I'm sure Mark's uncertainty about his future impacted on his performances on the pitch. The eventual sale of Hughes to Barcelona in the summer was hugely controversial and the fans were incensed – Hughes was an enormously popular player, something of a cult hero who had risen through the youth ranks and been very influential for us.

The truth is we didn't want Hughes to go. Ron Atkinson never said to me, 'I want to sell Mark Hughes.' But it was a difficult situation because Barcelona had shown an interest and Mark's contract was up at the end of the season. We couldn't run the risk of him leaving on what would have been an extremely modest fee in the region of £200,000, based on the European multiplier system, which was the same thing as our football tribunal and was calculated from the player's wages. Because Mark's were low at the time, Barcelona could have got him for just £200,000. To protect ourselves, we presented Mark and his agent with a new contract, which included an increase in wages and a 'buyout clause' that they insisted on. They also accepted the new wages, which we were happy to pay because it meant we had control of the player on a new contract. Barcelona eventually paid the 'buyout', which was £1.8 million. I took the brunt of criticism for Mark's move – everybody blamed me – yet I didn't want him to go. He was the last player I wanted to leave – but I also needed to protect the club and if we'd just left it the way it was and let him get to the end of his contract, we'd have got very little. So I couldn't win on that one. In the end it was Mark's decision to leave. He had the option to stay and complete his new contract.

The season ended miserably for United with a draw away at Watford. Ron and I were both in the gents' at the end of the match when Ron turned to me. 'Chairman,' he said, 'I think maybe my time's up. Maybe it's time to go.' I told him not to rush into anything, to just think about it. Okay, we were in a slump at that moment, but I thought it was too early for him to think about quitting. Yes, it had been a disappointing season, ending up in fourth place, a depressing twelve points behind champions Liverpool, but that great start we made showed what we could do as a team when we were at full strength.

11 GOODBYE RON, HELLO FERGIE

Just two days before the last game of the season, on 1 May 1986, the Manchester United museum opened for the first time to the public. The idea of a museum came initially from my uncle, Denzil Haroun, and had been under consideration for a number of years. As a rule the club didn't keep a great deal of memorabilia. We had a few things on show in various lounges or stored away, items like programmes and photographs, but as building work began on the museum we had staff going out to buy all manner of things, and we placed adverts in the match-day programme and in local newspapers asking for material. We also had a lot of items donated to us from families of players that had represented the club in the past. We ended up with an amazing collection, including items from players who played for us in our first FA Cup final and when we won the league for the very first time in 1908. We even managed to get our hands on material going back to the 1880s. The part of the museum that has the most emotional resonance for me is the Munich section because we have items such as the passports of some of the players and the blazer worn by Duncan Edwards on the plane on show, and other pieces that were taken from the wreckage.

The museum's grand opening was a memorable occasion and I was very pleased to cut the ribbon on the £100,000 development. Sir Matt was on hand, along with present and former players, and special guests including Duncan Edwards' mother, who came to see the display cabinet in the museum specially dedicated to her son. Later on, the museum was to play an important role in making Old Trafford a leisure destination during the week, not just match days. Whether you went on the stadium tour, or to the museum, or had a meal at the Red Café, it was all part of a conscious effort to make Manchester United a special day out.

So successful did the museum become that after ten years it had outgrown itself and at a cost of £4 million was substantially enlarged; it is now spread over three levels. In April 1998 we invited Pelé to come over to Manchester to open the new museum for us. I had never met him before so it was a privilege when we had dinner together and I must say I enjoyed his company enormously. He's a very likeable character. Bobby Charlton told me that Pelé is late for everything, but when he eventually arrives he's very engaging. Being the great star he is and lauded wherever he goes, he's got that aura of confidence about him. Yet he wasn't at all standoffish but jovial and quite lively. And I was delighted when he agreed to loan the museum some of his shirts and medals for a special section we put into the museum in his honour.

The mid-1980s saw a lot of development around Old Trafford. Something like £2.5 million was spent during this period. There was substantial development at the scoreboard end of the ground, a lot of new seating was put in, a new ticket office was built, along with a new office complex, a replacement floodlighting system and a new main entrance. Whenever we made plans for a new stand, or any other improvements to the stadium, I always liked to get involved with the architects. I saw that as one of my responsibilities. I'd spend hours, days, going through all the nitty-gritty detail, planning everything: how many executive seats we wanted there; how many extra boxes; whether they were going to be five-seater, six-seater or eight-seater boxes; whether catering should be in the boxes or in the central lounge; was an executive suite wanted in there?

The 'family stand' was also officially opened. With hooliganism still blighting the game I felt this was an important move because I wanted to make Old Trafford a more friendly and family-orientated place to watch football. I believed it was quite an innovative step, with adults only gaining admission to the stand if accompanied by a child. I also thought it would be an encouragement to the United supporters of the future.

With the ground undergoing something of a facelift, we did not neglect the pitch and installed an under-soil heating system. For a number of years there had been considerable discussion over whether First Division clubs should all have under-soil heating because it was ridiculous in this day and age that a football match could be cancelled because of adverse weather conditions. This situation had happened far too many times at Old Trafford, much to our embarrassment, but we wanted to get our pitch right first before investing in under-soil heating. That took quite a bit of time, due to the fact that we had to re-lay the surface several times. Finally we were in a position to install under-soil heating, only for the system we chose to prove a dismal failure. It had to be dug up, and the whole rigmarole of finding another system to replace it gone through again.

These are the kinds of problems you face and have to deal with as a chief executive. It was an intensive job and with my having a young family at the time it was sometimes difficult juggling work and home life. I got married in 1968 when I was in the meat business, which was more of a nine-to-five job. But from 1980, when I became United chairman, I had to be away from home much more. During the season I would be working weekends, of course, and sometimes we'd be playing midweek. There was all the travel for away matches and Europe, too, along with all the league meetings in London. I was probably a bit selfish that I didn't always consider the impact it might have at home. But if you're married to the job, that's one of the sacrifices you make. I made the decision that I was going to go full time at United and make it a success. I had my goals. In the end the rewards were very good, but it was tough at the beginning. I did miss out on a lot of home life, and if you were to ask my wife and children they would probably say they missed out on some family life, too – birthdays and other important dates. I did try to balance things – you always do – but I rarely got home before seven at night and very often when the children were young they were already in bed. Most businessmen have to go through a similar thing. It can be very challenging at times.

In the summer of 1986 Ron went off to the World Cup in Mexico to work as a pundit for ITV. I understood why he had agreed to take this job because Ron was a well-known media personality, but I felt that his place ought to have been at Old Trafford planning for the next season. When he came back, for example, Ron said he wanted to buy Terry Butcher, but everyone on the board, not just me, felt we should have been doing that in May, June or July, rather than near the start of the season – it was all a bit too rushed. So that transfer didn't happen. Then we made a dismal start to the new campaign, losing a lot of games and finding ourselves in mid-table. The team was struggling and Ron wasn't getting the response from the dressing room that he had when he arrived.

The final straw came on 4 November after a 4–1 hammering away at Southampton in the Littlewoods Cup. I knew instinctively it was the end for Ron. That evening Mike Edelson and I flew back to Manchester in a private plane deep in conversation about what to do next. The following day, we called a meeting for one o'clock in my office. Mike was with me and we called in Bobby Charlton and Maurice Watkins. It was then that we decided to make the change. My candidate to replace Ron was Alex Ferguson. My encounter with him during the Strachan negotiation had left a huge impression, and I'd had my eye on Alex for a while. You couldn't miss his achievements with Aberdeen: a nine-trophy haul, including three Scottish league titles, during an eight-year reign that saw him break up the age-long dominance of the big two Glasgow clubs, Celtic and Rangers. But what really put Alex on the map was beating Real Madrid to win the European Cup Winners' Cup in 1983.

My thinking was: *If he can do that at Aberdeen, what can he achieve at Manchester United?* What's more, he was young and ambitious and had a reputation for being a strong manager. You could just see the fire and enthusiasm in him.

When I brought up Alex's name it was met with unreserved enthusiasm. Nobody needed convincing that he was the right man. One other name that did come into our deliberations was Terry Venables, who had guided Barcelona to the European Cup final a few months earlier, having won the Spanish league the previous season. But he wasn't discussed for long; Alex Ferguson was always my preferred choice and we quickly agreed to go for him.

The first thing we needed to do was to find out whether Alex was of the same mind before we went ahead and dismissed Ron. The one thing I wanted to avoid was a repeat of what happened back in 1981 when Lawrie McMenemy, Bobby Robson and Ron Saunders all turned me down and I was left scrambling round to find a replacement for Dave Sexton. I didn't want to go through all that again. That's why it was so important to find out if Alex was willing to come on board before we made any official approach to Aberdeen.

But how to make the approach. I couldn't very well get on the phone to Aberdeen and say, 'Hello, this is Martin Edwards from Manchester United. Can I speak with Alex Ferguson?' It was Mike Edelson who suggested putting on a fake Scottish accent claiming to be Alan Gordon, Strachan's accountant. When the receptionist started asking personal questions about his wife and family we thought we might get rumbled, but Mike eventually got through to Alex, explained who he really was and passed the phone over to me. I quickly introduced myself and asked if he would be willing to meet up with us. I didn't have to spell out anything; Alex knew straightaway what I meant. Why else would I be calling him? He said yes and we arranged to come up that evening to see him. Our rendezvous point was the car park at Hamilton services on the M74.

At 4 p.m. that afternoon Bobby, Maurice and I all piled into Mike's Jaguar XJ6 and made our way north. It was around 7 p.m. when we arrived and it was pitch black. Because Alex didn't have a car phone we'd had to exchange registration numbers in order to recognize each other in the dark. It was all a bit cloak and dagger. When we spotted Alex I jumped out of the Jaguar and climbed into the seat next to him. Mike followed on behind, just barely keeping up. Our destination was Alex's sister-in-law's house in Bishopbriggs, on the outskirts of Glasgow, where a very nice spread had been laid out for us. After the usual pleasantries we told Alex that we wanted him to be the next manager of Manchester United and he said that he was interested. We didn't have to pitch the club to him. Everybody in Scotland knew Manchester United and their reputation because of Matt Busby, the style of football that Matt played and the Busby Babes; Alex was steeped in football history. It was not a hard sell.

And that was it really; it wasn't an interview. When we met Alex we weren't going up there to judge him. We knew him already and we knew we wanted him. We just wanted to make certain he would take the job. We didn't discuss terms or anything like that. And Alex didn't make any demands of us. Although I do remember him telling us that his chairman, Dick Donald, had once said to him, 'Alex, the only club you are leaving here for is Manchester United', because a few years before Tottenham had tried to prise him away and he had turned them down. When Alex told us that, we knew this deal was going to happen; we knew that Dick Donald wouldn't stop him coming to United.

We drove back to Manchester that night in a buoyant mood. But there was grim work to be done in the morning and I wasn't looking forward to it. It was now 6 November. Ron was out training with the team when word was sent out that we wanted to see him in the boardroom. I think by Ron's reaction when we told him of our decision to let him go he wasn't totally surprised. I think it must have been on his mind and he had considered the possibility. He accepted it with a single shrug and a placatory handshake. It wasn't an easy decision because after five years we had built up a good relationship. But the club had to come first. That evening Ron invited all his players and staff round to his house for a farewell drink.

I have to say I thought Ron took his dismissal very well and he has always appreciated the fact that he was given the opportunity to manage

Manchester United. As far as I know he has never held any personal grudge against me or the club. Whenever I've seen him he's always been very pleasant and courteous, and I've never heard him ever be critical about the fact that we didn't retain him. I always thought Ron and I got on pretty well, and I think he enjoyed his years at Old Trafford; it was an exciting period both in the style of football we played and in the players he brought in. Ron was attack minded: he liked wingers, he liked the team to play attacking football and always encouraged the players to express themselves. I felt he did a good job; we were never out of the top four and won two FA cups. But in the end, third or fourth place wasn't enough. We were close but just not quite there. It needed Alex to take us that one step further. So I don't look on Ron's tenure as a failure at all. It was a stepping-stone to great things in the 1990s.

That afternoon Maurice Watkins and I caught a flight back up to Aberdeen for a meeting with Dick Donald. Donald had been chairman of Aberdeen since 1970 and was quite a robust man, a little bit imposing, but a fatherly figure with a rosy bald head. I remember Alex telling me that he was a former world champion ballroom dancer. I'd met Dick once before and got on well with him. Maurice and I were very courteous: 'Mr Donald,' we said, 'we've come here to say that we'd like to formally approach you concerning Alex Ferguson.' I don't think he was surprised. He'd probably always known that one day he'd get a call from us. As a matter of fact, his son Ian, who was a key member of the Pittodrie board, had played a few times for Manchester United, as left back, and I think that helped a bit, too. Also, Dick had a great respect for Manchester United, and for Matt Busby as well, and must have thought, *Well, it's the biggest club in England coming for Alex and I can't stand in his way.* I got the impression that Alex was a bit like a son to Dick. So the negotiation went quite smoothly. One thing Dick was concerned about was the future of Archie Knox, who was Alex's number 2 and confidant; he feared that if they both walked out at the same time it would leave the club in a bit of a mess. It was agreed that Archie wouldn't go immediately, but Dick realized that Archie would eventually follow Alex, which indeed he did three weeks later.

It was all done very quickly: we identified Alex as our next manager on 5 November and by the morning of the 7th I was giving Alex a tour of the training ground and introducing him to all the staff and players. Then at 2.30 p.m. that afternoon he was introduced to the press. I've been asked many times if we made an illegal approach for Alex. Technically it was, but it was the sensible way of going about things. We had to make sure Alex wanted to come before we sacked Ron. At the end of the day we didn't do anything underhand, all we asked of Alex was would he be willing to come if I could negotiate his release, which I did. I then went up to see Dick Donald to ask permission to speak to Alex formally and we were given that permission. Obviously we had to agree compensation because Alex was under contract and we arrived at the figure of £60,000. It was an amicable solution.

When you bring a new manager into a club your hope is always that they will stay a long time and build a dynasty. I never thought in the short term, always long term, both in the appointment of the manager and of the players we brought in. Of course, there is inevitably that desire for instant success, but you can't always achieve it. When Alex became manager we hadn't won the league since 1967, and it was my view that with Alex being a young manager, and me a young chairman, we had the chance to lay a solid foundation for future success.

In hindsight, though, taking on the manager's role at United was probably a much harder job for Alex than he thought it was going to be. It took four years to win a trophy and seven years to win the league, and I imagine that Alex in his own mind would have expected to achieve those objectives sooner. Maybe he didn't know the English game and the players in the English league as well as he thought he did. And there is quite a step up from Scottish to English football in terms of the pace and quality of the game, although in those days it probably wasn't as great as it is today. With the money currently in the Premier League and the players the Premier League can attract because of this, the gap has definitely widened. Look at Rangers, who aren't the force they once were, having dropped down three divisions in 2012 (although they are now back in the top division), or at Celtic, who if they do get into the

Champions League rarely get beyond the qualifying stage. It's simply because the money isn't there. Coming to England, with the growing divide between the two countries, must have been quite a culture shock for Alex and meant it took longer than he anticipated to bring success to Manchester United

As I remember it, the reaction of both fans and the media to the arrival of Alex was mixed. There certainly wasn't a sense of euphoria; I don't think the supporters knew much about him. It wasn't like a big name today such as José Mourinho suddenly becoming manager of Manchester United. One thing Alex did have, though, was a reputation for being combative. In some ways that's not a bad thing in a manager, as long as it's controlled. It was Gordon Strachan who warned the other players about Alex's temper and all those flying teacups: 'Bloody hell, things are going to change a bit now,' he said. 'You think it was tough before; wait till you get this fella down here.' Poor Gordon must have thought he'd got away from Alex after their time together at Aberdeen; now after just one season at Old Trafford he'd turned up as manager again.

The teacups didn't start flying straightaway, although Alex was strong on discipline right from the beginning. He intensified training, wanted the players to look presentable – short haircuts, clean-shaven, and when on club duty to sport formal blazers. He expected every player to conduct himself in a professional manner and behave in a way befitting a club of the size and image of Manchester United. He was quite strong on all that, and as the manager you need to be because if you allow standards to slip you're going to have problems elsewhere. So I was fully supportive of him on this.

All a chairman can do for their manager is be supportive, especially in terms of team building. Alex had to find his feet, find out what he'd got, and that probably took him the rest of that opening season. Don't forget, Alex was thrown in at the deep end. We weren't well placed in the league when he arrived; we were four places off the bottom and eventually managed to finish eleventh. It's always a gamble changing managers well into a season, but desperate times call for drastic measures. So it was a difficult situation that Alex had to cope with and in those early days I would have regular meetings with him. If he had any problems he would always come to talk to me. Most of the conversations between us revolved around players: who he wanted in his squad and who he didn't want.

Pretty soon Alex identified a whole bunch of Ron Atkinson's stalwarts as surplus to requirements: Frank Stapleton, Arthur Albiston, Kevin Moran and Graeme Hogg all went. More often than not you're going to take a hit on those players going out because you've paid transfer fees for them. But if the current manager doesn't rate them he will want to sell them and it's not as easy to make money selling players on the market compared to when somebody really wants them and makes an approach. If Alex wanted a player it was my job to go and negotiate the transfer.

Two players on Alex's wish list in that summer of 1987 were Viv Anderson and Brian McClair, and they became his first signings for Manchester United. Viv was playing for Arsenal at the time but had agreed to come to us. I offered £250,000 for him. The Arsenal board wanted £500,000, but I stuck with my original offer and it went to a tribunal, just as it had done with Frank Stapleton. Once again the outcome was the same: I got the player for exactly the price I offered. Although this was the second time in recent years Arsenal had taken us to a tribunal, I never fell out with the club. They obviously had higher valuations of both players than I did, and if they wanted to go to a tribunal that was fine: you accept the rules of the game. But it's quite interesting that in both cases I was spot-on with my valuations.

Brian McClair came from Celtic and had been the leading scorer in the Scottish league in what turned out to be his last season. We paid £850,000 for him, the figure determined once again by a tribunal. When McClair first arrived he came as an out-and-out striker and played up front. Indeed, in his first season he was the first player since George Best to score over twenty league goals for United in a single season. Eventually, however, he ended up in midfield and went on to win a lot of medals during the eleven years he was with us as a player. Then, after cutting his teeth on the coaching staff of Motherwell and Blackburn, Brian returned to United in 2001 as reserve-team coach before eventually taking over control of the club's academy players. Both as a player and as a coach,

McClair gave great service to Manchester United.

McClair and Viv Anderson were great additions to the team but that summer unfortunately we missed out on one of England's brightest talents. Over at Watford, Graham Taylor knew that it was only a matter of time before his exciting young winger, John Barnes, was snapped up by one of the top teams. He called Alex and offered the player to him for £900,000. Alex said no, preferring to stick with current winger Jesper Olsen. I know Alex has always regretted that decision. To be fair to him, he had only been at United a few months, not long enough to judge whether Jesper was the better option. Jesper was perhaps a bit too lightweight for the rigours of English football. Barnes on the other hand was much more suited to it and of course went on to have a brilliant career at Liverpool. Maybe the Barnes deal came too early. Had it been a year later I'm sure we would have made a move for him.

Midway through the season, in December, we signed defender Steve Bruce for £825,000. I remember a few years before we signed Steve seeing him play in the Cup for Gillingham against Everton at Goodison Park and he was absolutely magnificent, racing up and down the pitch, in defence and attack. When I told Ron Atkinson that we ought to be in for him, Ron agreed that Steve had potential. The next thing we heard was that he'd gone to Norwich. Then Alex saw him in action and wanted him. Robert Chase was the chairman of Norwich at the time and he wasn't the easiest person to deal with, so it was a difficult negotiation. The real problem, though, was his medical: it was horrendous. Steve's knees were especially bad, and the recommendation from the Old Trafford medical team was that we should not take the player. I rang Alex and explained the situation. 'Look,' Alex said, 'all I can tell you is that he plays every bloody game for Norwich.' So we decided to take a chance and never regretted it. Steve never let us down; he was a terrific stalwart and rarely missed a game. Very often he appeared for us when he was injured or in pain and played through it. He was a tough character. He just wanted to play football.

With McClair banging in the goals, United managed to finish runners-up in Alex's second season, his first full year in charge, but we were nine points behind the eventual winners, Liverpool. Obviously to come second was a huge improvement over the previous season's poor position, but really we were nowhere near Liverpool.

I'm sometimes asked if Alex understood the challenge facing him when he first arrived at United. Most certainly he did. If you remember, it was very early on in his United career that he gave his now famous quote about wanting to knock Liverpool off their perch. I think that was his driving ambition. He wanted to make Manchester United number one.

Liverpool were winning practically everything and were really rubbing our noses in it. And I had to go to league meetings with Sir John Smith, the Liverpool chairman, and Peter Robinson, their chief executive. I remember David Dein saying to Sir John once, when Liverpool had won the league that weekend and we had a league meeting on the following Tuesday, 'Congratulations', and Sir John replied, 'What for?' 'Winning the league,' said David. 'Oh that,' replied Sir John. That's how dominant Liverpool were.

Going back to 1983, my first Wembley final as chairman had been against Liverpool and Sir John had approached me at lunch. 'Martin,' he said. 'Would you like me to show you the way to the dressing rooms?' I didn't like to say I'd seen them a few times when my father was chairman so I just said, 'Thank you, Sir John.' After lunch he came to get me and we walked down the touchline together and I got terrible abuse from the Liverpool supporters. When we got to the dressing rooms Sir John turned to me and said, 'Do you know, I've done this walk more times than I've walked to the bottom of my garden.' It was that kind of attitude that I wanted to overcome. Liverpool was the arch-enemy and we were constantly striving to beat them and dominate the league in the way they had been doing for years. That was always my ambition. Alex and I had that in common.

12 FIGHTING ON ALL FRONTS

On 8 February 1988 Tottenham's Irving Scholar, Peter Robinson of Liverpool and I were invited to London for dinner by Trevor Phillips, head of the Football League commercial department. The reason for the meeting was not made clear to us and we arrived completely in the dark. During dinner Phillips revealed that the league had received an offer from British Satellite Broadcasting (BSB) to cover live league matches on an exclusive basis and he wanted our views on it. While we welcomed the chance to at last break up the cartel operated by the BBC and ITV, we expressed extreme caution. We thought it was far too risky. BSB was still in its infancy, its audience share was small and there was no guarantee that the new channel would succeed.

In spite of our reservations the league was determined to press ahead and sell its rights to BSB and, after receiving overwhelming support from most of the ninety-two clubs, announced the deal to the press on 12 May. The figures involved were certainly impressive: £200 million over the next ten years. BSB wanted to launch its own dedicated sports channel and had identified football, along with movies, as the subscription driver it needed to secure an audience. But a spanner was about to be thrown into the works.

Over at London Weekend Television, then the ITV network franchise holder for Greater London and the Home Counties at weekends, their new head of programmes, Greg Dyke, saw the BSB deal as a major blow. Facing the prospect of no football on terrestrial television for the foreseeable future he contacted me and the other chairmen of the division's biggest clubs. We agreed to meet him in London on 16 June. In attendance was me, Irving Scholar, David Dein and Sir John Smith, along with Peter Robinson, and Philip Carter. It was here that Dyke unveiled his plan to disrupt the BSB deal by signing us all up exclusively for ITV. As far as Dyke was concerned, BSB could have the rest. It was an audacious gambit. Then Dyke played his ace. As it stood, the BSB offer was worth something like £150,000 a year to each of our clubs. ITV, said Dyke, was prepared to pay £1 million a year to each of the big five clubs for a period of four years. It was an extraordinary amount of money and an affirmation that the power base in the English game lay with the big clubs. After years of feeling cheated out of our fair share, at last we were being offered the type of money that we believed football was really worth. We also realized that we could not realistically accept the offer without upsetting all the other clubs in the First Division. So Dyke asked us to suggest a further five clubs who we felt should be included.

Pleased with our response, Dyke wrote to all five of us on 23 June with a formal offer. From there things began to speed up. On 6 July I chaired a meeting at Old Trafford during which Dyke put forward a new set of proposals that extended to ten First Division clubs. With the number of clubs involved now doubled, we realized that this would inevitably mean a reduction in money. Indeed, the offer now stood at £600,000 over four years. The ten clubs were made up of the original five plus Aston Villa, Newcastle, Nottingham Forest, Sheffield Wednesday and West Ham. ITV agreed to televise up to twenty live games in a season. Also, in the final year of the contract, ITV would have an option to negotiate for television broadcasting rights for the four years beyond 1991–92 and a right to match the best bid.

In an attempt to extricate ourselves from the BSB deal we all drafted a letter to the secretary of the Football League. It read: 'We have no wish to participate in the proposed arrangements with BSB, but, on the contrary, intend to make our own separate arrangements with alternative broadcasters. Please confirm that the league will not place any obstacles in the way of the making and implementation of any independent arrangements by the signatories to this letter.' We couldn't have made our position any clearer.

Now we had to persuade the other First Division clubs that they had made the wrong decision signing up with BSB. It didn't prove too difficult as they were open to our persuasive argument that ITV was by far the more established broadcaster, was offering more money and had a national audience. And when you're trying to sell a product, you want it to be seen by the largest possible number of people. By contrast, nobody really knew exactly where BSB was going. There were no guarantees with them. It was a brand new organization. Was it going to be around in ten years' time? Nobody knew.

As more and more First Division clubs moved into our camp, the reverberations were felt right across the English game and Football League chiefs came out fighting. They declared we had no right to negotiate our own TV deals, and that any deal we wished to reach had, by virtue of the league regulations, to go through the Football League management committee. They even went so far as to call us rebels, and when you think about it, we, the five big clubs, were challenging the authority of the Football League, so I suppose you can understand why. They also tried to take out an injunction against us from negotiating with ITV. Legal documents were flying around. But behind closed doors they were in a panic, fearing we might break away and form a super league, which in fact was something we were once again considering and had taken legal advice on.

In a bid to pacify us and hopefully bring us back into the fold, Graham Kelly, secretary of the Football League, wrote to both me and my fellow 'rebel' chairmen on 12 July. His suggestion was that 80 per cent of the BSB monies could go to the First Division clubs, with 10 per cent to the Second Division and 10 per cent to the Third and Fourth Divisions collectively. The gesture was too late; we had no intention of backing down now.

On 2 August I received a letter from BSB confirming that they had withdrawn their offer to televise football. Although they still had the support of the Second, Third and Fourth Divisions, without the top teams they knew that they simply didn't have an attractive enough package. With ITV the only player in town, a deal was agreed on 8 August when the representatives of all the clubs in the Football League gathered at the Cumberland Hotel in London. It granted ITV exclusive rights to show up to eighteen league matches per season, along with a recorded highlights package. The agreement was worth £11 million a year over a period of four years.

As far as I was concerned we made the right decision going with ITV, especially when you look at the financial trouble BSB got into just a few years later, which necessitated them having to merge with their great rival, Sky. We certainly stuck to our guns and forced the Football League to change their minds on a deal we never had any faith in. Looking back on it today, if we hadn't been able to persuade the Football League not to go with BSB, the breakaway of the top clubs to form the Premier League may very well have happened back in 1988.

⚽

Back in 1985 United invested in a local basketball team, the Warrington Vikings, later renamed The Manchester Giants. If you look at all the top teams in Europe, such as Real Madrid and Barcelona, also a lot of the Eastern European clubs, they've all got a basketball team that competes in their national basketball leagues. So when we were approached to buy the Vikings I felt that it would be an interesting addition, and we ran it for three years, during which time the team became national champions.

While the team itself had been relatively cheap to buy, the stars of the English basketball league were mainly American players who hadn't made the cut back home so had come over here, and some of them were on relatively big wages. Unfortunately, we didn't get big enough crowds to make the thing pay for itself. Our supporters never really took to it because they felt we were taking our eye off the target with something that wasn't related to football. And as time went on, team losses crept up to such an extent that finally we just didn't see any long-term future in it.

The team played its home matches at the Stretford Sports Centre in Trafford, Greater Manchester, and at one point we looked at the idea of building an 8,000-seater sports hall next door to Old Trafford. The idea was that it could also be a home for United reserve-team matches and maybe the occasional pop concert. However, with the European football ban still in force we had to keep a close watch on our financial situation and I felt the cost involved was a luxury we just couldn't afford.

Over the years we had looked into numerous projects, such as the possibility of building a hotel next to the ground, pretty much where the Hotel Football stands today, but what always took precedence over such ideas was the stadium. Every time we looked at a building project of this type we said: hang on a minute, shouldn't we be using this money to improve Old Trafford or spend on the team? I'm sure if the fans had a choice they would rather we spent the money on a good striker than a hotel or a basketball stadium.

The chairman of the basketball team was a man by the name of Amer Al Midani. Born in Beirut, Al Midani was the son of a Lebanese millionaire property developer, had been to Manchester business school and also lived in the area. We felt he could be another useful addition to the board and he stayed with us for quite a few years, in that time becoming one of the club's biggest shareholders.

Al Midani wasn't the only new face in the United boardroom in 1988. Nigel Burrows worked in finance, specializing in pensions, and was introduced to me by our commercial manager, Danny McGregor. Danny thought that Burrows might be interested in buying some shares and coming on the board. I met Nigel a few times; he'd been a huge Manchester United supporter ever since he was a kid living in Blackpool, from where he would travel over for games. He was also a patron of United's luncheon club. Nigel was quite young at the time, but a successful businessman, and I saw him as a useful addition.

Another important recent development was the introduction of a club membership scheme. This was our response to the government announcing its intention to pass legislation demanding football fans be made to carry ID cards. This issue was raised at a lot of league meetings and the general view was extremely negative. Personally I was totally against it. I could understand the government's desire to stamp out hooliganism and make grounds safer but this was the wrong way to go about it. The process of everybody going through the turnstiles with ID cards felt as though it would be infringing on personal freedom, and would have been extremely time consuming. And, of course, the cost of implementing the scheme would have fallen on individual clubs. We just couldn't see how it was going to benefit anybody. We felt that a club membership scheme would be the best way to monitor who was buying the tickets. The fans weren't happy about it, probably because they felt it was another way of United taking money off them. It cost £5 to join but there were additional benefits such as reduced admission to league games and priority Cup tickets.

As the 1988–89 season began, we slipped behind our main competitors and there were early rumblings of discontent about Alex, particularly over some of the players he had brought in like Ralph Milne, who came from Bristol City at a cost of £170,000, so hardly a *galáctico*. I think the fans felt that these kinds of players just weren't Manchester United quality. We had to more or less tough it out that season.

The fans were equally unhappy with some of the players Alex seemed happy to let go, like Gordon Strachan. There had been problems between Alex and Strachan for a while, not helped by a curious series of events the previous season. Alex had made it very clear to me that he wanted to retain Strachan's services, so I met with the player and negotiated a new deal that Gordon told me he was happy to sign. The next thing I heard, Strachan had revealed his intention to leave for the French club Lens. Alex called me to ask what was going on. I told him that it was my understanding we had agreed terms with Strachan and I was more than surprised to learn that he wanted to sign for Lens. As it happened, Lens promptly sacked their manager and the deal fell through. Strachan was back at Old Trafford, but his relationship with Alex had irretrievably broken down and when Leeds made an approach Alex quickly offloaded the player.

Norman Whiteside and Paul McGrath had gone for very different reasons. From the start of his reign Alex was determined to stamp out the drinking culture that resided in the club. Whiteside and McGrath were the main culprits, but there were one or two others as well. As chairman I was never made fully aware of how serious the problem was because Ron Atkinson never raised the issue with me. McGrath later wrote a book in which he talked openly and honestly about his battle with alcoholism. Both McGrath and Whiteside were terrace favourites but that didn't save them when Alex lost patience with their drinking antics and out they both went. Whiteside was sold to Everton where, sadly, he was to last just the one season before his troublesome knees forced him to retire from the game at the age of twenty-six. McGrath fared much better, managing to rejuvenate his career at Aston Villa while at the same time become a vital member of Jack Charlton's Republic of Ireland side.

Despite results not going our way and the supporters beginning to turn, I retained full confidence in Alex. He'd begun to stamp his own mark on the team and we'd made some good signings, starting with Anderson, McClair and Bruce, even if we weren't currently getting the results we'd hoped for. Alex made another change at the back, bringing in his old goalkeeper from Aberdeen, Jim Leighton, for £450,000, even though he had promised Dick Donald not to poach any of his players. But needs must, as our current goalie Gary Walsh had suffered a bad injury and his future was uncertain. Fully aware that we could not be seen talking to the player, who was still under contract, Alex and I drove up to Scotland, having arranged to meet with Leighton just off the M73 near Cumbernauld. When Leighton spotted us, he jumped into the car and we drove to the house of one of Alex's relatives. As we passed along the quiet street, Alex pointed out the house and told us the back door was open, saying he would join us later. It was all very cloak and dagger.

There had also been the return of fan favourite Mark Hughes. He'd gone off to Barcelona but hadn't been a particular success there so they'd loaned him out to Bayern Munich. The German club were very happy with Mark, but he wanted to come back and Alex saw Hughes and McClair as our front pair. It was like the prodigal son returning; everyone was happy. We paid £1.6 million to get him back, having sold him to Barcelona for £1.8. It doesn't happen very often that you sell a player and then buy him back again, but Mark was very young when he left, so it made sense and we needed him. Plus we never wanted him to go in the first place.

We had also hoped to make a marquee signing that summer. Alex knew we had proven goal scorers up front but lacked real creative flair to give them any proper service, so had identified Paul Gascoigne as the player to rectify that problem. And Paul was all lined up; we'd agreed a fee with Newcastle, I'd spoken to their chairman at the time, Gordon McKeag, and we had talked to Paul's agent about personal terms. Alex had also spoken personally to Paul before going on holiday and was confident the player was on his way to Old Trafford. Then we got a telephone call to say that he was going to Tottenham. We heard later that Tottenham had thrown in a car and a house for his parents; they were prepared to offer the earth at the last minute to get him.

We were very keen to get Gascoigne, but he slipped through the net. This happens a lot in football: you win some, you lose some – you just have to make sure that you win more than you lose because you're not going to get every player you go for. Gascoigne, however, was something of an exception, a special player, and you do wonder how things would have turned out if he had come to United instead of Tottenham, under the managerial control of Alex.

One of the few bright spots of what turned into another disappointing season – we finished in eleventh place – was the emergence of a group of young players whom the press dubbed 'Fergie's Fledglings'. Among them are names that still resonate with fans today. There was Tony Gill, a handy utility player, midfielder Russell Beardsmore, Lee Martin, who made an excellent left back, Giuliano Maiorana, an exciting winger brought in from Eastern Counties League club Histon – the £30,000 transfer fee saving the part-timers from going bust – and Mark Robins, a nineteen-year-old striker.

The pick of the bunch was probably Lee Sharpe, who came from Torquay for £180,000, which was a lot of money for a seventeen-year-old back then. Alex and Archie Knox had seen him play and obviously recognized the lad's talent and ability. The manager of Torquay at the time was Cyril Knowles, who had played full back for Spurs, and we were afraid that he might alert the London club to Sharpe's potential, so the deal was done quickly. Lee was very successful for us, becoming our first-choice left-winger for several years. He was strong, athletic and a good crosser. I'll always remember his hat-trick against Arsenal at Highbury in the League Cup fourth round in 1990. He was absolutely outstanding that night.

Lee was a bit of a Jack the Lad, a good-looking boy whom the girls went for – there was plenty going on in his personal life. Alex was a bit wary of some of his social activities; Lee was probably the first high-profile player of Alex's reign – pre-Giggs and pre-Beckham in the pin-up stakes – but unfortunately he became something of a favourite for tabloid writers and, combined with injury setbacks, he never scaled the heights that perhaps his talent deserved.

Such is the legend of the Busby Babes that no club relates so strongly to the success of youth as Manchester United. Alex certainly understood that when he first arrived at Old Trafford and, after watching the youth teams and seeing how they performed, he reached the opinion that the scouting system and the club's youth policy was in need of repair. I'd had my concerns for some time about the issues that Alex subsequently highlighted because Ron, like a lot of managers, tended to concentrate on the first team. Mind you, Ron's legacy with the youth set-up was by no means bad: he was responsible for bringing Eric Harrison to the club as youth team manager.

During Alex's early days, he called Eric into his office to inform him of his dissatisfaction with the club's development of young players. Defending his record, Eric pointed to successes like Norman Whiteside and Mark Hughes. Alex accepted those were fine players but wanted more young players coming through. You could see his desire to bring talent through the ranks from the start; his understanding that a strong youth policy means a strong first team down the line.

At the time Alex felt that Manchester City were way ahead of us in terms of recruitment and development of local young talent. His solution was to dramatically increase the number of scouts, the idea being to control Manchester first and then widen it to the rest of the country. This is where Alex was excellent at the beginning – motivating the scouts, getting the best young players – and I was fully behind him on this. Whatever Alex wanted for the youth team, we gave him. And he was ably supported in this endeavour by Brian Kidd, who returned to the club in 1988 as Youth Development Officer. I got along well with Brian and always found him enthusiastic. He was instrumental in helping to recruit a lot of kids, thanks to his name and pedigree as an ex-Manchester United player, one of the 1968 European Cup-winning heroes. It had been his nineteenth birthday on that day, so Brian was very much the youngster of that team and Manchester through and through. Consequently he was well positioned to know what youth had brought and could bring to a club. Nobby Stiles was also working for us at that time in the youth team set-up. It's always good to have old boys on board, people who are part of the history of the club. It's something that the supporters can associate with and young players relate to – they could potentially be looking at their future.

Some of the so-called 'Fergie Fledglings' never got to become first-team regulars, but they did represent something that was exciting and important. It showed that Alex was prepared to put young players into the team and give them a chance. It was a statement. And it was part of the ethos of the club, going back to the old Busby days, when the FA youth cup was first introduced and United used to win it regularly with home-grown youngsters playing in a certain way. United supporters have always liked to see young local players given a chance, even if in the long term they don't make it. Alex fully embraced the Manchester United way in terms of youth policy, and in the long term that paid huge dividends.

13 SELLING UNITED

On 15 April 1989 United were playing at home against Derby County. We lost 2–0, a result that sort of summed up where we were at the time, a mid-table side struggling for a bit of form. For once though the result was totally insignificant. Not that long into the match, news came through that there were problems at the FA Cup semi-final between Liverpool and Nottingham Forest, which was taking place at Sheffield Wednesday's Hillsborough stadium. The full scale of what was transpiring wasn't fully known until much later and when we finally realized what had happened it was horrendous. Ninety-six Liverpool fans had died as a result of overcrowding that led to a horrible crush. At the time, many people thought it was the fault of the Liverpool supporters coming in late and drunk. Of course, since then we've learnt a lot more. The police were plainly on the defensive – they clearly made big mistakes on the day – but it took years for all that to come out and for the supporters to be finally vindicated.

Alex and I made a special point of visiting Anfield shortly after the Hillsborough disaster to show our grief and personal support for Liverpool Football Club on behalf of everybody associated with Manchester United.

We arrived quietly to pay our respects, away from the media glare, and brought with us a sizable donation to the Hillsborough disaster appeal fund. This terrible tragedy could have befallen any team's supporters. Indeed, had we not lost to Nottingham Forest in the previous round, it would have been us facing Liverpool on that fateful afternoon and our own fans who could have been caught up in that terrible tragedy. This was one of the reasons why before the start of the following season I made the decision to reduce ground capacity at Old Trafford by over five and a half thousand as a safety measure. The big fear was that what had happened at Hillsborough due to overcrowding could happen anywhere. Obviously we were going to lose some revenue but I felt we had to do something.

The government reacted to the disaster quickly, too, instigating a full review overseen by Lord Justice Taylor. His interim report was published in August 1989 and the final report followed in January 1990. It sought to establish the causes of what had happened and to make recommendations regarding the provision of safety at sporting events in future.

The Taylor Report had huge consequences for football in the UK, with its main recommendation that all major stadiums should convert to all seating. It was a decision that proved very unpopular with many supporters, who had always preferred to stand, but I think it was the right decision because there hasn't been a major tragedy since. Of course, this was going to mean a huge cost to the clubs, and while there was some governmental assistance in the way of various grants United didn't get very much. Indeed, the Sports Ministry went so far as to stop a football trust's grant of £2 million going towards the redevelopment of the Stretford End. The government considered us wealthy enough to fund the project ourselves. Because of good housekeeping we were considered to be cash rich, and now we were being penalized for it.

In reality we were hardly cash rich at the time and my overriding concern was just how we were going to pay for all these improvements. Then, out of the blue, the answer appeared to arrive in the unlikely form of an ex-teacher by the name of Michael Knighton.

I was in my office one day attending to regular business when I got a call from Barry Chaytow, chairman of Bolton Wanderers and a friend of Mike Edelson. Barry said he had someone he'd like me to meet and asked if he could bring him over for lunch at Old Trafford. At that time I wasn't looking to sell my stake in Manchester United, but the climate in football was looking bleak. We'd had the Bradford fire and the Heysel disaster in 1985, clubs were still banned from European competition so we weren't getting any money from European football, and then we'd just had Hillsborough, along with the knowledge that we were going to have to spend all this extra money on the stadium. Clubs were struggling – it was a real low point in English football – so Knighton probably felt it was an opportune moment for what he was about to propose.

Frankly I'd never heard of Michael Knighton so knew nothing about him. He was young, just thirty-seven, had once been a teacher, had then made his money in property and had recently retired. He was also very interested in owning a football club, which I found out when we met on 30 June 1989.

I'll never forget that meeting. As we talked I began to see that what Knighton was proposing seemed too good to be true. He was promising that he would personally pay for the rebuilding of the Stretford End, and was prepared to buy me out completely – at that time my shareholding was around 50 per cent. With the Taylor Report imminent I knew that we would have to knock down the Stretford End to convert it into all seating – there had been enough educated speculation that this would be the verdict. All seating was surely on the way. Except for a few seats at the back, the Stretford End at the time was all standing, and we had estimated it was going to cost in the region of £10 million to completely rebuild it. As we were close to our year end, we knew our profit for the year was going to be £1.4 million; any sort of major redevelopment on that sort of profit was going to be difficult. Knighton's proposal to cover the cost – at a stroke eradicating any fears we had concerning ensuring the safety of our fans and conforming to new ground regulations – not to mention buying my shares in the process, was consequently an attractive deal – and not just for the club. He was offering to wipe out the debt I had carried since 1978. Eleven years later that debt had grown to over £900,000 with interest payments, a figure that obviously weighed on my mind. What with this and the promise to finance the new Stretford End, I understandably wanted to hear more.

After the meeting was concluded we agreed to hold further talks on my return from holiday. That second meeting took place on 21 July. I travelled up to Glasgow and Knighton picked me up in his private helicopter to fly me to his house, Killochan Castle. There we talked long into the night, as I wanted to gauge just how serious his interest was. At around midnight we shook hands on a deal that valued my shares at £10 million. Knighton now had an option to buy them.

At this stage nobody beyond me and Knighton knew anything about the proposed deal. The first person I confided in was Maurice Watkins, who immediately wanted to meet with Knighton. Three days after my visit to Killochan Castle I introduced the two of them. I must say that Maurice was surprised by the course of events, but understood my motives in considering Knighton's offer. He also agreed to stay silent, but when the team went on a pre-season tour of Japan, Nigel Burrows overheard a conversation between us concerning Knighton and queried me about it. Rather than lie I took Nigel into my confidence, on the proviso that, since I hadn't yet told the other directors, he keep it to himself, which he did.

On our return from Japan I decided the time was right to tell the remaining board members, which I did on 18 August. I met with each of them individually and their reactions were much the same as Maurice's: a mixture of surprise and shock, as none of them had any idea of what was going on. It had been my prerogative to do it that way. After my experience with Maxwell I had no intention of going through that media circus again. That's why I thought it was better to keep it in-house until I was certain what was going to happen and that Knighton had the finance in place to do the deal. Not only had I been assured that this was the case, I had also taken independent legal advice that funds were indeed there. Knighton was being supported by two serious and powerful backers, businessmen Stanley Cohen of Parker pens and Robert Thornton, the former chairman of Debenhams and a man well respected in the City. So I was quietly confident that I had made the right decision. However, within a week, one of the most infamous events in the history of Manchester United made me think that perhaps I had made a dreadful mistake.

Our first game of the 1989–90 season was on 24 August, at home to Arsenal. A couple of days beforehand, I'd held a press conference to announce that Knighton had an option to buy my shares. Even though we weren't a public company at the time, I felt that it was in the public interest to reveal what was happening, and to pre-empt any possible leaks. On the morning of the Arsenal match, Knighton, who was eager to introduce himself to the Old Trafford faithful, had told me of his intention to go out on to the pitch. I advised strongly against it. I was very nervous about the whole thing. Although the proposed deal had gone public, nothing had been finalized yet, so my advice was no, not yet, don't do anything. He didn't listen. Just minutes before kick-off he asked the PA to announce him over the Tannoy as the new owner of Manchester United and, resplendent in a United kit, he ran on to the pitch, surrounded by photographers, juggled with a ball and kicked it into an empty net. This performance was met with cheers from the crowd, but backstage the reaction was very different. I didn't actually see Knighton's shenanigans – I was still in the directors' room entertaining visiting guests – but I caught it later on the news. It's become an iconic moment but at the time I was fuming. The deal hadn't been finalized yet. He was jumping the gun.

That was really the first sign that something wasn't quite right about Knighton – it was reckless and his decision making really worried me; others felt the same way. It was one of the worst possible moves he could have made. Even Knighton himself, in hindsight, has admitted it was a mistake. Why did he do it? Who knows? Maybe for publicity purposes. Whatever the reason, it raised huge questions in my mind, such that I now had severe doubts.

As for our supporters, many of them probably welcomed Knighton at first – it was someone new coming in and making promises. Let's face it, a lot of them weren't big fans of Martin Edwards. They probably thought: *We haven't won anything in four years, so Edwards isn't the answer, maybe this guy is.* Maybe some of them thought: *Edwards, the greedy bastard – he's done nothing for us and he's walking away with £10 million.* A lot of the fans weren't happy with Alex either at the time and maybe they thought Knighton would come in and change the manager.

For the most part, though, *I* tended to be the object of protest from fans, and that's fair enough: as chairman you take full responsibility for what's happening at the club. Some of my friends in the game felt it went too far sometimes. In his autobiography, Irving Scholar described me as the club's 'whipping boy' and recalled one incident during a match at Old Trafford when he saw two United fans try to physically get at me. I do remember that occasion: they came up to the directors' box screaming and hurling abuse, but I used to get quite a bit of that so wasn't phased. It even got to the point by the mid-1990s that I tried to avoid as much as possible making public appearances and presentations on the pitch because of the level of abuse from fans.

I used to get a lot of hate mail, too, some very abusive, and sometimes aimed at my family. Unfortunately personal abuse goes with the territory. Some people thrive on it, but I can't say I do – I'm not that thick skinned – but there's nothing you can actually do about it other than carry on with the job to the best of your ability. That's all you can do. And as chairman you can't hide yourself away behind the scenes; you're in full view of the fans, who can vent their frustration, and believe me they do.

Not long after the ball-juggling debacle, Knighton's credibility, along with his attempt to take over Manchester United, began to unravel. Just a week before Knighton was due to confirm the deal, Cohen and Thornton dramatically pulled out. Why they withdrew their support was never made clear but my feeling is that they didn't want Knighton to take sole charge of United. I think they wanted more power than Knighton was prepared to give them and that's the reason they fell out. Whatever the truth may be, Knighton was left with no choice but to find new backers. To this end his accountants compiled a report on Manchester United, which was sent out to several potential investors. When we heard what was happening we were appalled. This report, which Knighton was essentially hawking around, contained confidential information about the club and there was a real risk of it falling into the hands of our competitors. All this from a man who did not yet own the club. It was a very serious matter and the final straw for both me and the board. Once we knew he was struggling to raise the money to pay me, we couldn't help but ask ourselves how on earth he was going to deliver on the promise to finance the new Stretford End. It was a mess and I wanted him to withdraw his option.

Quickly we took legal action to stop Knighton releasing his confidential report, and a judge granted the club an interim ruling. His hawking the document around trying to raise the necessary money to take over could have resulted in just about anybody ending up owning Manchester United. It was dragging the name of the club down. Relieved by the court's decision, the board now looked at a way of stopping Knighton exercising his option. The feeling by this time was so strong that if Knighton had taken over, some of the board members were going to resign.

It was suggested that the directors take independent legal advice and Maurice Watkins was charged with finding a suitable barrister. By this stage, matters were more or less out of my hands. Because I had personally handled the contract with Knighton, the board had to take separate legal advice, although they kept me fully informed and I fully supported their action. Funnily enough, when the directors all came back to report to me what had happened, Maurice said, 'It's very interesting, Martin, because the barrister we met said he was at prep school with you.' 'Oh really?' I said. 'What's his name?' 'Grimes,' Maurice answered. 'Evidently you used to make him eat your cabbage.'

The directors also called in the services of the merchant bank Ansbachers to assist them. Ansbachers were to help the club during its flotation on the stock market a few years later. All of this served to heap more and more pressure on Knighton. Not only was everybody at the club against him, but the fans now didn't want the takeover to go through after the months of speculation in the media about whether the deal would happen or if he had the finance. On 9 October I met with Knighton at the Novotel hotel on the M63, on the outskirts of Manchester. I was accompanied by Maurice Watkins. Although Knighton insisted that he had the money to complete the deal, I told him that events had now gone too far and I suggested he tear up the contract. If he did that I was prepared to offer him a seat on the board. That's very likely what swung it, because after a brief pause for thought he agreed. By then I think Knighton was tired of it all. He'd been through the pain barrier and had a lot of opposition and bad press. He'd been receiving hate mail as well. So I suspect the offer to give up the option and come on the board was a relief to him. He probably thought, *Well, I can battle on, I might even win this, but I'm coming in on the wrong foot, people don't want me now, and I probably won't be able to turn them all around*. In the end it was the right thing to do.

Knighton ended up staying on the United board for three years. One or two of his fellow directors never really took to him, mainly because of what he'd done, but personally I never fell out with him. As a character I found him quite affable. He was a bit of a maverick and also a bit of a dreamer.

Inevitably I took a lot of stick over the Knighton episode. It was a low point, no question. It was hugely disruptive, courted a lot of bad publicity and gave my critics plenty of ammunition. It's not a time I'm particularly proud of or look back on with any particular fondness. That said, it was an offer that I had to take seriously. It was a chance to write off my debt, and for the other shareholders to cash in if they wanted to. Also, what would the fans have done to me if they learnt I'd turned down the offer of huge investment to rebuild the Stretford End? I simply couldn't dismiss it out of hand. I had the best interests of Manchester United at heart, even though it was never received that way.

14 SEEDS OF SUCCESS

After the Knighton fiasco the club was back in the doldrums. We all needed a boost and the decision was made to invest heavily in the team to avoid a repeat of the struggles of the previous season. In that summer of 1989 five players were brought in – almost half a team. It was a major shakeup and an important moment, because many of these players were to play a huge part in the success United went on to enjoy in the early 1990s.

Gary Pallister was certainly a pivotal buy. Strangely enough, that was the only deal I didn't personally negotiate. I was on holiday at the time and got quite a surprise when I learnt how much we'd ended up paying. Pallister was at Middlesbrough and they didn't want to sell. Alex, though, was desperate to land Gary and before I left for my holiday we'd agreed he could go and get him. Alex went with Maurice Watkins to do the negotiations. Gary was under contract and Middlesbrough held out for £2.3 million, the largest sum United had ever paid for a player and then a record fee for a British defender. When they rang me on holiday to say what they'd paid I thought, *bloody hell!* It was a bit of a shock. In hindsight it turned out to be a great bit of business. Together with Steve Bruce, the pair formed one of the best defensive partnerships in United's history.

Paul Ince was another vitally important player for us. He played in the FA Cup final in 1990, the Cup Winners' Cup final in 1991 and the League Cup victory in 1992, and was also in the first league championship-winning side– the all-important one – in 1992–93, as well as the Double-winning side in 1994. Ince, then, was very much part of that early success. We bought him for £1.7 million from West Ham, Paul hardly endearing himself to his old club or its supporters when he appeared in a United shirt before the deal was actually completed. I remember that whenever we went down to play West Ham, Ince was invariably subjected to vicious abuse.

At United, Paul was the self-styled 'Guv'nor', which I don't think Alex liked at all. There's one amusing story when we played Glasgow Rangers in a pre-season game. Sean Connery was very friendly with David Murray, the Rangers chairman, and was there that day as Murray's guest. When the United lads heard that Connery was in the directors' lounge, they asked if I could bring him down to meet them. So I got hold of Sean, took him into the dressing room and introduced him to all the players. Sean had heard that Ince called himself the 'Guv'nor', so when I introduced them, Sean said to Paul, 'I'd like to meet the "Guv'nor",' continuing, after a short pause, 'Is your wife here today?' He was obviously taking the piss. The players absolutely loved it and got a huge buzz out of meeting the James Bond star.

Another player we bought that summer was Mike Phelan, who came to us from Norwich for £750,000. A utility player who was equally adept at playing in defence or midfield, Mike played more than a hundred games in five years at United and was appointed assistant manager to Alex when Carlos Queiroz left the club to take over the Portuguese national side in 2008.

Danny Wallace was probably the most disappointing of the new signings. He'd been a prolific goal-scoring winger for Southampton and came to United for £1.2 million, where it was hoped he would realize his potential. Sadly it didn't work out for him. He was plagued by injuries and, as we were later to learn, he was battling spinal multiple sclerosis, which I think may possibly have started to have an effect during those years he was at United. Full diagnosis of his condition didn't come until 1996, by which time he'd been forced into early retirement.

Finally there was Neil Webb, a skilful goal-scoring midfielder from Nottingham Forest. As I remember it, Brian Clough didn't want him to go, so we couldn't reach an agreement and it went to tribunal. We ended up paying £1.5 million. Neil made his United debut on the day Knighton did his ball-juggling act. Like Danny Wallace, we never saw the best of Neil because, not long after joining us, he snapped his Achilles tendon while on England duty and was out for seven months. I don't think he was ever the same cultured player after that, which was a real shame for someone so talented.

Some time earlier, we'd tried to buy Stuart Pearce, another Forest player. Alex had made enquiries, which hadn't got very far, and so, one afternoon when we were passing through, we turned up at the City Ground on the off chance that Clough would accept a meeting with us. We both recognized his car parked outside the office but were told that he was playing squash; as we couldn't really hang around, we left.

Over the years Clough made one or two derogatory comments about United; I think he slightly resented the fact that we never asked him to be our manager. Regardless of that, I got on all right with him. When we played Forest I'd go into his office after the game and have a drink with him – he was always very hospitable with me.

⊕

Unfortunately the massive outlay on new players failed to deliver instant results, with each of the new signings struggling to adapt early on. Gary Pallister, especially, didn't have a great start and came in for a lot of criticism. But it was tough for all these players, coming as they did from smaller clubs. It takes time to get used to the pressures and expectations of playing for such a giant club as Manchester United. Yet there was very little patience around, and you could not blame the supporters for being angry because our performances were so inconsistent. Without doubt, rock bottom was the 5–1 defeat at Manchester City in September 1989.

It was a poor display, it's true, but every shot City struck that day went in – it was one of those games. I felt 5–1 flattered them a bit, not that I'm defending a 5–1 defeat. It was humiliating.

I habitually visited the dressing room before and after games, but on that particular day the dressing-room door was firmly closed, and I suspect Alex was going berserk. I can still remember that weekend clearly. Alex didn't leave his house the whole time; he was absolutely devastated by that result.

Alex and I never felt the need to talk after every game. We would discuss things in the office during the week or in the car going somewhere or sitting next to each other at away matches. After all, I knew how Alex was feeling and the way he was thinking. I knew what his ambitions were, what type of players he was looking for. We were in tune with each other.

After that woeful City game the team suffered several more bad results. I remember them being booed off after losing against Spurs at home, and there were a few remarks made to the directors' box by people leaving the ground, and at me personally as well. I shared the frustration of the supporters. As chairman, when your team is losing matches and you're drifting down the league it is of course a concern. Attendances were dropping, too, for one game as low as 33,000, which is desperately poor when you're used to sell-outs. But I was also conscious of the fact that we had brought in a lot of new players and that they needed time not only to gel together but also to prove themselves, one way or the other. I just felt it was too early to be making sweeping changes. We'd invested a lot of money in the team and now had to give it a chance to come right.

As well as the odd verbal blast from disgruntled fans I was also receiving a lot of angry letters. Most of them were critical of Alex. The general gist of them was: he's been in the job now for three or four years, we're going backwards rather than forwards, he might have been successful north of the border but he's struggling down south. He doesn't understand the English game, the players he's bought aren't good enough, and we've wasted £2.3 million on a useless centre half. That sort of stuff.

Newspapers and media pundits had their say, too, damning Alex's record. Even some ex-players said he wasn't the right man for United and should go. And then, of course, there was the famous home defeat to Crystal Palace on 9 December, when a disgruntled supporter unfurled a banner declaring: 'Three years of excuses and it's still crap. Ta'ra Fergie.'

I had not lost faith in Alex. We knew how hard he was working behind the scenes and the progress he was making with the coaching staff, the scouting and especially the youth players. We could see the club was moving in the right direction under his guidance. So despite the clamour for change I can honestly say that we never sat down as a board and discussed Alex's future. Not once did we ever discuss replacing him. I was just hoping and praying that something would happen that would turn things round. Luckily that arrived in the third round of the FA Cup. We were facing a difficult away tie against Nottingham Forest on 10 January 1990. This was a game everyone expected us to lose and the knives were already out for Alex. Could he survive another bad result? What people didn't know was that I had approached Alex that week and told him that his future was not dependent on us winning that game.

United folklore tells a different story: that it was Mark Robins' goal that saved Alex from the chop. Of course, it was a relief to win – had we lost the game it would most certainly have heaped more difficulties on Alex, so it helped enormously. It took the immediate pressure off and we went on to make the FA Cup final.

Our opponents were Crystal Palace, managed by former United hero Steve Coppell, and it was a real rollercoaster of a match. Palace took the lead with a deflected header that looped over the despairing Leighton. Then Robson equalized and Mark Hughes put us ahead. With us looking on course for victory, Coppell made an inspired substitution when he brought on the young Ian Wright. He had an immediate impact, scoring within three minutes of his introduction and with almost his first touch. The game went into extra time. It was Wright again who popped up at the far post in the ninety-second minute to slot in his second of the match and what looked like Palace's winner. But we kept our composure and with seven minutes to go Danny Wallace slipped a pass through to Hughes who slid the ball into the net. The match ended 3–3.

By comparison the replay was quite dull, although Alex took a massive gamble by dropping Jim Leighton and replacing him with Les Sealey, a goalkeeper we had on loan from Luton. I wasn't told about the decision prior to kick-off, nor would I expect to have been told. To me that was a footballing decision: the manager picks the team with no interference from me or the board. Obviously Alex felt that Leighton was at fault with those two late goals in the Cup final and that he needed to make the change. It was a huge decision because Leighton had played the majority of our games that season, but ultimately it was proven to be the right one because the result justified the action.

It was a very tight game, as I remember, with the Palace players trying to kick us off the ball all night. Lee Martin scored the only goal of the game and we were reasonably comfortable throughout. Still, it was a huge relief when I heard the final whistle. It was vital that we won that match because even though I wanted to protect Alex and see him succeed, there comes a point when you can't keep defending someone. If we had gone to the end of that season and not improved – indeed, if things had got even worse and we hadn't had that Cup run – I might have been forced to take action. Really it was winning the FA Cup that saved Alex because looking at our league form it was still wildly indifferent – we finished up a disappointing thirteenth.

Looking back now it's hard not to underestimate just how important it was to win that first trophy under Alex. If circumstances had played out differently, Alex might very well have been pushed out of United and all that success we subsequently went on to enjoy might never have happened. So, in hindsight, that FA Cup win was an even more important result than we realized at the time. In a way that Cup run not only saved Alex, it saved the team; it gave them confidence and built real momentum going into the following season.

15 FLOATING UNITED

Looking back on my time with Manchester United I've always said that my best two buys were Eric Cantona and Peter Schmeichel, but if I had to pick a third, Denis Irwin would definitely be the one. He was a fantastic signing for us – a huge part of all those trophies we went on to win throughout the 1990s. As left back, Denis was Mr Consistency, very rarely having a bad game. I'd say he was the model professional footballer: very neat and tidy on and off the field. He had first come to our attention the previous season when we played Oldham twice in the semi-final of our victorious FA Cup run, and he was particularly impressive. The former Arsenal player Frank McLintock represented Denis at the time and handled the negotiation. The fee was an absolute bargain at £700,000.

Despite Denis coming in to strengthen the defence, our league form continued to be erratic, and while we improved upon the previous season's thirteenth-place finish, we failed to mount a title challenge and ended up sixth. Arsenal were crowned champions that year, despite having two points deducted by the FA after a stormy encounter with us at Old Trafford that ended in a mass brawl.

I remember it well. Denis Irwin was scythed down by Nigel Winterburn, and Brian McClair followed through on Winterburn in none too subtle a fashion. There was bad blood between those two going back a couple of seasons to when McClair missed a penalty at Highbury during an FA Cup tie and Winterburn purposely jogged over to voice a few choice words in his direction. The rivalry between Arsenal and Manchester United was quite intense in those days anyway, so everything just kicked off and twenty-one players were involved, most, it must be said, trying to calm things down. The FA took the incident very seriously and docked Arsenal two points and United one point, the first and only time United have had points deducted for not controlling their players. To my knowledge no club in the Premier League era has ever been punished in the same way for a similar offence. In hindsight, I think that maybe the FA's punishment was correct. The players were out of control, it was a free-for-all, and you just can't have that as an advertisement for top-level football.

On a positive note, one of the bright spots of that season was the emergence of a seventeen-year-old winger by the name of Ryan Giggs, who made his league debut in March 1991 against Everton as a substitute. People were talking about how good a player Ryan Giggs was when he was still at schoolboy level. The son of a Welsh Rugby League player, Ryan was on Manchester City's books when one of our scouts mentioned that there was this wonder kid there who was a United supporter and that we should really try to get our hands on him. I have to say that Alex worked tirelessly to persuade Ryan's parents, especially Ryan's mother, that the best home for their son was Old Trafford rather than Maine Road. Once that was done we enrolled Ryan into our School of Excellence and then, on his fourteenth birthday, in November 1987, we signed him on a schoolboy form.

The first time Ryan really came to my attention was watching him captain Salford in the 1989 English schools trophy final against St Helens, which took place at Old Trafford. He was absolutely outstanding that day. He controlled the game with his all-round ability and athleticism, and was up and down that pitch the whole time, and the team won 4–0. In many respects Ryan was our best prospect since George Best. Everybody talked about Best at fifteen on the training ground, and it was the same with Ryan. We all knew he was going to be something very special. When you think about it, thirteen championship medals is just incredible. I can't see that ever being beaten.

His arrival in the first team was perfectly timed, just as United were at the start of something extraordinary, although we didn't know it then. And Ryan was pivotal to all those successes – every single one. He was a wonderfully exciting player to watch, a true footballing superstar who put bums on seats. Obviously as he matured his role changed in the team. No longer able to make those blistering runs down the side of the pitch, he relied instead on his experience and moved inside a little bit, but he remained hugely influential on the game and off the pitch. I certainly count Ryan among United's all-time greats, and I've seen a few.

Coupled with our patchy league form that year, our defence of the FA Cup also ended disappointingly in the fifth round, with a 2–1 loss to Norwich City. And though we made it to the League Cup final we suffered a shock defeat to a Sheffield Wednesday side managed by Ron Atkinson. Our salvation that year turned out to be Europe, as we reached the final of the Cup Winners' Cup. After five long years, the European ban on English clubs imposed after Heysel had been lifted and Old Trafford was buzzing with excitement at the prospect of playing in European competition again.

In all honesty, the road to the final was relatively easy, our opponents being quite inferior teams: Pécsi Munkás of Hungary, and Wrexham, who we managed to put five goals past over two legs, Montpellier in the quarters, then Legia Warsaw in the semi-final, who we beat fairly comfortably.

The final itself, held on 15 May 1991, was a very different prospect; one we went into as slight underdogs as we faced a Barcelona team that included the likes of Ronald Koeman and Michael Laudrup and that was coached by the great Johan Cruyff. When you think that Barça had just won the Spanish league and would win the European Cup a year later, it just shows the quality of the side that we beat in the final – and we beat them well.

It was a fantastic night with a wonderful atmosphere inside the Feyenoord Stadium in Rotterdam. We filled about three-quarters of the ground, and without doubt our fans' vocal encouragement gave our players a real lift. Although I felt we were worthy winners, towards the end it got a little hairy. Barcelona got a free kick and who else but Koeman stepped up to smash it in from distance to put them right back in the tie. The Spanish team were really pressing and had a goal ruled out for being offside. They kept coming. Clayton Blackmore cleared a ball off the line to preserve our lead. For us watching, it got increasingly nerve-wracking late on but the team managed to hang on to get over the finishing line and claim our first bit of European silverware since 1968's European Cup.

Although Mark Hughes grabbed all the headlines for his goals – he scored both of them that night – for me the real hero was Les Sealey, who played in goal with stitches in his leg.

Less than four weeks earlier Les had gashed his leg badly playing at Wembley in the League Cup final when he collided with Sheffield Wednesday's Paul Williams. The leg was cut almost to the bone but he refused to go off and, after he hobbled through the last twelve minutes of that game, it was stitched in the dressing room.

As the team prepared to return to Manchester after the match, Les collapsed and was rushed to hospital for emergency surgery. The wound had become infected and he came very close to losing his leg. Now, amazingly, here he was facing Barcelona in the Cup Winners' Cup final. Les had managed to assure Alex that he was fit enough to play, but right near the end he got another knock and was almost playing on one leg. If he'd been fully fit he might have saved Koeman's free kick, which would have given us a much more relaxing time on the sidelines.

I was very sad to hear in 2001 of Les's untimely death from a heart attack while working as West Ham's goalkeeping coach. He was only forty-three. He was a great character and will always be something of a cult hero among United fans for his heroics at the end of that 1990–91 season.

That night we all had a fantastic party in the hotel. Mick Hucknall, a big United fan, was there with us, in jubilant mood, and danced until the early hours of the morning. It was quite the celebration and hopefully signalled that we would be able to compete with the biggest teams in Europe in the future.

Our triumph in the Cup Winners' Cup could not have been better timed, since a couple of weeks later we floated the club on the Stock Exchange. The original date had been set for the beginning of May but we thought we'd leave it to see if we won the final, which we thought could only help with the flotation. It was a bit of a gamble but one that certainly paid off when we beat Barcelona.

The decision to float Manchester United's shares on the stock market was a controversial one, but after the Knighton fiasco in 1989 it seemed the only option left to raise the sums of money needed to push the club forward. It was something we'd considered before.

Back in 1983 Tottenham became the first English football club to float on the stock market. I had met the Spurs chairman Irving Scholar earlier that year when United and Tottenham travelled to Swaziland to play in a series of friendly matches and we'd become friendly. One evening I called Irving to invite him to dinner. I wanted to see if United could follow Tottenham's lead and go for a flotation. It was certainly an option, but there was clearly a cost involved in going down that road. After all, I knew what being in a public company was like. I'd worked for one. My father and uncle floated Louis C. Edwards & Sons in the early 1960s and their lives changed as a result. Suddenly, from being their own bosses, able to do what they wanted, paying themselves a bonus or buying a Rolls Royce if they fancied one, a whole raft of restrictions were placed on them. Being a public company is totally different to being private; you're answerable to the Stock Exchange. There are all sorts of Stock Exchange rules and regulations that you need to comply with, and you have to make financial reports to them; it really does change how you do things. That's why in the end we decided against the idea. It wasn't something United needed or wanted to do at that time.

In the aftermath of Knighton some members of the board again raised the question of floating the club. Again I was unconvinced. The pitfalls remained the same, not least the fact that as a public company you have to be constantly mindful of shareholders' interests and pay dividends.

Prior to the float, United did pay dividends but only when we'd had a good financial year. Whenever we made a loss, a dividend was not forthcoming. The point is that we always had that option. If we floated, that would all have to change. Of course, if you lost money you could still refuse to pay a dividend, but that would have an adverse effect on your share price. As a plc you have a much bigger responsibility to your shareholders than if you are private. And where before the major shareholders affected were mostly the board members themselves, once you've floated there are a lot more shares in public hands.

You also have to be very careful what you say in public or to the media. In some ways the back-page press don't help a plc because they're reporting all the time on multi-million-pound deals, speculating on who we might be selling or buying, and that all has a big impact on the profits of the club and therefore an effect on the share price. And City-regulated businesses don't like all this inaccurate speculation. In short, the pitfalls were myriad, which was why I was undecided.

Yet we needed money, and we had a situation where I was the majority shareholder, holding 50 per cent of the shares; in order to create the money we required, I needed to liquidate my position. The alternative, instead of selling to an individual, was to go public. After Knighton made a play for United he essentially opened the gates for people to think they could have a bit of the club. There was a chap called Gordon Bishop, a Cheshire property developer and United supporter, who actually went on Granada Television saying he was going to buy the club. Even Al Midani toyed with the idea of buying United but in the end never made an offer. However, the board persuaded me that the float was the right route to take and once that happened all talk of takeovers died.

We agreed on a prospectus that set out four reasons for deciding to float United as a plc. These were to raise the money needed for the redevelopment of the Stretford End; to widen the ownership of Manchester United; to provide increased liquidity to shareholders; and to give employees and supporters of Manchester United greater opportunity to invest in the club.

As it happened, we already had the merchant bankers in place for what we intended to do – Ansbacher, who earlier had advised the directors on how to stop the Knighton deal. We found ourselves working with Glenn Cooper, their Head of Corporate Finance and a vastly experienced City man. I remember inviting Glenn to a board meeting and as we discussed the flotation I went round the table asking for opinions until finally it was Glenn's turn. 'Glenn,' I said, 'can we float Manchester United?' Mulling the question over in his mind for what seemed like several minutes Glenn finally gave me an answer: 'Just.' It was scarcely a ringing endorsement, but it was enough.

Much later Glenn admitted that he was not at all confident of the deal succeeding and feared that it might all end up a ghastly mistake. He was right to have reservations. Tottenham remained the only major football club that had floated, but eight years after making their debut on the Stock Exchange they were in big financial trouble. They hadn't been paying regular dividends, the share price had gone south and they'd overextended themselves on the merchandising side of things. All this would sadly culminate in the departure of Irving from Tottenham and the sale of the club to Alan Sugar and the then Spurs manager Terry Venables.

That's what we were up against and that's why Glenn was so cautious with his answer. As a result he had a torrid time trying to get a stockbroker to handle the issue; nobody wanted to touch it. Finally, after being turned down by something like seven brokers, Glenn managed to persuade someone to take us on. Why the hesitancy? After the Spurs experience the City looked upon football as far too risky a proposition. They didn't believe that a football club could generate profits on a regular basis, or that football club directors would be disciplined enough to pay dividends on a regular basis and generally act as proper plc custodians of the business. As far as they were concerned, football was too precarious in terms of success and failure. We had a prime example of this in that year's FA Cup final when Paul Gascoigne ruptured his cruciate ligament; investors were saying: 'Look, that's what can happen, your star player and main asset can get a serious injury and be out for months.' Even doing well in league and cup competitions doesn't guarantee earnings growth, and transfer fees in a single season can wipe out profits.

I had a very good relationship with Glenn: he was just a year older than me and an Old Harrovian, so we had a public school background in common. He also knew the City well, having worked there in several capacities. But what I liked most about Glenn was his honesty: he never promised the earth; if he told you something was going to be hard, you knew it was going to be hard. And he was very practical and keen to know how the business worked from the inside out. He spent ages going through things like how much money we made per game, how much we made from catering, how we set the pricing for season ticket holders and the executive boxes. Glenn wanted to know everything. He was very thorough and of enormous help when we floated, especially in terms of helping me prepare. As I was chief executive, it was up to me to make the presentations to the City, so we had several dummy runs in which Glenn would ask me all the questions that were likely to be raised and that I needed to have answers for.

I was well aware that by floating I could also finally clear my debt, which I was simply not prepared to carry for the rest of my life. It had caused me too much worry for too long, and getting rid of it would be a welcome side effect of creating funds for the development the club needed.

But before we floated, Glenn was insistent that my role as chairman and chief executive had to be split. 'You can't do both,' he said. 'You have to make a choice. And if I were you I'd stay as chief exec. You will get paid more as chief exec, and it's the most important role.' I agreed, which left us with the task of finding a new chairman. We concluded that our chairman needed to be high profile and preferably from the north. Even better if it was someone with a connection to the club.

It was an easy decision for me: Sir Roland Smith. Roland held nine directorships and was chairman of British Aerospace, he had good connections with the Stock Exchange and was a lifelong Manchester United supporter with his own table on match days in the Stretford Suite overlooking the pitch.

There's an amusing story of when Roland was hospitalized after being taken ill at Old Trafford in 1994. He asked a man in blue scrubs approaching him with a pair of defibrillators, 'You're not a Man City supporter, are you?'

Roland had also been a friend of my father's and had held the position of vice chairman on the board at Louis C. Edwards & Sons. He was the perfect candidate and Glenn fully agreed with my choice.

Over the years I think I worked well with Roland. He always thought his role as chairman was to support me as the chief exec, which I always felt he did. He couldn't really help me with the running of the club, with the manager and the players, things like that, because that wasn't his background. But Roland was very useful with all his City connections, especially when I had to make City presentations. These entailed you making a financial presentation on your results to a bunch of city analysts and Roland would come along as chairman of the plc, and was great at setting the scene and the right tone. He was like a warm-up act for both me and the finance director, and it helped that he would know most of the people in the room. He was very good with financial PR, too – things I didn't really want to get involved with. He was also about six-foot-four and his somewhat imposing demeanour always reminded me of the eagle in *The Muppet Show*, although with a much better sense of humour.

Next on the agenda before floating the club was the acquisition of a finance director. A qualified finance director, able to do City presentations, is a major requirement of a company that's going public, and although we had good accountants internally at the club they weren't sufficiently qualified to do the job we would be asking of them. We advertised the position and received a large number of applications, the list of candidates eventually being whittled down to four possibilities. Eventually we picked a man called Robin Launders.

As with Roland, I think Robin was an excellent appointment. He had studied engineering at Manchester University. He had also been finance director at the car dealership Reg Vardy, which he had helped bring to the stock market. It was a good combination of skills, with the engineering degree coming in especially handy when I asked Robin to supervise the building of the Stretford End and later the North Stand – projects that were completed on schedule and didn't go over the budget. There were, however, issues with Robin. He was very bright and I think when people couldn't match his intelligence Robin could on occasion be a bit short with them, which led to him upsetting quite a few of the staff. But we certainly got the best out of Robin, and as a finance director he was extremely disciplined and organized.

One of the things that Robin came up with was the idea of a transfer fee reserve account. We felt that to be taken seriously, and to reassure City investors that we wouldn't spend all the money we made on new players, we should have this transfer reserve fund, which in good years we could put money into so that when we did need to buy players it wouldn't impact on the balance sheet because the reserve fund was always listed as a separate entry in the accounts. At the same time, dividends would be protected. The scheme wasn't to everyone's liking. David Gill dropped it when he came in as the new finance director; he thought it was a bit of a nonsense, manufactured: that the figures in the reserve were purely an accounting entry, never representing hard cash. But the City had responded positively to this because they thought that we were showing that we did take transfer fees into consideration and we were putting money to one side for it, even though it was only on an accounting basis. I think, at the time, because no football club had successfully floated before, that it gave the right impression, signalling the right intent, so it served its purpose.

Just as Tottenham had done when they floated back in 1983, we had to create a plc. The structural device of creating a new plc was a fairly standard procedure: all you had to do was buy an off-the-shelf company. This is a company that has already been formed and registered but is not active and can be bought in order to place your assets into it. We purchased Voteasset Public Limited in December 1990 and a month later its name was changed to Manchester United plc. The football club, which continued to function with its own board to manage footballing matters, of which I remained chairman (indeed, I was often still referred to as 'Chairman', especially by the players, throughout my time as chief executive), now became a wholly owned subsidiary of the newly created plc.

Much more problematic was choosing the right faces for the plc board – faces that we hoped the City would find acceptable and have confidence in. It was required that Roland Smith and I be on the board; so too Robin Launders as the finance director. We also needed some non-executive directors. All public companies have to have non-executive directors; this is so that the executives can't just do whatever they want. Therefore you have to create non-executive directors, and the more professional they are or the more experience they've got, the more confidence that gives people you want to buy your shares. Glenn asked if I wanted to recommend anyone. There was a little bit of friction among some of the directors over who was chosen but I felt that the one person I needed with me was Maurice Watkins. He was the club solicitor and involved in many aspects of the day-to-day running of the club. It was Glenn himself who chose the other non-exec, Al Midani, due to the fact that he was the club's second-highest shareholder.

After the float, the relationship between the football club board and the plc board actually worked well. All the major financial decisions had to be taken by the plc board because they were responsible to the shareholders and the City for profit and loss. That included all transfer dealings. The club board could still discuss players and make their recommendations of who we should buy and sell but the plc always had the last word. I don't think the club board resented that; there was plenty of other work for the club directors to do without impinging on the plc board. For instance, dealing with the FA and the League, together with logistics around Old Trafford, and representing the club on various committees. I thought the two boards complemented each other very well.

I must say there was quite a buzz of excitement around Old Trafford as the date of the float approached, although I don't think it was particularly shared by Alex. I have a feeling his lack of enthusiasm was based on a concern that after United went public the finances would be more controlled and there might be restrictions on the purchase of players. I think he was also worried that too many layers of management would slow down the financial decision making. Over the years such concerns have been given as the reason why Alex did not take up the club's offer of share options. The truth is very different.

We had decided that all heads of department and senior managers would each receive 25,000 shares in the float – completely free. We did not make a distinction, so the catering manager, the commercial manager, the secretary, the assistant secretary and others, including Alex, all got 25,000 shares each, free. The one exception to this was the financial director, who was given 100,000 shares. It was agreed that I would not take any shares due to the fact that I already had a substantial holding.

All seemed fine until Alex learnt that Robin Launders was getting four times more than him. This was because as finance director Robin had a big responsibility for the success of the float. Although Glenn and I had already done the job of selling the club to the City, Robin's job was to make future financial presentations to investors in order to maintain their interest and to keep the share price up. Alex interpreted this as a slight against him and refused to take his free shares. But when you think about it, Alex's salary would have been much greater than Robin's, and he had the opportunity to earn a big bonus if the team was successful. Robin didn't get a bonus when the team won the league or a cup. I felt the whole thing was a misunderstanding, really.

The float itself took place in late May 1991 and was pretty manic. We didn't leave Manchester until the early hours of the morning of 22 May because we'd been up all night doing last-minute paperwork. I don't think we arrived at Glenn's London offices until 5 a.m., and the press conferences and interviews started at six. It was one of those days when you forget how tired you are; you just battle through it and crash out at the end. And by the end I was absolutely shattered, but it had been a totally exhilarating experience. We'd been working on the float for several months and in that time it had completely overtaken my life.

However, a figure returning from the not too distant past did his damndest to put a spanner in the works. It was known by us that Robert Maxwell had bought a large number of shares in Manchester United: around 500,000. He still retained that shareholding, so Glenn spoke with Maxwell's son Kevin to enquire what the family intended to do with it. Did they want to sell? If so we'd buy them before the float; that way we could take them out of the equation. But no, the Maxwells wanted to hang on to them, though they assured Glenn that it was not their intention to interfere in or hinder the float in any way. Well, within just a few days of the flotation Maxwell dumped his shares on the market. The club had been valued at £46 million, substantially more than the £20 million tag attached to the abortive takeover offer by Knighton, and the shares began trading at £3.85. Within a week, however, the share price had fallen to £2.60, although they did eventually rally again. In terms of price I can't say the float was an immediate success, but that was purely because of those shares dumped by Maxwell. I still don't know why he did it because he could have earned a lot more if he'd hung on to them.

Another big disappointment for me was the reaction of the supporters. Before the float we had to decide how many shares would be made available to business institutions and how many would be open to the general public, most of which we hoped would be United supporters. In the end we leant more towards the supporters than the institutions; of the 4,674 million shares, a figure that includes the shares the directors and I put into the float, 2,077 million were offered to institutions and 2,597 million to the public. Not only was this good PR but it was also the right thing to do. However, while the institutions took up their full allocation, the supporters didn't, and the underwriters – Ansbacher themselves – had to take up the slack, ending up with a batch of shares they didn't particularly want. I must admit I was surprised. After us having just won the Cup Winners' Cup I thought we had a fair wind behind us, but the fans' response to the float was muted, to say the least. They must have known from all the publicity that the principal reason for obtaining a stock market listing was to raise money towards the redevelopment of the Stretford End.

Additionally, as individual directors we all put shares into the float in order to make it a success. If you're floating and the directors or the board still own the majority of shares, there could be an argument that it's not a proper float. Glenn was anxious that we were all seen to be putting some of our shares into the float, spreading the shareholder base with institutions and individual shareholders. I was reducing my holdings in the club from 50 per cent to 27.8 per cent, so that should have pleased the supporters. What probably infuriated them, though, was the fact that I personally raised £6.4 million from selling my shares, a million of which I used immediately to pay off my debt, but the only way I personally could raise money for the club was through selling those shares.

It's probably true to say that the supporters didn't want Manchester United to be publicly owned. I had some sympathy with this view because once you've floated you're up for grabs – anyone can come in and buy you. It's not like when you're in private hands and it's up to you to agree any sale; if someone comes in with the right amount of money it's very difficult to stop it. Most companies are up for grabs if somebody's prepared to pay the right price. Nothing's sacred in business. I have to point out, though, that when fans complained later about United being a public company it was a bit harsh because they had been given an opportunity to own a much bigger holding, and therefore to have a much bigger say in the running of the club and its future.

Even though I was against the float initially, I cannot say that it wasn't successful, because it was. From the time we floated in 1991 to when I stepped down from my position at United in 2003, the club went from one triumph to another, both on and off the field. In my opinion it was a good, solid investment. Not only did the share price go up in that time, but shareholders were getting an increased dividend every year. City institutions were also beginning to change their opinion about the profitability of football and coming on board, because we were delivering. We set a template for success.

By 1996 a majority of stock, 60 per cent, was in the hands of City institutions. The BBC pension fund, for example, was quite a large shareholder, and you'd expect it to be very conservative in its investments, so it must have felt our shares were a good buy.

By 2000, United were one of the very few clubs anywhere in the world recommended by stockbrokers as a blue chip investment. Certainly after we made a success of floating there was a rush by other clubs to use the stock market as a means to acquire fresh funds. By the end of the 1990s more than twenty clubs had taken this same route. This was a vindication of our decision which, although a risk, helped make the club what it is today.

16 OLD TRAFFORD GETS A FACELIFT

A significant side effect of United floating was the change of emphasis it had on my relationship with Alex. In the early days I used to meet with Alex quite a bit, but after the float I had many more responsibilities and, because we were expanding rapidly at the time – all the heads of department were answerable to me and they all wanted a direct link to my office – I was a lot busier than before. I had to spread my time around a lot more and consequently it was difficult to maintain the constant dialogue Alex and I had earlier enjoyed. There are only so many hours in the day.

I'd also learnt an important lesson from my father's time and from his relationship with his managers, notably Tommy Docherty. My father got too friendly with Tommy: they used to go to the races and other social activities together, which made things difficult when Tommy had to be sacked. Over the years I think I had a very good working relationship with Alex – we had a common goal and we worked towards that – but if you ask if we went out socially together, no we didn't. We didn't need to be buddies. Besides, we had very different personalities.

In fact, I didn't make particularly great friendships with anyone at Old Trafford. I don't believe that you can be too matey with the people working under you. It does not necessarily work. I have seen it go wrong so many times. It can cause problems because friends can fall out with each other. It doesn't mean you can't have a laugh or get on with people in the workplace. But don't become best pals with somebody you're dealing with on a day-to-day basis, because there are bound to be times when you have opposing views, which can cause problems when you have too much personal baggage attached to your relationship, meaning you can't be honest for fear of damaging a friendship. Especially when you have to sit down at the end of the year and negotiate a bonus and that person thinks they're worth more than you do; that their salary should be bigger or they should have a better pension.

The fear of some supporters that the float would take money out of the club and therefore stymie investment was put to bed when we brought in three new players in the summer of 1991: Andrei Kanchelskis, Paul Parker and Peter Schmeichel. Alex had been urgently looking for a wide right player when somebody brought up the name of Kanchelskis. After studying videos of Andrei, Alex and I flew out to Frankfurt to watch him play for Russia in a friendly against Germany. We were so impressed by both his strength and speed that after the match we sought a deal for him. It turned out that Andrei was represented by three agents, including a Russian by the name of Grigory Essaoulenko, who had been given authority by Andrei's club Shakhtar Donetsk to conclude the transaction. It all went quite smoothly and the full payment was £1.2 million.

It took much longer to land Schmeichel. His club Brøndby wanted £1 million for him, but because he was coming to the end of his contract I was determined to pay a lower price. The club were also refusing to let Schmeichel go until his contract ended in October, well after the start of our season, and we wanted him for the first match. Maurice and I flew over to Copenhagen at the end of June, met with representatives from Brøndby and spent the whole afternoon negotiating. We argued for hours on end. I knew Alex was desperate to get Schmeichel but I refused to pay the million. So we stuck it out and finally they agreed he could come to us for £505,000, and we could have him for the start of the season. I felt that was money well spent, because we'd have had to pay £325,000 for him anyway if the transfer went to the European multiplier system. Peter joined us on 6 August, the same day we signed Paul Parker for £1.7 million from Queens Park Rangers.

Without doubt the Schmeichel deal is one of the best bits of business I ever did during my time at Manchester United. During the years he was with us Peter developed into the best goalkeeper in world football and his contribution to everything we achieved is immeasurable. With Peter in goal we won two Doubles and a Treble. I liked Peter as a person enormously and had great respect for him. He was very much his own man. He was quite tough when it came to salary and contract negotiations – no pushover – but he was always very straight and honest in my dealings with him. A true United legend.

The start of the 1991–92 season was disrupted slightly by the departure of Archie Knox to Rangers. Walter Smith had just been made manager there and wanted Archie as his assistant. I know Alex was very disappointed in Archie's decision to leave. They'd both worked so hard to create a winning team, but now they were achieving success Archie had gone. With his boundless enthusiasm Archie was quite instrumental in sorting out the coaching side and the scouting system with Alex in those early days. They really worked well as a team.

Alex's choice of replacement was a sound one. He promoted Brian Kidd from the youth set-up to be his new number two. I'd known Brian since he was a young lad – he was in the team when my father was chairman – and we got on very well. Brian has always been something of a nervous character, a bit of a worrier, but a real grafter – he worked very hard and loved his training and schedules. He took to his new position immediately and, together, he and Alex made a brilliant new team.

Thanks to our confidence-boosting cup win in Europe everyone at United believed we were finally capable of mounting a credible title challenge, and with just six games to go we were top of the league, with our destiny in our own hands. Only Leeds could catch us if we did the unthinkable and slipped up. Which is exactly what we proceeded to do.

In defence of Alex, he was very unlucky with injuries. Bryan Robson and Mark Robins were already sidelined and then we lost Paul Ince,

Danny Wallace and Paul Parker during the run-in. What also crippled us was the FA's insistence on the season finishing early to allow the England squad time to prepare for the summer's European Championships. This led to a horrendous fixture congestion, which at one point forced us into playing four matches in seven days. We did ask the League for a bit of help with the fixtures but got nothing out of them, so in the end we just ran out of steam and Leeds caught us up.

Really that was the year we should have won the league. We'd beaten Leeds in both cup competitions, going on to lift the League Cup ourselves, but that only left them free to concentrate on the league. If we'd gone out of one of the cups earlier then we probably would have won it, but we just hadn't got the legs by the end.

Of course, it didn't help that officially we lost the league against Liverpool, who beat us 2–0 at Anfield. The Kop absolutely loved that. But I'll always remember Liverpool's chairman David Moores coming up to me at the end of that game to offer his commiserations, and he had tears in his eyes. Liverpool fans probably don't want to hear that, but I think he felt United had done everything that season but win it, that we'd been so close. He seemed genuinely sorry for me. I have to say I felt pretty sorry for myself, too. It wasn't a great feeling: we'd been trying for twenty-five years and that was our big opportunity and we lost it right at the death. And to Leeds.

Manchester United have enjoyed, if that's the right word, a massive rivalry with Leeds that goes back decades. Elland Road was always a daunting place to go because the fans absolutely hated us. When you drove into the directors' car park at Elland Road there was always an attendant there waiting for you. He had the Leeds blazer, badge and hat and always knew who you were. He'd stop your car and as you wound down the window he'd bend down to look at you. 'Good afternoon, Mr Edwards,' he'd say politely and take his hat off. 'On behalf of Leeds United and on behalf of Mr Leslie Silver, the chairman, OBE, and Mr William Fotherby, the chief executive, and on behalf of myself we would like to welcome you to Leeds United Football Club this afternoon.' I thanked him. 'If you would like to go to bay four over there and park your car, Mr Edwards,' he would continue, 'and make your way into the directors' suite.'

I remember that on one occasion we'd taken a load of abuse throughout the match from the Leeds supporters, as you can imagine. After the match I made my way back to my car and was just about to drive out of the car park when the attendant arrived. 'Mr Edwards,' he said. 'On behalf of Leeds United, on behalf of Mr Leslie Silver, OBE, on behalf of Mr William Fotherby and on behalf of myself, we hope you have had an enjoyable afternoon.' I looked at him and said, 'No, I haven't, and you can all f*** off!'

The final home game that season turned out to be the very last in front of the old Stretford End, as the bulldozers moved in to make way for a new all-seater stand, which would help us to meet the safety conditions set out in the Taylor Report. Moving to an all-seater stadium was inevitably going to mean a substantial loss of capacity. Back in the good old days of Best, Charlton and Law, crowds of up to 60,000 regularly watched United play. This figure had gradually reduced over the years and was going to be around 43,000 once the ground had been made all seated. The majority view among the fans was that we should be thinking of making Old Trafford bigger, not smaller, and for a time we were looking at a ground that could realistically hold 53,000, a figure that included the existing standing areas along with developing more of the stadium into seated sections. Hillsborough and the Taylor Report put paid to that.

We did understand the concerns of the supporters and were always exploring ways to increase capacity. At one time we looked into the possibility of a gallery or upper tier at the Stretford End. Also under consideration was the possibility of raising the roof all around the ground to give us an extra 8,000 seats. However, this would have impaired the view of people at the back of the stands, and with a price tag of £30 million it was ruled out as being too expensive. The whole situation was fraught with difficulties, but we were trying, and looked at everything along with our architects. At one point we even contemplated lowering the level of the pitch to enable more seating, although I quickly came to the conclusion that this was totally impractical. If we could have found a sound way to increase capacity we would have done so. As it was, Old Trafford remained the biggest club ground in the country and supporters needed to understand that we had to comply with the Taylor Report.

Temporarily losing the Stretford End inevitably led to even more disgruntlement among the fans, as capacity would have to come down to 34,000 while work was being carried out. And with fewer people coming through the turnstiles we had no choice but to raise ticket prices. Once you've done that, the new prices do tend to stick. But if we wanted to maintain the standards of the team, pay the players the same wages and be competitive in the transfer market, along with developing the ground, we needed the income to do it. It was really a case of supply and demand. Saying that, even with our increased prices we were still cheaper than most other First Division clubs, although not necessarily the cheapest in the North-West, which had traditionally been cheaper because it wasn't as affluent an area as the south.

I'd been watching United since I was a kid so I was constantly conscious of the fact that we shouldn't price out the ordinary fan. Obviously, as time went on, everybody started raising prices – today the cost of football is much greater – but we always made sure there was somewhere in the ground where supporters could get in reasonably cheaply.

Getting the balance right on pricing was important. I've always believed that if the supporters feel the pricing is reasonable they're more likely to support you in other ways, like buying a programme, for example. It's the same with replica kits and other merchandise: if you feel good about your club you'll buy more items than if you feel it's overpriced. Remember, supporters have no other choice but to pay for their seat if they want to attend a match, whereas they don't have to buy a programme or a shirt. Don't sting them on the things they can't do anything about, because ultimately you want a full house and for them to create an atmosphere.

The difficulty comes when you start getting full houses every week, which we did eventually; then it becomes a judgement call, because you know you can charge a high price and you'll still sell out. How greedy do you want to be, though? Sometimes I'd be in a meeting and some senior members of staff would ask why we weren't charging more; then I'd have an argument with them defending our pricing policy. The daft thing was that my name out there on the terraces was as a greedy bastard, but here I was fighting internally to keep a sensible price for our supporters.

In 1994 United's highest-priced season ticket was £280, while the average for the Premier League, excluding United, was £307. By 1998 this had risen to £361, when the average for the rest of the Premier League, excluding United, was £442. In 1998 ten clubs in the top flight had higher season ticket prices than United. And we were still fairly affordable in 2000, certainly compared to all the London clubs. We were providing winning football at a very reasonable price in the best stadium in the country.

In light of the work needed to make the Stretford End fully seated, we decided to put an executive suite in the middle of the stand, which was inevitably extremely contentious. Those supporters always thought of the Stretford End as the traditional standing area; that was the end that created the most atmosphere and noise during matches. But in building that stand I had to look at it not emotionally but logically and say, well, we've got to put seats in, it's going to be very expensive so we need some return on that investment. And one of the ways I could get a return on that investment was by putting an executive suite in there, along with a lounge and premium-priced seating.

A lot of those supporters still had hopes that football would one day return to standing, that it was only a temporary ban, but, as we know, the results of the Taylor Report are still with us. I never wanted to go back to standing anyway. Although I understand the passion some people have about standing at a match, if you are an owner of a football club why would you ever want to put yourself at risk again of a Hillsborough or anything approaching it? I suppose there will always be calls for its return, but when we were designing the new Stretford End we knew it wasn't going to happen. And if you're putting executive seats in, you can only put them in the middle of the stand – people don't want to be in an executive seat in the corner – but, boy, did we take some stick for it.

That ill feeling is still around today, in the shape of Roy Keane's idea of the 'prawn sandwich brigade'. People are still critical of all this commercialization, saying that it's ruined football. But who has it ruined it for? It's ruined it for the ones who want to go back to the days of shouting and swearing and throwing missiles on to the pitch, but for others it's created much more of a family atmosphere.

Indeed, another development was that we put an area designated for families, which was known as the family stand, in the new Stretford End and there was a lot of criticism about that, too: how dare you put a family stand in among all that bad language? Again, this was done not to upset anyone; it was mainly for the players' benefit. We had decided to move the dressing rooms, which had been situated below the main South Stand, to the new Stretford End, just behind the goal. We needed new dressing rooms anyway: our old ones were in real need of modernization. We also built the players' lounge there, so it made sense to put the family stand nearby so that the players and their wives, families and guests could have quick and easy access between the two.

In all, giving Old Trafford, and the Stretford End in particular, a facelift paved the way for what the ground is today: still the biggest in the country, and with the best facilities. We couldn't afford to be behind the times in 1992, and partly because of what we did then, Old Trafford is ahead of the times now.

17 THE PREMIERSHIP ARRIVES

Without question the English Premier League is the most exciting and most popular league in the world, broadcast in well over 200 territories with a TV audience not far off five billion people. It's an incredible success story.

The big five clubs at the time – Arsenal, Everton, Liverpool, Tottenham and United – had been threatening to break away and form their own super league for years. It could have happened in 1985. Instead they came up with a compromise agreement called 'the Ten-Point Plan', which kept the league structure in place. They thought about leaving again in 1988 over the league's proposed television deal with BSB, and even though their preferred bidder, ITV, won the contract they remained convinced that the league still needed change.

In June 1990, almost two years after he'd won the Football League contract for ITV, Greg Dyke wrote to me and the four other clubs. 'We think it is time for the five to sit down and meet with us again. There are a number of issues we should discuss, including the next Football League contract.' Although it took a few months to organize a date on which all of the five chairmen were available, in mid-November I travelled down to London for what was to prove a highly significant meeting. Besides me, Irving was there, David Dein, Philip Carter and Liverpool's new chairman, Noel White.

Greg was a genial host and wanted to know how everything was going with the ITV contract. We told him that we were happy and had no major grievances. The conversation carried on and then David Dein raised the topic of us breaking away from the other divisions to create a new league, and asked, if that were to ever happen, whether ITV would buy the TV rights. Honestly it could have been any one of us who raised the subject, given that we had all been talking about it for years, but the credit must go to David. We could tell that Greg found the idea appealing, so we asked him and the other ITV executives present to leave the room for twenty minutes while we had a discussion among ourselves. When Greg returned, a decision hadn't really been reached but I think it was clear that evening that we felt the time was ripe for a breakaway and that the right solution for football was an independent league comprised of the existing First Division clubs. This would form the tip of a new pyramid structure for English football.

Due to the fact that we'd been through so much hassle before with the Football League, we decided to approach the Football Association first with our proposal. Of course, we knew we couldn't just walk away from the Football League without some kind of negotiation, but if the FA, as the governing body, were to sanction our move, that would make things much easier going forward.

We weren't sure what the FA's reaction would be, but it was one that had to be tested. We were fortunate that Liverpool's chairman, Noel White, being a senior member on the FA council, had huge influence, so he, along with David Dein, was delegated to take our proposals to them early that December. The chairman of the FA at the time was Bert Millichip, who'd been around football a long while as a director and chairman of West Bromwich Albion. Funnily enough, Graham Kelly, who had been at the Football League during the BSB debacle, had since moved to the FA and was on our side right from the beginning. Bert wasn't against the idea either. Like us, they thought the time was right.

I think what helped us during our dealings with the FA was that we talked about cutting the size of the league down to eighteen clubs. This was something they were very keen on because it meant the top teams playing less games, which could only be beneficial to the national side. In the end that never happened. While Arsenal, Tottenham and United were prepared to go to eighteen, when it actually came to the voting later on Everton and Liverpool didn't support the idea; they wanted to stay at twenty-two because of the impact losing four home games would have on their gate receipts. By the mid-1990s, however, the Premier League was reduced, but only to twenty clubs.

With the FA on side we began to explore the practicalities of setting up a separate league. There was a lot to consider. We would need our own rulebook. We had to set up our own fixture list. There were players' registration and contracts to sort out, along with pension schemes and personal accident insurance. There was the selection of referees. Also, we would need offices and staff – a whole structure had to be put in place. There was a time constraint on it, too, because we wanted to break away in time for the 1992–93 season, so a lot of work had to be done in a very short period.

The first thing we did was set up sub-committees formed of key people from our own clubs. For example, Maurice Watkins at United had an interest in the legal side. Ken Friar, who was secretary at Arsenal, helped to compile the rulebook, while Jim Greenwood, who was secretary at Everton, worked on player contracts. These specialists were appointed to various committees and got on with all the administration work.

Another key appointment was Rick Parry as chief executive. Rick had no background in football, coming as he did from Ernst & Young, a firm of chartered accountants, but in 1985 he had been instrumental in preparing Manchester's Olympic bid. That's when I got to know him because both Phil Carter and I were on that Olympic bid committee and saw Rick first-hand and were convinced that he'd be a good choice as the Premier League's inaugural chief executive. We interviewed Rick very early on in the process and he agreed to come on board and stayed with us for many years before taking up the same post at Liverpool. I must say the Premier League has been very lucky with its chief executives; both Rick Parry and his successor Richard Scudamore have been excellent.

While we never lost sight of the sheer enormity of what we were attempting – by far the biggest change in the history of the English game – all of us were determined to stay resolute throughout. I can't remember ever having a discussion with my fellow chairmen about whether or not what we were doing was the right thing. Our only real doubt was: can we do it legally? One hurdle in our way had come about due to our own earlier threat to break away in 1988.

At their annual general meeting, the Football League passed a new rule that effectively meant that any club who wished to leave the league had to give at least three years' notice. That left us either with having to wait the three years or with finding a legal way to get around it. In the end it was Rick Parry who came up with the solution. Thumbing through the FA rulebook one day he saw that the FA's own ruling on club's giving notice to leave was actually just six months, thus rendering the Football League's three-year rule totally invalid.

Another key objective was getting the players' union, the PFA, on side. If they'd wanted to, the PFA could have caused major problems by discouraging their members from joining with us, and obviously, without the players, we didn't have a league. As it was, the PFA themselves had produced a paper about reorganizing the game, and although this didn't call for a breakaway, they were realistic enough to know that things needed to change. Then it was merely a question of negotiation, making sure that they looked after any of their members who were left behind in the event of a new league being set up.

What happened was that the PFA always got 10 per cent of any television contract. We all understood how important the PFA were in using this money to help players further down the leagues, or those who got injured or fell on hard times, and obviously they were anxious that this payment continued. In the end I was the one designated to go and negotiate with Gordon Taylor, the PFA's chief executive, on what fee they would receive in the future. Those negotiations were quite tough and at one point the PFA threatened a players' strike if they didn't get the same percentage as before. After a lot of brinkmanship, a compromise was eventually reached.

With both the FA and the PFA on board, a breakaway league looked a very real possibility. A lot of people criticized us at the time for pushing this forward, saying how it was the big five out to grab whatever they could get at the expense of the smaller clubs. Parts of the media, when they found out, also looked on it distrustfully. Even the *Manchester Evening News*, our local paper, was against it.

But this was never a dash for cash. All we ever wanted was autonomy, a chance to self-govern – something that we had wanted for a long time. The ninety-two-club voting structure had always made it difficult to get anything through for the big clubs. We wanted to vote on our own future. This issue was simmering below the surface for years and we'd only avoided clashes in the past through compromises that didn't really solve those underlying issues. With our own league we would be more in control of our destiny: able to negotiate our own TV and sponsorship deals and to decide among ourselves a fair distribution of the monies.

Of course, we understood the importance of the lower leagues and grass-roots football, which is why we agreed to continue playing in the League Cup and FA Cup. We also felt that it was extremely important to have promotion and relegation. We didn't want the Premier League to be a closed shop. That was never the intention. If you were good enough you could always get in and be part of it and aspire to be number one. Let's take a recent example: Leicester City. They were in the Championship for years before they were promoted back into the top flight in 2014. Then, against all the odds, they became Premier League champions in 2015–16: a remarkable achievement. That was always our aim: we didn't want to destroy any club's hopes of one day getting into the Premier League and doing well. It was all about aspiration.

We were also keen that anybody who was relegated from the Premier League wasn't left high and dry; that's why the parachute payments came in. These payments were always very generous but, over the years, as the TV contracts have gone up substantially, so too have the parachute payments, almost to the detriment of the other clubs in the Football

League because they give the newly relegated side a huge advantage. Having said that, teams in the Premier League do tend to pay higher wages, and you can't get rid of players' contracts overnight so they still need money to offset those expenses.

For much of 1991 numerous meetings took place relating to the setting up of the Premier League, many of which were held in secret so that the details weren't leaked to the press. Many times we booked rooms in hotels under assumed names. I remember at one meeting in a London hotel, Irving had to go early and left by the kitchens in the back so that no one would spot him.

It was, however, an open secret that the Football League were furious with the FA for sanctioning the new league, arguing that it would totally undermine the whole structure. Such was the Football League's intransigent opposition that they took court action to prevent the Premier League from going ahead. Fortunately for us, the judges in the case ruled in our favour. As for the clubs themselves, they never had any difficulty seeing the merits of our proposal and I can't remember any of them not wanting to be a part of it. Once they realized the new league represented no real changes for them: that they were still in it, that there was relegation and promotion as per normal, that we had our own committees and were making our own decisions, and that we had our own TV deal and sponsorship money, it was, for them, a no-brainer. Why would they say no? It wasn't a tough sell.

You could say that the first tangible foundations of the Premier League were laid on 17 July 1991 with the Founder Members' Agreement, which saw us give formal notice of withdrawal from the Football League. Then, on 23 September, came the tripartite agreement between the FA, the Football League and the newly formed Premier League. It's an agreement that is still in place today.

As to who would televise the new league, it was a straight fight between ITV and BSkyB. It was important to start the Premier League with a brand new TV deal. If we'd launched it any other time we'd have been into an existing television contract with the Football League and it couldn't have been done. As it was, ITV's current contract expired in 1992 and on 18 May 1992 we received a new bid from Greg Dyke, a minimum of £200 million over a four-year period for the rights to televise thirty live matches per season. If we preferred a five-year contract, said Greg, that was also on the table and was worth a quarter of a billion pounds.

BSkyB, backed by Rupert Murdoch, were desperate to land the rights to the Premier League. They saw live sport, especially top-flight football, as an integral part of their broadcasting going forward, and tabled an extraordinary £304 million for a five-year deal. I think the majority of clubs wanted to go with BSkyB, but out of loyalty to Greg Dyke I voted to stay with ITV, as did three of the original five big clubs. Tottenham's Alan Sugar voted for the BSkyB deal – I guess he had a lot of Squarial dishes to get rid of. Ultimately BSkyB won the contract and the BBC, who were part of the bid, were awarded the highlights package and revived the popular *Match of the Day* programme.

When the deal went public quite a few people were not happy at all. I think the majority of fans were unsure of quite what to expect from it. Alex Ferguson was enraged because the decision had been taken without consulting the managers or the players. Indeed, he went public in calling on his fellow managers to fight 'the most ludicrous and backward decision that football has taken'. He was particularly unhappy about BSkyB's plans to show live games on Sundays and a Monday night. This, he said, would handicap those teams involved in European competition because it meant having to play on a Sunday or Monday and then face a tough European tie midweek. It's a problem that to this day hasn't completely gone away.

Once the TV agreement with BSkyB had been finalized, it all became about deciding on a fair distribution of the TV monies. What we eventually came up with was that 50 per cent of the total pot would be shared equally between all the clubs in the division; 25 per cent would be on appearance so, depending on how many games you appeared in, you got a share of that 25 per cent; and the remaining 25 per cent was based on league position – the champions got the most, and then you worked your way down.

There were various other things put into the contract as well, such as a clause that guaranteed every club got a minimum number of games, so that it wasn't just the same big teams appearing all the time. We believed this was the fairest formula and over the years it has generally worked very well. The very fact that it hasn't been altered since it was set up tells you that it was a well-considered plan. It's a much fairer distribution of TV money says than in, say, Spain until recently, where individual clubs used to negotiate their own contracts.

I have to say that I don't see a day when big English clubs own their own TV rights, although I think that some foreign investors have come into the game believing that eventually they will be able to do so. If you were to talk to any of those founder members of the Premier League, none of us ever wanted to hold our own rights completely because that would absolutely destroy the league – you can't have the top clubs dictating it and taking all the money, otherwise it's not competitive. Some people today would argue that this is what the Champions League has done: distorted the Premier League because of the money it generates, giving those teams that appear in Europe on a regular basis an enormous benefit over the others; in other words, favouring the more successful and wealthier clubs.

Irving Scholar, David Dein, Philip Carter, Noel White and I were all football fans; we were not modern owners in it for what we could get. If we'd said at the beginning of the process to set up the Premier League that we want 1 per cent for the five of us personally setting up the league in perpetuity out of this, imagine what wealth we would have today (1 per cent of the current Sky contract would mean £50 million; that's £10 million each). None of us ever thought like that. All we were interested in was getting a fair deal.

We weren't just thinking about competing with each other, either: we were thinking about competing on a European level. My target was always Liverpool. When I came into the game, Liverpool were winning everything; overhauling them was the first priority. But once you get successful domestically you then want to beat Real Madrid, Barcelona or Bayern Munich, and the only way you can compete with those elite teams is if you are getting a fair return for your product. One of the ways we could do that as a league was by breaking away and making sure we negotiated our own TV deals. It didn't mean that the Third and Fourth Divisions would be any worse off, because they could negotiate their own TV and sponsorship deals. They're still there, no worse off than they were when we left. Instead of all suddenly going out of business, as everybody predicted, they have survived. And the fact that there is promotion and relegation means there is the opportunity for a club to rise through the divisions. They can do it, and do. The door to the Premier League is always open.

Our thinking was exactly the same when it came to sponsorship and overseas rights: all clubs in the Premier League would get an equal share. At the time, TV rights for foreign markets weren't really worth that much. Nobody quite foresaw the value they would eventually have. If we'd had any idea quite how much they'd come to be worth, we probably wouldn't have agreed that formula. But I've always argued that if you start toying with bits of the original founding members' agreement, then other things become subject to negotiation. That formula was fair and has lasted the test of time. It's twenty-five years since the Premier League started and it's become the biggest and most successful league in the world. Certainly as a revenue generator, although I'm not sure the way clubs spend their money is always the most sensible.

I must say that part of the success story of the Premier League is down to the expertise of Sky. Initially they didn't have many subscribers, but on the back of football they grew rapidly. They needed football to drive its subscriptions and they really went for it; as a result, every subsequent contract has increased substantially. Understandably, because of their huge investment, they wanted many more games. Now the two institutions are totally interlinked. When you think of the Premier League you automatically think of Sky as well. And yet they are always subject to being outbid every time we have a new bidding process. Sky have done a tremendous amount for football, especially in the analysis of the game and the punditry that has made every match even more interesting to watch.

Television exposure in overseas markets played a big part in promoting the Premier League, too. Due to the money Sky put into football, English teams could attract better players, ones who might otherwise have gone to play in the other major European leagues, and because of that fans around the world became more interested in our game, which in turn further drove the overseas market – to such an extent that the Premier League has gone on to surpass all the expectations we had when we first decided to break away all those years ago. If you look at the original TV contract, no one could have predicted that the value of the most recent deal in 2015, when the Premier League sold its television rights to Sky and BT, would be for a record £5.1 billion.

Looking back on what we achieved, I guess there is an element of quiet personal satisfaction. It took the combined efforts of all five of us – me, Irving Scholar, David Dein, Noel White and Philip Carter – to form the Premier League. I don't give prominence to any one person. We all wanted to do it, and if any of the five of us hadn't been there it would have been different. We all contributed in our own way. I guess that Irving Scholar, David Dein and I were the young bucks, being as we were in our mid-forties, while Noel White and Philip Carter were about ten or fifteen years older. We had the youth and the enthusiasm, but they had the experience. It was a good combination. We still meet up occasionally, although our numbers are now sadly one fewer since Philip's death back in 2015.

At the time we didn't celebrate at all when the Premier League launched, which is strange. We didn't even open a bottle of champagne to toast its success; we were all too busy working hard for our clubs. In time, as the Premier League became more successful, we started to realize what we had actually created. I think we take more satisfaction from it now than we did then. When we consider all the legal hoops we had to jump through to make it happen, it gives us even more satisfaction, making us appreciate all the more what we accomplished.

18 CANTONA

The inaugural Premier League season turned out to be a momentous one for Manchester United, but it couldn't have started any worse.

After playing in just three games, our brand new £1 million summer signing, striker Dion Dublin, lay on the Old Trafford pitch writhing in agony having broken his leg in a tackle with one of Crystal Palace's centre halves. The Eagles player just went straight through him. Obviously it wasn't deliberate, but it was a nasty tackle. Dion had made quite an impact since arriving from Cambridge United, having scored on his debut and impressing his teammates with his commitment.

Poor Dion was out for over six months and effectively his United career was over. He never really established himself in the first team after that, and decided to move on, subsequently enjoying a good career with Coventry and Aston Villa. It was a shame things didn't work out for him at United, but when we won the league that season, even though Dion hadn't played the required number of games to qualify, I made sure that he received his winners' medal.

After the loss of Dion we struggled to find the net and it was obvious that a new striker was urgently required. An attempt to prise David Hirst away from Sheffield Wednesday was rejected, yet it wasn't long before a player arrived at Manchester United who would prove to be the catalyst for the club's dominance of British football for the rest of the decade.

I first heard about Eric Cantona from Irving Scholar, who since stepping down as chairman of Tottenham was living in Monaco. Irving saw a lot of French football and used to rave about Cantona: 'You must see this player, he's fantastic,' he'd say. Early in 1992, Cantona moved to England for a transfer fee of just under £1 million. His destination was Leeds United, where he was instrumental in them winning the league that year at United's expense.

One day in November 1992 I was in my office when the phone rang. It was Bill Fotherby, the managing director of Leeds United. 'Hi, Martin, how are you?' he said, beginning the usual pleasantries. 'Howard Wilkinson [the Leeds manager] is interested in buying Denis Irwin. Would you be prepared to sell him?'

I must admit to being taken slightly aback by this, since Denis was a key player for us. 'I don't think so, Bill,' I replied. 'I can ask Alex, but I doubt it.'

Then a thought flashed through my mind. I'd heard rumours that all was not well at Leeds with Eric Cantona; that he and Howard Wilkinson didn't have the best of relationships. So I decided to try my luck and asked if they would be prepared to sell Cantona. There was a short pause. 'You know, that's not as stupid as it may sound,' said Bill. 'Let me find out. I'll come back to you.'

In the meantime I rang Alex Ferguson. 'Alex, if I can get Eric Cantona, would you take him?' Alex didn't need much encouragement. 'Oh yes,' he said. 'I certainly would.' I told him to leave it with me and that we might have a chance.

The next day Bill Fotherby called back to see if we were prepared to sell Denis Irwin.

'No, we won't sell him, Bill,' I said. 'But we're definitely interested in Eric. Can we do the deal?'

'Well, I've spoken to Howard,' said Bill. 'And we would be prepared to do a deal. But we would have to do it very quickly because the supporters absolutely love him here and if it gets out we're selling him there'll be an uproar. What would you be prepared to pay?'

'One million,' I said.

'I can't sell him for a million,' said Bill. 'I'd get slaughtered. What about 1.6?'

'No,' I said. 'I can't do 1.6.'

'How about 1.5?' asked Bill. 'You'll give me 1.5.'

'Look,' I said. 'You want to get rid of him and we are prepared to take him. He's a big gamble, Bill.'

Well, the price kept coming down: 1.4, 1.3, 1.2, until finally we agreed on a million. 'But can we say it's 1.6?' said Bill.

'You can say what you like,' I said. And that's how we did the deal. Coming off the phone I immediately rang Alex at the training ground. He asked how much we'd paid. 'A million,' I said. He couldn't believe it. He couldn't believe we'd got Cantona for a million.

Then, of course, we had to meet Eric to agree personal terms, which wasn't difficult because he was very keen to come to United. The meeting was held at The Midland Hotel in Manchester and his agent was a man by the name of Jean-Jacques Bertrand. Both of them wanted the deal done immediately, which suited us, so it was all wrapped up very quickly and announced to the press.

There probably hadn't been a player like Eric Cantona at United since the days of George Best – that kind of talismanic figure, a showman. What made Eric even more special was that, while that famous 1960s team had three great players in it – Best, Law and Charlton – all European footballers of the year, Eric was undeniably the star; he stood out from the rest of the side.

I knew that we had a good enough team to win the league, especially with him, but I wasn't especially confident; there was no feeling that this was our year. If anything, there was an element of fear because the season before we'd got so close to it and yet had fallen away at the end. This time around we were really in the thick of it again, fighting a three-horse race for much of the season with both Aston Villa and Norwich City. In the end we won by ten clear points, having finished with a sequence of seven successive wins.

Normally you associate fantastic single moments with a cup win because you're there on the day, but to win the league after twenty-six years the way that we did was terrific. It was an unbelievable feeling because I had been involved in the whole of that long wait and it became more and more agonizing as the years went by. I was there the last time we won the league, going all the way back to 1967, and now to win it again as chairman was a very special feeling. And being champions changed the whole atmosphere at Old Trafford. It was as though an enormous weight was lifted off our shoulders.

I firmly believe that Cantona arriving when he did, playing his debut match for us early that December in the Manchester derby, provided the momentum that took United to the championship title. There's a famous football saying that managers are always looking for that one player to complete the jigsaw. Well, Eric was that one player we needed. He was the one who unlocked the door for us; the difference between just missing out and winning. Over the next five seasons we won the league four times with Eric in the team. Winning became a habit. But it was that first championship that was so important – eventually getting us over the line.

I'm sure also that the fact we had stability at the club played a huge part in our success. Not only had I been chairman since 1980 but Alex had been there since 1986, and here we both were in 1993, seven years later. It was an ongoing project we were willing to see through and we had supported Alex in very tough times. That is what was so pleasing about winning the league in 1993: it justified our patience and support.

That championship trophy was not the pinnacle for Manchester United, as history would tell. It represented the beginning rather than the end. My ambition now was to go on and lift the European Cup, or as it had just become known, the UEFA Champions League. I wanted Alex and this team to emulate the great success achieved by Matt and be crowned kings of Europe. Saying that, I didn't want the pursuit of the European Cup to become a millstone around our necks. The importance of winning the national league would always be paramount. That was to be our bread and butter.

19 BRAND UNITED

Back on 9 June 1992, I was in my office when Danny McGregor, our commercial manager, came in to tell me that Edward Freedman was arriving at Old Trafford to give a talk about merchandising and did I want to attend.

At the time, Edward Freedman was in charge of merchandising at Tottenham, where he had revolutionized their whole approach to marketing. For years the practice at United was to license out our products. For example, a company would approach us and say, we want to put your crest on a mug. We'd draw up a contract with a minimum guarantee and they would go off to make the product and then pay us a royalty on whatever they sold. Of course, with that you never quite knew what's going on. Are you always getting the correct royalty? Are they selling more than they're saying? Are they just paying a licence fee and then going off and doing their own thing, meaning that's the last you see of it?

Tottenham under Freedman wasn't giving out licences; he was sourcing everything himself, dealing directly with manufacturers, getting the T-shirts, putting the Tottenham crest on them and doing it all in-house.

He was way ahead of everyone, so I wanted to hear what he had to say.

I went along and listened to the presentation, and afterwards told Edward that if he had a spare moment before he left I wanted to see him in my office for a chat. When he arrived I wasted little time in offering him a job with United. At first he turned me down, but I remained resolute and suggested another meeting. He returned the following week and this time accepted my offer. I don't think he was happy any more at Tottenham; he was finding it difficult working under the new regime of Alan Sugar and Terry Venables, which made it that much easier bringing him over to United. I certainly wouldn't have considered head hunting Edward if Irving had still been in charge at Spurs.

The appointment of Freedman was by no means an instinctive decision. I'd known for some while that we needed to bring somebody in to improve our marketing, and one look at what Tottenham were doing showed Freedman was obviously the man to do it – at the time, their merchandising sales were something like 50 per cent up on United's, despite having less success than us on the pitch. And Irving had always spoken very highly of him.

In fact, I had met Edward a couple of times in Irving's office in London. There was also a conversation I remembered having with Peter Kenyon, who was then at Umbro. Having already begun to consider enlarging our merchandising set-up, I wanted to pick Peter's brains. 'If you were looking for somebody to run the merchandising side of things,' I asked him, 'who would you go for?' 'I'd get Edward Freedman at Tottenham,' he said, without hesitation.

Edward spent years in the textile and retail business before coming into football; he had lots of contacts and some good ideas about moving forward and increasing trade. The principal problem as I saw it with United was structural. When Edward arrived, marketing was the club shop and that was about it. We didn't have a marketing man. We had a commercial manager but most of his time was spent on things like match-day sponsorships and promotions. He wasn't really a retailer.

The club shop had been in the hands of Matt Busby since 1968, on a twenty-one-year lease. When he purchased it there was a clause in the contract to the effect that should he wish to sell the business it could only be sold back to the club. Sometime in 1987, with the lease due to run out in a couple of years, I had approached the Busby family with a view to buying the shop from them. Over the last few years it hadn't been doing very well and my thinking was that we could do a better job with it. The deal made sense on both sides because the Busby family would want to sell out before the lease ended, after which they might not get as much money. The last thing I wanted, though, was to be accused of ripping off the Busby family, so in the end I probably paid over the odds for the shop at £146,500.

As part of the deal we had agreed to give Matt's son, Sandy, a five-year consultancy job at the club with a salary of £13,000 a year. That added another £65,000 on top of the purchase price, so you could say that in total we paid over £200,000 for the shop. But we believed it was an important asset to own and it was one that we intended to build upon over the coming years.

Pretty soon we had two shops that opened on match days: one at the front of the stadium, the other at the back. Eventually when we redeveloped the East Stand we put the megastore in there. We were always expanding the shop or looking for more space.

Building up the stores was only part of what Edward wanted to do. One of his first instructions was to stop the licensing of products. He said that we should be more efficient with them; that we couldn't just be giving out licences left, right and centre because it undermines their value. We had to take these things on board ourselves and start doing our own production – producing our own goods, like branding our own clothing in the shop.

He also got to grips with our mail-order business, which was almost negligible. If I recall rightly, we had something like one person manning a telephone. Soon Edward was placing ads for items of clothing in the club programme, and you could send in order forms. He didn't much like the club programme either, so we gave him a run on the design of that and soon started selling more programmes. He was a terrific marketing man.

One of Edward's most high-profile innovations was the launch of

Manchester United magazine, the first time a football club had its own individual magazine. There wasn't a lot of support for it at first when Edward initially came to me with the idea. 'What's the risk?' I asked. He told me we might sell a few thousand. I thought it was worth a gamble and the first issue came out in November 1992. Over the course of the 1990s, the magazine became the most popular football monthly in the world, selling about 80–90,000 a month. It was unbelievable.

Next we started a video magazine that came out every two months, which contained match highlights, player interviews and other features. The club already had an agreement with a company to produce videos for us, and they paid us about a pound, I think, for every video sold. Edward said no to that; we'll do our own videos. Again, it was a huge success: we sold thousands of them.

As the merchandising side of things expanded, people would approach us with all manner of product ideas, some of them totally unsuitable. There were things like ladies' underwear with 'I scored at the Stretford End' on them. Ultimately you just had to rely on a bit of common sense. There were also a huge number of counterfeit goods; we did our best to chase them down, but it was hugely expensive and we weren't always successful in getting a prosecution.

Over time, Edward built up an excellent team around him that understood marketing. And having chosen Edward, I fully supported him, as I had done with Alex, by simply letting him get on with his job. If he wanted to spend money he would come to see me about it. For example, when he wanted to build a new shop or warehouse, he needed my approval. But on everything else I gave him a free hand and I think it worked out very well. Edward did, though, have a clash of personality with Robin Launders. Robin wanted to know everything that was going on and Edward wasn't the type of person who liked to be questioned all the time. It drove him mad. He came to see me and asked if I could get Robin off his back. So that had to be sorted out and in the end I made sure that Edward was only answerable to me.

We also decided to run the merchandising as a separate business, much the same way as the Pools and lottery and the catering were subsidiaries of the plc. The catering had its own managing director, Michael Whetton, and had its own structure and staff; it was a completely separate company, producing its own monthly reports and management figures. We did exactly the same with the merchandising. We made it Manchester United Merchandising Limited, Edward was managing director and I chaired it. As chief executive of the plc I chaired all the subsidiary boards.

Of course it helped Edward's marketing drive enormously that, from being also-rans, United suddenly were champions in the very first year of the Premier League and went on to be hugely successful for a sustained period. That's really when we began to take advantage of all the merchandising opportunities, and that's where our timing was good in bringing in Edward when we did. Inevitably, this led to certain critics remarking that Manchester United were no longer a football club; that we were more like a brand, a business, a money-making operation. Yet this marketing success helped turn us into a superpower able to rival the likes of Real Madrid, Barcelona and Bayern Munich.

It also added significantly to the club's turnover. The net margin was probably 10 or 11 per cent. If Edward was taking £38 million in sales – that was the best year he ever did – he made around £4 million net profit. Now, that's £4 million profit from pretty much nothing, which is where our merchandising was before he arrived. As well as being valuable for the club, that was also extremely useful in terms of the share price in the City, which liked the turnover and publicity generated from merchandising.

Merchandising players' shirts is also big business. Which player's shirt sells the most always gets a lot of publicity. Yet a lot of it is overplayed. I hear statements like, 'You've got to buy so and so because you'll get your money back on shirt sales.' In reality, there's no chance of getting your money back on shirts if you're paying a player top wages. Of course you get some money back, but it's more about what that player is going to do on the field than whether his face is going to sell in the shop. It's more about the results; those are what are really going to bring in the money.

Merchandising does have a cost attached to it, hence the lower margins than you might expect; if you make 10 per cent net profit on turnover then you're doing well. Whereas something like television is straight to the bottom line. There's no cost to television: you get a cheque from Sky through the League for several million pounds each year – it's straight to profit. Shirt sponsorship is also very profitable.

Almost everything else has a cost to its sale. Take catering, for example: you've got to have somebody to cook the food and then staff to serve it. Even sales at the stadium have a cost attached. On a match day, you've got to print the tickets, have somebody on the turnstiles, and then have people to clean up the stands after everyone is gone. All of these different turnover aspects of the business have costs attached to them, yet they still made strong margins for us. But merchandising gets an unparalleled amount of publicity considering the value to the business. Don't get me wrong, it was very important – it put pence on the share price and was a good indicator of how popular United were becoming, particularly in global terms – so I'm not undervaluing its impact. However, in the context of the whole business, the team winning a cup, getting into Europe, the next TV negotiation, were all worth much more. Merchandising had its place though, and Edward was excellent at it.

I believe we were the most forward-thinking club in terms of merchandising, very much leading the way among our competitors. At the same time it set us on the road to becoming a worldwide brand.

Back in October 1993 Old Trafford played host to one of the most talked-about British boxing bouts of the decade when Nigel Benn took on Chris Eubank for the World Super Middleweight crown. While I was keen to use Old Trafford to put the fight on, there was a slight nervousness on our part because these sorts of events had been known to get very rowdy at times, and the last thing we wanted was for anything to go wrong and damage the reputation of the club.

I held several meetings with the promoters and the police, and the whole thing turned out to be a huge success, with over 40,000 fight fans showing up for what the press called 'Judgement Day'. I was there that night, and it was a hell of a fight and a great atmosphere under the floodlights. Nigel Benn actually had a link to United because Paul Ince was his cousin, so I suppose our allegiance was to him, but in the end the fight was a draw.

I always wanted to make Old Trafford a venue for a whole host of sporting events. Back in 1981 we put on a cricket seven-a-side tournament under the floodlights. Then in 1986 we were asked to stage the first Whitbread Trophy Bitter Rugby League Test match between Great Britain and Australia. It was a prestigious event covered live on BBC's flagship sports programme *Grandstand*, and a crowd of over 50,000 came to watch. It proved so successful that the Rugby League approached us to see if they could hold their Super League Grand Final at Old Trafford, which we were happy to do, and that has become a regular event to this day. Putting on these kinds of events not only gained the club extra revenue, but also associating the United brand with big sporting events was another great way to sell the club to a wider public and increase our visibility around the sporting world. This, for me, was very important.

Another important element of selling the Manchester United brand and making it better known around the world were the pre-season tours.

Just prior to the 1993–94 campaign we took the team out to South Africa, which was a particularly memorable tour for me. Playing a match in Cape Town, I had the privilege of sitting next to Nelson Mandela and chatting to him throughout the course of the game. One incongruous thing I couldn't help but notice was that he had these huge muscular thighs. When I plucked up the temerity to ask him about this he told me that when he was in prison he used to train with weights every day to alleviate the boredom. He also loved boxing and often used to practise it; his all-time hero, he revealed to me, was Muhammad Ali. The people you meet and the stories you hear from people interested in your club when travelling are often remarkable, and it's then, when football takes you out of the circles you usually move in, that you really appreciate the industry. Of course, the bigger the club becomes, the more high-profile fans you get asking to come to your matches. It's great for the club's brand, because of the exposure – to be seen with famous fans or visitors – not to mention thrilling on a personal level.

As you might imagine, United get invitations to tour from all over the world. We always tried to pick places that would give us some competition. It's vitally important that the manager is happy with the pre-season arrangements and that the games provide his players with some kind of test. Latterly, of course, marketing came into the equation. You want to go to places where you know you're going to be well received because you've got a lot of supporters there or to a country where you can help build up the brand. Managers can get concerned sometimes if the pre-season becomes too stretched or too ambitious and involves asking too much of the team during what is important preparation for the season to come. You've got to be careful you don't overdo things. It's about striking a balance.

Back in my father's time the team often went abroad on pre-season tours. I remember in 1967 my father going off to Australia and New Zealand and the team playing ten matches. Strangely enough, the team would go off somewhere at the end of the season, too. When I became chairman I cut those games out altogether because I felt they were becoming unnecessary. Some of your key players were off on international duty anyway, that being the time of year that World Cups and European Championships were played. You would only disappoint the fans by not having your star players feature – always a bone of contention with the organizers.

I also found that players didn't take the post-season tours very seriously. They were winding down and wanted to have a bit of fun rather than focus on the games. They were in relaxation mode and on occasions that led to a bit of trouble. Coupled with the increasing number of games in Europe and playing too many matches anyway, I felt it best to abandon the end of season tours to concentrate purely on pre-season. The fans are serious about their clubs, and every match should therefore be taken as seriously. You can't undersell the people who are your lifeblood.

20 VICTORIOUS UNITED

As we prepared for the 1993–94 season it had become clear to us that one of United's most influential and popular players was coming to the end of his remarkable career. Bryan Robson was still playing but his appearances were getting fewer, due either to injury or to competition for places. The man identified as the perfect long-term replacement for Bryan was a young player at Nottingham Forest called Roy Keane. We'd watched him for a while and were well aware of his potential, but Roy had already spoken with Blackburn's manager Kenny Dalglish and had verbally agreed terms. Determined not to lose out on the player, Alex spoke to Roy personally, told him that United wanted him at the club and in the end persuaded him that we were by far the better option.

Alex then went on holiday and it was left to me to get the Forest chairman Fred Reacher to sell us Keane. When I called Fred he was on the golf course – he always took his phone with him in his golf bag. The price he quoted for Roy was £4 million, a pretty hefty figure at the time. In the end I managed to get the fee down to £3.75 million. And what a buy it was! It was also a big statement to our rivals that we had absolutely no intention of resting on our laurels as we aimed to defend our first league title since the 1960s.

Without doubt Roy must be included in anyone's list of United greats. He can lay claim to seven Premiership medals, and how many players can say they were part of two Double-winning teams and a Treble? Roy was a winner, pure and simple, and a leader capable of grabbing the team by the collective throat and hauling them over the finishing line. I don't think we've had that kind of player since. He was uncompromising and a strong personality. He had very high standards and didn't like it when others failed to come up to them. In some ways he was a perfect representative for Alex on the field. He set the benchmark.

Towards the end of his career at United, Roy knew exactly how valuable he was to the club. I think he would almost certainly have been prepared to leave on principle if he hadn't got what he thought he was worth.

Keane quickly made his presence felt in that United midfield and we went on to totally dominate the league that year, playing aggressive, fast and stylish football. Looking back I think that side was as good as any United has ever had. When the first-choice eleven played together we never lost a game. Schmeichel was in goal. Parker and Irwin were the full backs, both of whom played in that position for their respective countries and were excellent at coming forward. Brucie and Pallister were in the centre of defence, solid as a rock. In the midfield there were Ince and Keane, two battlers, but also capable of a great deal of flair. On the wide right, Kanchelskis, who was an absolute flyer and could score goals, and on the left, Giggs, tearing the opposition defence to bits. Finally, up front, you had Cantona and Hughes. What a side, crafted over the previous few seasons. It was magical. There's no weak link there whatsoever.

The tragedy is that Alex was never able to field this side in Europe due to a UEFA ruling restricting teams to only three foreign players. For some absurd reason the rule also applied to Irish, Scottish and Welsh players, so in addition to Cantona, Kanchelskis and Schmeichel, Giggs, Hughes, Irwin, Keane and McClair were also affected. That's almost an entire team. I firmly believe that if it weren't for that UEFA ruling the team would have got very close to winning the Champions League. As it was, they never got the chance to prove themselves in Europe. The ruling was eventually lifted in 1996.

Our first European cup campaign after an absence of over a quarter of a century in the top flight of European competition ended in November 1993 in chaotic scenes against Galatasaray in Istanbul. The atmosphere on that trip was horrendous from the moment we arrived at the airport, being exposed to the familiar greeting of the Galatasaray fans mockingly slitting their throats. That kind of thing doesn't have any place in football.

There was an awful atmosphere during the game, too. Cantona managed to get himself red-carded after the final whistle and as our players made their way off the pitch several of them were manhandled by the Turkish police, who were supposed to be there to protect us from the home fans. In the end we were just glad to get out of the place.

On 20 January 1994 we all learnt of the sad passing of Matt Busby. I was at home at the time and spent a good portion of the day fielding telephone calls from the press. When I arrived at Old Trafford I couldn't help but feel moved by all the flowers, scarves and other United memorabilia that fans had left outside the stadium.

Until quite recently Matt was still a familiar face around Old Trafford. I used to see him fairly regularly. Although Matt was in his eighties he liked to come down for the occasional lunch to meet up with old friends. Over the last few years his visits had begun to dwindle but he would still be seen in his seat for home matches.

On 22 January United played Everton at Old Trafford. Before the match there was a minute's silence, which I have to say was wonderfully respected. It was only natural for the board themselves to want to pay their own special respect to Matt's memory and it was a unanimous decision that the best way to do that was to erect a statue in his honour. It stands there today in front of the East Stand.

I'm so glad that Matt lived long enough to see his beloved Manchester United win the league again. Sadly he missed one of the club's greatest ever achievements when we won the domestic Double in that 1993–94 season, the first Double in the club's history; it would have been a suitable final memory for a man who gave United so much. We really should have won the Double back in 1957 before Munich, when we won the league but lost the Cup final to Aston Villa after our goalkeeper Ray Wood was injured after five minutes in a collision that left him with a broken cheekbone. Of course, those were the days before substitutes were allowed. This time we made no mistake and did it in style, too. We might even have won the domestic Treble if not for a defeat at the hands of Ron Atkinson's Aston Villa in the League Cup final. But we dominated the league, with our talisman Eric Cantona up front, and in the FA Cup final brushed Chelsea aside 4–0, the Frenchman scoring two penalties, with Hughes and McClair also on the scoresheet.

We almost didn't make it to Wembley at all. Having drawn relegation-threatened Oldham in the semi-final, it was only a spectacular late goal from Hughes that forced a replay, where a goal scored by Bryan Robson (alongside others from Irwin, Kanchelskis and Giggs) helped us to a 4–1 victory. When Bryan wasn't selected for the final, not even making the bench, he was no doubt bitterly disappointed but probably realized he was coming to the end of his playing career. By this time he was in his mid-thirties and was very much a squad player, coming in for the odd game, and had already been approached to go to Middlesbrough as player-manager. Thankfully Bryan's career extended long enough to be part of the United side that won the league in 1993 and 1994, so he received two championship medals, which he fully deserved for all his years of service.

Our successes over those two seasons had created something of a backlash in how the footballing public viewed Manchester United; a state of affairs that persists to this day. For years following the Munich disaster we were many people's second-favourite team; now we were intensely disliked. It was a movement epitomized by the terrace chants of 'stand up if you hate Man United' that almost became a national anthem for rival supporters. People felt we were arrogant, which I don't think we were. Our success had bred confidence. We did have strong, single-minded players like Keane, Ince and Hughes, who could look after themselves on the pitch and mix it with the opposition. Cantona was also known to rile a few players. Perhaps it could be said that the style of the team, and the aggression, turned a few people off.

Also, we were making a lot of money. Not only had United started to dominate league football but our turnover on merchandise and other business activities was so much higher than everyone else's. There was a lot of jealousy around. And the process becomes self-perpetuating: the more profit you make the more you can invest in the team and the more successful you become, much to the annoyance of supporters of other clubs. Perhaps this is really where all that hatred for United comes from. Success can breed envy in some.

The accusation has always been that United sold out to the dollar; that we became overly commercialized. But every major club was doing the same thing; it was only because United were the most successful at it that we caught the brunt of the criticism. Personally I don't agree that United became too commercialized; I think we got the balance right. All we were doing was capitalizing on our success on the field in order to consolidate it, and every football club knows it has to do that if it wants to stay out in front. When Alex arrived at United our first objective was to win the domestic league title, to be number one in our own country. To achieve that we had to overtake Liverpool. Once we'd done that our next objective was to be number one in Europe, to win the European Cup. After that you want to go on and win the World Club Championship. You want to win everything. You can only do that with a strong underlying financial base.

While I was running Manchester United we never ever had a fairy godmother. We never had a situation like Chelsea's where a wealthy individual takes over and starts throwing money around, and drastically changes their footballing fortunes in a short time. We never had a handout from anybody. Everything we generated was off our own back through floating on the stock market, good management, creating successful teams, and backing it up by capitalizing on the success of that team with our commercial success. That was always my focus.

Things are a little bit different today. I don't like to be too critical of what's going on now but I think from a financial point of view football has got out of hand. The last two or three television deals were a huge opportunity for football clubs to give something back to the fans, but football takes the money every time and spends it on players and wages. It goes straight from the TV companies into wages, transfer fees and the pockets of agents; hardly anything ever goes back to the fans. One just has to look at the record figures spent on transfers and agents in the 2016–17 season, the latter up 38 per cent from £160 million to £220 million.

To my mind football clubs, chief executives and to a lesser extent managers have allowed agents in particular to get away with what they do today. I was always quite strong on agents. I felt that if an agent brought a player to our club he was entitled to something. I used to think that £250,000 for an agent was more than reasonable, and that figure was always spread out over the life of the contract. If an agent was getting £50,000 a year he was doing very, very well by the standards of the 1990s. Nowadays it's just gone mad: they're into the millions. I know the transfer fees have gone up, but the agent's percentage of those transfer fees has gone up even more. It's up to football clubs to control the agents, in exactly the same way as it is to control wages, else it's anyone's guess as to where power will eventually lie.

21 KUNG-FU ERIC

We knew when we bought Eric that there was a risk attached to him because of the disciplinary problems he'd had in France, which included him being banned from international matches for one year after insulting the national coach on television. Alex obviously thought that he would be able to control his volatile personality, and for the most part he succeeded. However, in March 1994 Eric was dismissed in successive Premier League games; one he was unlucky with, the other he wasn't, when he stamped on an opponent's chest at Swindon.

Then, the following season, came that infamous night at Crystal Palace on 25 January 1995. I watched the whole thing unfold. Eric had got himself sent off for a petulant kick-out at a Crystal Palace player, and as he was marching down the touchline you could see this Palace supporter giving him abuse. Suddenly Eric veered off towards the crowd and performed a kung-fu kick on the fan, following it up with a series of punches. It was unbelievable. There was complete silence in the directors' box; we all looked at each other as if to say, did that just happen? We knew straightaway that this was very serious and that the consequences were going to be severe.

As you can imagine, the fallout the next day was spectacular. Everybody wanted their say about the incident, the newspapers were full of the story and it was all over the television; people wanted to know what Manchester United were going to do about it.

Before returning to Manchester I met with the FA's director of public affairs David Davies and told him that the club were quite prepared to take action. I mentioned that I might be able to persuade the United board to ban Eric until the end of the season; would that be enough to appease the FA? 'We're not talking a life ban here, are we?' I asked. The club were a bit worried that the footballing authorities were going to throw the book at Eric. 'That would be very helpful,' David assured me.

That evening back up north, Roland, Maurice and I met Alex and we all agreed to ban Eric until the end of the season, thinking that would be the end of the matter with the FA. In other words, we'd done our bit, we'd come down fairly heavily on him, and hopefully that would stop the FA from taking even more punitive action.

The next day we held a press conference to explain the reason for our decision. In the meantime the FA set up their own commission to consider the incident, and they decided to ban Eric until the end of September, which meant he wouldn't be available to us for any pre-season training or the start of the 1995–96 season. We were very disappointed with this judgement because I thought we had taken strong disciplinary action ourselves. There have been instances with players since when I believe clubs haven't taken the necessary action themselves. I felt we had acted responsibly and that the measures we'd taken should have been accepted as a reasonable and fair resolution to the matter.

Such was the severity of the incident that Eric was charged with actual bodily harm and had to attend a court hearing, where he was sentenced to a two-week prison sentence. It was Maurice Watkins who got him out on bail and then, on appeal, his sentence was reduced to 120 hours of community service.

Eric never explained what happened on the pitch that day or why he did what he did, but everyone remembers his famous 'sardines' quote. After winning his appeal Eric broke his silence by taking centre stage at a packed press conference. 'When the seagulls,' he said, pausing for effect to take a sip of water, 'follow the trawler, it is because they think sardines will be thrown into the sea. Thank you very much.' With that he got up and strode out of the room.

Everyone was left mystified, and the debate raged about what he meant. All that Eric was trying to do was make a point about the press hounding people and looking for stories in his own inimitable French way. In fact, before that press conference, Eric asked Maurice Watkins, who could speak French, to translate into English what he wanted to say.

That whole affair was a complete nightmare, and culminated in Eric saying that he was finished with English football, leading to Alex having to go out to Paris to persuade him to come back. The main concern for Alex was that he didn't want this to be the end of Eric's Manchester United career. Indeed, around this time we had to fight off an approach by Inter Milan to prise Eric away from Old Trafford. Alex was very much on the defensive, wondering what he could do to bring him back and get him motivated again. Eric was so important to the team that Alex didn't want to lose him. Ultimately, managers want the best players so they tend to be a bit more forgiving.

Naturally, the rest of the team were disappointed that Eric wasn't going to be around for the rest of the season – he was their talisman – but I felt we had enough strength in depth to compensate. Especially since we had only recently smashed the British transfer record to buy a new striker. With Mark Hughes now thirty-one, Alex had been on the lookout for a long-term successor, and halfway through the season had identified two likely targets in Stan Collymore of Nottingham Forest and Newcastle's Andy Cole. Alex had already begun negotiations with Forest's manager Frank Clark but it appeared to him that the club were prevaricating, unable to make up their minds over the deal.

At the beginning of January Alex rang me to say he could get Cole. Newcastle's manager Kevin Keegan was prepared to let him go for £6 million, plus our young winger Keith Gillespie, who we valued at one million, so that pushed the whole deal up to around the £7 million mark. It was a lot of money at the time but I knew it was the right thing to do.

I don't remember losing any sleep over the fee. Cole was hot property at the time and scoring for fun at Newcastle. And he became a big success for us, ending his career with a goal every other game. He was a good professional. I'll always remember him scoring five goals in our 9–0 demolition of Ipswich just a couple of months into his United career. As extrovert as he was on the pitch in terms of his goal scoring, as a person, Andy was rather shy and quite introverted – a good foil for the louder characters in the dressing room.

We had also strengthened our defence at the start of the season with the acquisition of David May for £1.2 million from Blackburn. But while we came close to reaching the same dizzy heights as the previous season we ended up second best all round, losing both the league and the FA Cup in May. Blackburn had been top of the table for the majority of the year but on the last day of the season the destination of the title had still to be decided. Blackburn were two points ahead facing a tricky match against Liverpool at Anfield. We had to win at West Ham and hope our old foes could do us a favour. Against the run of play West Ham went ahead but in the second half our overwhelming domination finally earned us an equalizer from Brian McClair. In the final fifteen minutes we bombarded the West Ham goal and had numerous opportunities to score. Needless to say their keeper played a blinder and we were denied a stonewall penalty. That's the way things go sometimes. Matters were made even worse after we learnt Liverpool had beaten Blackburn. Losing the title under those circumstances was the worst feeling I ever had in football.

There was almost an inevitability about our FA Cup final loss. Having missed out on the league the week before, we were all pretty down, the spirit just wasn't there, and Everton beat us 1–0 in an unremarkable match.

All in all it was a bad season. Losing Eric as we did halfway through had a profound effect and I have no doubt that with Eric in the team we'd have done the Double again. We did the Double in 1994, Eric had his moment of madness in the 1994–95 season and we won nothing, then we went on to do the Double again in 1996 after he came back. It's amazing to think that with Eric in the team we would probably have won three Doubles on the trot. That's how influential he was.

22 'YOU CAN'T WIN ANYTHING WITH KIDS'

Soon after winning the league for the first time, Alex came to see me to ask for a pay rise. He wasn't happy at learning that his salary was less than George Graham was receiving over at Arsenal. He was, however, on a big bonus each time he won us a trophy. In the end I offered Alex an improved contract, which he signed.

At the close of the 1994–95 season, Alex was still aggrieved over being paid less than George Graham, and although we'd won nothing that year he asked me for another pay rise. As far as I was concerned this was really a matter better dealt with by Roland Smith and Maurice Watkins: I didn't think that it would be healthy for the chief exec and the manager to fall out over salary negotiations. The issue wasn't resolved to Alex's liking, however, and it would be bubbling under the surface for much of the coming season.

There were more pressing matters in the summer of 1995, when my suspicions were raised that Old Trafford was being bugged. Certain things had appeared in the press that made us question how they had come by that information. Especially since we always tried to keep confidential matters very much in-house. I decided to carry out a search of the premises and we discovered wires, a tape recorder and several tapes in the ceiling of my office. It was a shocking discovery that left me feeling more than a little unsettled, since the culprit must have been able to gain access to my office in order to put the equipment there and collect the recorded information. Someone was getting in somehow. Although an internal investigation was carried out, we never did find out who was responsible.

That summer, United offloaded three of its most experienced and high-profile players in Paul Ince, Mark Hughes and Andrei Kanchelskis, much to the consternation and bewilderment of the supporters.

I must say that a lot of people at Old Trafford were surprised, in particular, when at the end of the season Alex announced that he wanted to sell Paul Ince. A popular player among the fans, Paul was still quite young at the time. I remember Brian Kidd approached me and said, 'Bloody hell, chairman, what's happening? Why are we selling Paul?' I did query it with the manager but Alex was adamant that he wanted him to go. The reason he gave was that in some of the big games that season Paul hadn't carried out his instructions. Alex had given Paul certain defensive responsibilities and felt that he had been let down. I think Alex blamed Ince for a couple of key losses. A very good offer had come in from Inter Milan and Alex believed that he had more than enough quality coming through the ranks to cover his position in the shapes of Paul Scholes, although he initially played in a more advanced role, and Nicky Butt.

The fans didn't quite see it like that; they viewed it as a purely commercial deal and I took all the flack for it. There were all sorts of phone-ins about it and even a programme on Manchester's Radio Piccadilly. But I couldn't ask a manager to keep a player he didn't want. It was Alex's call to make that decision and we stood by him.

The sale of Mark Hughes was a different matter. Alex didn't want the player to leave but Mark was coming to the end of his contract and refused to put pen to paper on a new one. We'd already signed Andy Cole in January so Mark must have thought his chances of playing first-team football were going to be limited. Chelsea took full advantage of the situation and approached Mark; we eventually agreed to let him go to them for a fee of £1.5 million, and Mark went on to do well there.

It was a little bit more complicated with Kanchelskis. During the last season Andrei had complained of a knee injury and Alex basically didn't believe him, because the club physio and consultants couldn't detect anything. In the end, Andrei did need an operation and the player and manager fell out as a consequence; the trust had gone. In the summer Andrei asked for a transfer; Everton were interested and were prepared to pay £5 million.

Andrei's agent Grigory Essaoulenko arrived at Old Trafford to conduct the negotiations. His was a face I recognized from our previous dealings with him when we first signed Andrei from Shakhtar Donetsk, but Alex had more cause to remember the Russian after a recent bizarre incident at Manchester Airport.

Following a 1–1 draw at Nottingham Forest, Alex had driven back to Old Trafford, arriving there at one o'clock in the morning. He was surprised to see Essaoulenko waiting in the car park. The agent told Alex he had something for him and asked if could collect it at the Excelsior hotel at Manchester Airport. Alex protested, but Essaoulenko would not take no for an answer. When Alex walked into the hotel foyer he was presented with a gift-wrapped package which he later discovered to be stuffed with £40,000 in cash.

Mystified about why he had been given this money – was it an attempted bung or a way of currying favour – Alex arrived the next morning at Old Trafford and revealed what had happened to club secretary Ken Merrett, who then telephoned Maurice Watkins. I was also made aware of it. Obviously Alex had done the right thing telling us and Ken put the £40,000 into his office safe, where it remained untouched for almost twelve months. Essaoulenko's arrival for the Kanchelskis deal represented the perfect opportunity to return the money. The only thing was, he didn't want it. When I insisted he take it, things became very heated and veiled threats were made concerning my physical wellbeing. It was a load of nonsense really; in the end he took back the money and we sold Andrei.

Of course, the fans didn't know what was really happening behind the scenes; all they could see was Manchester United releasing three important players and not replacing them. We went into the 1995–96 season with no major signings, such was the faith Alex had in a batch of young players that were soon to write themselves into the history books at United.

For the past couple of years it had been enormously satisfying watching this group of youngsters, soon to be dubbed 'The Class of 92', break through and cement their place in the first team. Back in September 1994 United had courted controversy by fielding a supposedly 'weakened' team in the League Cup at Port Vale. Alex had made several changes from the side that had played just five days earlier in the league, bringing in some names that were then largely unfamiliar, like Gary Neville, David Beckham, Nicky Butt and Paul Scholes. Alex got a lot of criticism for that decision but Scholes, on his senior debut, scored both goals as we went on to win 2–1. And that was the start really, the first time the wider public became aware of this class of very talented young players.

We'd known for some time they were a special bunch. I remember when Bryan Robson went to play in the reserve team with a lot of them and came back complaining that he wasn't even allowed to take a throw-in. They were so organized, he said, each of them having their own separate role in the team, that when he went to take a throw-in, the ball was taken off him and Gary Neville took it instead.

Gary was the captain of that youth team and very much the leader on the field. He was extremely mature for his age. Some people thought that his brother Phil was the better player but both of them were excellent footballers, and also very good cricketers. Indeed, Phil was so highly rated that he captained England at Under-15 level. I'll always remember talking to Ray Illingworth, the former England captain and manager, who told me that Phil was an absolute certainty to play for England at cricket. They were sorry to lose him to football.

As for Nicky Butt, everybody knew, when he was still at an early age, that he was going to make the grade. There were no doubts about him at all. At seventeen he was very strong for his age, a hard tackler, combative

– you really didn't mess with him. He was streetwise in that sense, and he could read the game well. Like all of that youth team, Nicky had real hunger and desire, and was a great worker.

Without doubt, though, it was David Beckham who became the most famous of them all, largely because of his marriage to Posh Spice. I actually played a part in the two of them becoming a couple. Edward Freedman called me up one day asking for a favour. He was discussing some business with Simon Fuller, the manager of the Spice Girls, and Fuller wanted to come to a game. He was bringing Victoria Adams and Melanie Chisholm with him, so asked if I could accommodate them in the directors' room. I was happy to do this and after the match the girls asked if they could go down and meet the team. I escorted them both to the players' lounge, and that's where Victoria met David for the very first time.

Despite the media circus that often surrounded David, he was a very exciting young player. The main parts of his game were his energy and dead ball skills, his vision and his supreme passing ability. Originally David was a junior at Tottenham, but his father was a huge United fan and brought him up to Manchester to enrol in one of Bobby Charlton's soccer schools, and that's where it all started for him. Everyone knew who Beckham was in the dressing room because Alex, when he was courting David and making sure he signed for us, used to bring him to home matches. I always used to see this little blonde kid in the dressing room and wonder who it was – it turned out to be the young Beckham.

Then of course there was Ryan Giggs, who had already established himself in the first team. But I always remember Brian Kidd saying to me around this time that of all the young players breaking through, for him the jewel in the crown was Paul Scholes. Paul went on to have a magnificent career, winning eleven Premier League championship medals. Only Giggs has won more in domestic football. And what a footballer Scholesey was! He was a very influential player on the field – when he wasn't there you really noticed it. Not only was he highly creative, with a fantastic range of passing, but he could score goals as well as make them. He was a quiet lad. I'm not sure he was that quiet with his peers, but he was certainly media shy in those early days. Without question Paul ranks among my favourite players from my time as chairman.

There were other players, too, who might have made the grade. Ben Thornley was a very useful winger but sadly broke his leg in a reserve game against Blackburn. There was also Robbie Savage, who went on to have a good career elsewhere. The fact that you didn't always make it at United didn't mean you weren't a good footballer and weren't going to succeed at another club.

When you mention the Class of 92 you have to talk about Les Kershaw and Eric Harrison. Eric gets the credit for bringing the players through the system, of gelling them all together into a team. But it was Les, who is often forgotten in the story, who found and recruited them all, along with his network of scouts. Les also had to deal with the parents, making sure they were comfortable about their son coming to United, and building up a good relationship between the club and the players' families. He was very important to United. Later he became director of the academy and I still see him at Old Trafford on match days.

During the development of Scholes, Beckham, Neville and co., I was kept very much in the loop. I'd go to watch as many of the youth team games as I could, and following the matches it was customary for the parents to be invited for a meal in one of the suites. In this way I got to know a lot of the players' parents, including Ted Beckham. Scholesey's family used to turn up. I remember Nicky Butt's dad and Giggsy's mum Lynn. It was very much a family-type atmosphere at those matches; almost a return to the 1950s style of doing things. What Alex was trying to achieve at Manchester United was a successful team playing the United way, from youth level right up to the first eleven. It was a throwback to how things were done under Matt Busby and everybody at the club bought into that philosophy. Les and Eric were key to a lot of that.

I had quite a bit of contact with Les, especially since his office was at Old Trafford and not at the training ground. Very often during the day I would pop in to see him for a coffee and a chat, so I knew what was going on with the youth team. And I wanted to know what was going on. I was always keen to learn how the youth were faring, who was coming through and who was going to be the next star, so it was especially gratifying to watch that very special generation of players make the impact that they did.

But was it too early to blood them? That was the question a lot of people were asking, especially after we lost our opening game of the season 3–1 at Aston Villa. It was a defeat that led to the now infamous quote from Alan Hansen on that evening's *Match of the Day*: 'You can't win anything with kids.' He wasn't the only one thinking that. I was probably as worried as anybody that we might be a bit short. Of course I knew these players were all exciting prospects, but it was only if you were involved with them on the training ground day in day out that you would have been confident they were ready to step up to the plate. I couldn't tell that from the boardroom. Most of the supporters, too, would not have been aware of the quality of these players; they'd have seen them on occasions but to suddenly rely on youth to that extent was a brave decision on Alex's part. You have to give him huge credit for his vision and his understanding of the players, because not only did we win the league that year but we also won the FA Cup, achieving our second Double in just three years. It was an astonishing achievement.

Of course, the return of Eric Cantona in early October helped us enormously. Indeed, such was his influence that season that he was named Footballer of the Year by the Football Writers' Association. Eric added experience and gravitas to our team. In those vital last months of the season we won seven of our matches 1–0 and in five of them Cantona scored the vital goal. He was also a great example to those young players around him. He used to stay behind after training in the afternoon and Beckham and all the rest of them thought, *well if it's good enough for Cantona we'll do a bit extra as well*.

When Eric returned from his suspension, I renegotiated a new three-year contract with his agent Jean-Jacques Bertrand. I played it canny: 'Look, we've got to be protective towards the club here, because if Eric does anything crazy again we can't be paying big wages with him sitting on the touchline for eight months.' So the idea was for the new contract to be related to results. Eric would still get a wage, although there would be no monetary increase, but if we won the league he'd get a big bonus. And it would be the same if we won the Cup.

Eric was training the day Jean-Jacques Bertrand and I were going through this new contract, and I could see that the agent was not entirely won over by it. 'Eric could end up with less than he was getting before,' Jean-Jacques pointed out.

'But if we win things, he'll get more,' I replied. 'And we have been winning things.'

'We'll have to put this to Eric when he's finished training,' said Jean-Jacques.

After training, Eric arrived at my office and I began to explain what we had done; that if we lost the league he could end up with less, but if we won it he got more. 'So what do you think for the next three years, Eric?' I asked. 'How many times do you think we'll win the league?' His reply was immediate. 'Three times,' he said. Jean-Jacques Bertrand's face fell. 'Eric, no, be quiet, it is not in your interest to say that; there is no guarantee that you will win the league.' But Eric looked at me: 'Of course we are going to win the league three times.' Even though it was against his own bargaining position, Eric couldn't bring himself to say anything less. No, we will win the league three times in the next three years. That's how confident he was.

While he was with us, Eric was among the highest-paid players at the club, and he was worth every penny, but throughout my time as chief executive I considered it vital to keep control over wages. I felt that if you were too generous on wages it affected everything else, including ticket pricing, how much you could spend on the stadium and the purchase of other players. Don't forget we were a plc as well, so it was normal business practice to control the wages.

There wasn't a wage cap as such at United; more like a wage ceiling that could rise when a particularly important player's contract came up for negotiation. Obviously the players weren't all on the same wage and only a select few were in the top bracket. I remember that when we renegotiated with Keane, he became the highest paid. At one time Andy Cole was on the biggest salary. So now and again you had to raise the ceiling, meaning that certain players could jump past others in terms of salary.

I had a specific formula when it came to calculating wages for new contracts. I looked at what a player cost in terms of transfer, signing on fees and overall costs and then divided that by the number of years of his contract, so I knew what was sensible, what we could afford. Often people would try to bargain, but you don't have to agree to their demands. You pay what you can afford. If you pay way over the odds on transfer fees or on wages, there comes a day of reckoning. Clubs will get into financial trouble, wage and transfer templates become meaningless. Even in my time, lots of clubs were in the red, but they still went on spending money they couldn't afford to. I never put Manchester United into that position. My responsibility was the long-term stability of the club. We had been around for 100 years and I wanted us to be still around in another 100 years. I was never going to put the club into jeopardy because the manager wanted this or that player or the supporters wanted something. I had a duty of care to make the club profitable and successful.

Alex came to me once and asked if we could get Gabriel Batistuta, but his wage demands were just ridiculous and I told Alex that there was no way we could afford them. There would have been a huge knock-on effect and it would have destroyed our wage structure. You've got a squad of players, all with varying ability; if you start paying ludicrous wages to some, and others feel they are better players, you're going to run into problems. Put simply, if you give players what they want you'll be bust in no time. It's a constant battle with managers and players. They are highly remunerated but when they get success they want more. You have to remember, I was running a business, a public company. Prudence may not have won me any favour with the supporters on the terraces, but you have to look at the bigger picture, and that is what I have always done.

Consequently, wages were always negotiated individually with the player concerned, who would come to see me and we'd thrash out a new deal. Match bonuses were different and encompassed everything from wins or draws in league games; progression in cup competitions, escalating with each round; and success in the Champions League, starting with getting through the group stage and then further rewards for advancing through subsequent ties. These were negotiated every two or three seasons with the players. They would come in and say, 'Hey, what about the bonuses; they've not been touched for a while', and we'd sit down and do them. The players would invariably appoint a committee of four to handle these negotiations. Gary Neville was always on the committee, so too Denis Irwin and Roy Keane – the usual suspects. And, of course, Eric.

I remember one specific occasion when I'd gone through and altered the bonuses to what I thought they should be for the coming season. I presented a copy of my proposal to each member of the players' committee to discuss among themselves. Eric chatted to the others and then looked me straight in the eyes. 'Chairman,' he said. 'The bonuses are an opportunity for the directors to show some respect to the players.' Dramatic pause. 'I do not think these bonuses are showing enough respect.' It was pure Eric.

On another occasion, a couple of years later in 1998, the bonuses still hadn't been agreed by the day of our first league match at Old Trafford against Leicester City. That morning the secretary Ken Merrett came to me and said, 'Chairman, the players are saying you haven't settled the bonuses and they're talking about not going out.' I sent a message down, saying: 'There's going to be a capacity crowd here today, and there's going to be a lot of disappointed faces out there this afternoon if the team don't come down the tunnel.' In the end the players accepted the deal. When you're running a football club, you can't afford to lose in a power struggle over money.

The 1995–96 season was one of the most exciting in years. Almost from the start, Kevin Keegan's Newcastle side emerged as front-runners and were twelve points clear of the rest of the field by mid-January. However, slowly but surely we managed to claw them back.

One of the most eventful games that season, for all the wrong reasons, was an away trip to Southampton. Losing 3–0 at half time, Alex ditched the grey kit the team were wearing and made them all change into our blue and white strip for the second half. His reasoning was that the players had found it difficult to pick each other out. I felt it was a bit of an excuse, really – we were getting hammered – but blaming the kit took the pressure off the players, and we won the second half 1–0, although the match still ended as a loss. I know that Edward Freedman wasn't at all happy because it killed the sales of the grey kit stone dead. The team never wore it again.

The match against Newcastle in March at St James' Park, where they had yet to drop a point, had already been touted as a title decider, and the tension between both sets of fans was almost palpable. It was Cantona's deft strike that won it after Schmeichel had made a series of outstanding saves to deny Les Ferdinand. After that we went from strength to strength and Newcastle faltered. It was the start of their wobble, which culminated in Keegan's now famous rant on television. Alex employed his deadly mind games by suggesting the likes of Leeds and Nottingham Forest might not put in the same effort against Newcastle as they had against us, and Keegan took the bait. It was an emotional outburst and gave the appearance of a manager who had lost it. I felt it showed quite a bit of weakness on Keegan's part and the United fans lapped it up. The feeling was that we've got them now. And indeed we had.

Having secured the league we made our way to Wembley to face our old adversaries Liverpool in the FA Cup final. Famously the Liverpool lads arrived for the match in cream-coloured suits designed by Giorgio Armani. By contrast our boys were dressed in black suits and looked as if they meant business. A rather dull match was decided in the end by a moment of individual brilliance by Cantona. The ninety minutes were almost up and we seemed to be heading into extra time when Beckham crossed the ball and Liverpool's goalkeeper, David James, punched it out to the edge of the penalty area, where Cantona was lurking. Most players wouldn't have been able to control that ball, and any attempted shot would probably have gone sailing miles over the bar, but Eric leant back, caressed it beautifully, and it tore into the back of the net. It was a wonderful way to win a final.

It took a little while for Alex to achieve success at United, his first trophy being the 1990 FA Cup (above), followed by the Cup Winners' Cup the next year. Alex would go on to outstrip even the successes of Sir Matt Busby (pictured with Alex, left).

Our acquisition of some of the greatest players to ever wear the United shirt was one of the main reasons for our extended period of success. Bryan Robson (top), Viv Anderson and Brian McClair (middle) and Mark Hughes (left) were all key to those 1990 and 1991 triumphs.

And Eric
Cantona (top),
Roy Keane
(right) and Andy
Cole (below)
were three key
players who
helped secure
dominance for
the rest of the
decade.

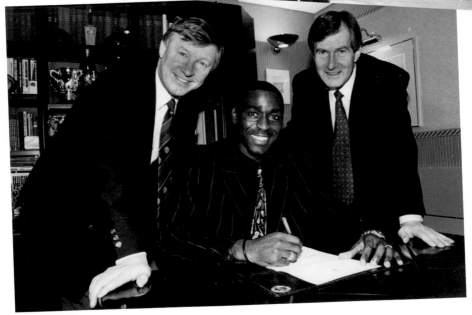

CARLING

The Treble: winning the Premiership (above), congratulating goalscorer Teddy Sheringham after our FA Cup win (below), acclimatizing to the Nou Camp (opposite, top) and a few hours later winning the biggest of the lot, the Champions League (opposite, bottom).

The celebrations after that Champions League triumph lasted a long time! As you can see, everyone from the players to the board members were ecstatic.

And we celebrated in style with an open-top bus parade through Manchester.
This was something all United fans wanted a piece of.

(Above) My legacy: an
Old Trafford equipped
for the future, as the
biggest club ground in
the country.
(Right) Having retired
in 2003, I'm now one
of many former United
servants nervously
watching our matches.

Not only had we achieved our second Double in three years but United were the first English team ever to win the Double twice. A great accomplishment, yet I didn't feel that this was in any way the end of the run. With our team filled with young players who had years ahead of them, my thinking was that this could be the start of something really big; we could dominate English football in much the same way as Liverpool did in the 1980s. But would Alex Ferguson be leading the team out next season?

In the days leading up to the FA Cup final the question of Alex's salary raised its head again. I took the same position as before, leaving the negotiations to Maurice and Roland Smith, who were happy to sit down with Alex to discuss a new deal. Although I was not privy to what went on, I heard later from Maurice that things got very heated and that Alex, frustrated at what was being offered, threatened not to perform the manager's traditional Cup final role of leading his team out on to the Wembley pitch (although he did in the end). I don't know why Alex was in such a rush to complete the talks before the Cup final. I'd have expected him to want to get the season out of the way first. After all, we had the whole summer to sit down and sort things out. As it was, the following week Alex did put pen to paper on a new and much-improved deal.

I don't believe there was ever any real possibility of Alex walking out on United over his pay dispute with us, but I think the FA smelt blood in the water and as a result wanted Alex to replace Terry Venables as England manager after that summer's European Championships. I remember Jimmy Armfield and the FA's chief executive Graham Kelly coming to see me about it, and I told them firmly that in my view Alex would never take the position. Anyway, he was our manager and I didn't think he was ready for the national job because he still had plenty of life left in him as a club manager. Of course I couldn't stop them approaching Alex and I believe they did approach him at some point, but in the end nothing came of it. I never discussed the matter with Alex, nor did he ever raise the subject with me. I was confident, though, that he wouldn't take it. A Scotsman managing England! Not a chance.

23 THE LEGENDS THAT ARE AND MIGHT HAVE BEEN

After winning another Double in 1996 the team was now enjoying unprecedented success and popularity. Old Trafford was regularly sold out for games, official membership figures were approaching 103,000, more people than ever before were taking advantage of the museum and stadium tours, and business was brisk at the ground's newly opened megastore. It was clear that if the club was to keep on growing, the stadium needed to expand.

First we looked at totally redeveloping the South Stand, but that would have meant building over the railway line that runs past the stadium on that side. It would have been feasible but in the end the cost was just too prohibitive. That left the East Stand or the North Stand. The North Stand was by far the biggest and also probably the most old-fashioned stand by then. It had been built in 1966 in time for the World Cup matches and here we were thirty years later. If we were going to press ahead with the redevelopment of the North Stand, which was to extend much further outwards than its predecessor and require a drive-through access road, much depended on the availability of the land owned by Trafford Park

Estates, which was situated adjacent to the United Road and consisted of businesses and warehouses. Failure to purchase this land would have meant we could only have developed the North Stand within the confines of what we had there already, which was a total non-starter. Negotiations went on for the best part of a year and proved quite difficult, but in the end we paid £9.3 million for the land, which was considerably more than the commercial rate, but in all honesty less than we were prepared to pay.

While we had the land, all the business tenants remained in situ and we had to buy some of them out, starting with those closest to the stand, so that work could start. We were prepared to be reasonably generous and those that wanted to accept our offer could. If we couldn't do a deal with them we were prepared to wait until the end of their lease. All in all it was quite a big undertaking.

Going back to my father's time, our architects had always been Atherden Fuller; they knew the ground inside out and were excellent at their job. As for the building work itself, that always went out to tender and for two reasons: first, we wanted the best price possible, and second, we wanted to avoid any accusations of backhanders.

In June 1995 the North Stand was demolished and construction began on the biggest, most costly and most ambitious development ever undertaken by the club. What always happens when you're building a new stand is that you hope the seats become available for matches as quickly as possible. You have to be very careful, though, from a safety point of view; there's quite a bit of effort involved in stopping the work and making new areas of seating suitable for match days. This is where Robin Launders was very good, liaising with the contractors to get as many seats back per game as possible while they were developing the new stand.

By May 1996, and the end of that season, the new three-tiered North Stand was completed at a cost of £18.65 million. Combined with the purchase of the land, the total amount spent was close to £30 million. That was a huge investment, but the refurbishment and expansion raised the capacity of the entire ground to more than 55,000. Thanks to this increase, United could now expect to take £1.2 million per game.

Having spent so much on the new stand, it was important to get the best payback possible on it, which meant that we had to increase the number of private boxes, executive seating and lounges. Back in 1966 those boxes could accommodate six seats; this time we put ten-seaters in and put them in both the middle level and the upper level. And we put a big executive suite right in the middle of the stand, with dining rooms behind it where we could do match-day catering. This was the Manchester Suite, the biggest dining room in Manchester, which could cater for a thousand people. We also opened the Red Café, a themed restaurant that over the years has become an extremely popular destination for fans.

I have to applaud the work of Robin Launders here. He had already delivered the Stretford End on time and on cost, which gave us enormous confidence when we came to do the North Stand, and again he delivered. United were probably the first football club ever to deliver a stand on time and on budget. And that was important, because Old Trafford had been allocated several games at Euro 96, including group matches, a quarter-final and a semi-final. As the biggest ground in the country outside of Wembley, Old Trafford was always going to be a venue for such a prestigious event. It was also probably the best-policed ground in the country. Manchester police were used to handling big crowds, consequently the FA had a lot of confidence about using us. However, there was a massive scare around the start of Euro 96 when an IRA bomb went off in the city centre of Manchester. The fact that nobody was seriously injured was astonishing when you saw pictures of the aftermath. Naturally that caused huge consternation among the organizers and security had to be stepped up along with extra policing. Thankfully the games at Old Trafford passed off without incident and the new stand proved a great success when it took its bow.

⚽

Due to our triumphs on the field, numerous businesses now wanted to be associated with Manchester United, especially since we had just become the first football club to join the list of top 250 companies. A good example of one of these interested parties was Nike, who were keen to win the kit contract from Umbro and develop a long-term relationship with the club. Edward Freedman, Danny McGregor and I were flown to the States by Nike to look over their operation in December 1995. We were shown round one of their Niketown shops in Chicago and then taken to their headquarters in Beaverton, Oregon.

When Nike first approached us, I told Edward about it and we both decided that the best course of action would be to put a valuation on any prospective deal, so we went out to the States with some idea of what we wanted. Edward produced a full and extensive report, based on previous kit sales, the club's fan base, how much it cost to produce the kit, and other things. The value he came up with was £15 million a year. Nike gave us a full presentation about how many kits they could sell through their various branches and shops and how United could expand into the American market. But when they asked us what value we put on it, and we produced the £15 million figure, the number they came up with was well south of that.

Umbro meanwhile were anxious to continue their relationship with United, having beaten Adidas to the kit deal back in 1992. That contract was now due for renewal. Obviously Umbro didn't know what Nike were prepared to offer; all they knew was that Nike were interested enough to fly us over to the States to wine and dine us. At our meeting we obviously didn't tell Umbro that Nike's offer had fallen well short, and I can remember saying to Edward that we should show them our report. Edward agreed and passed his report over to their chief executive, Peter Kenyon. He read it and Umbro agreed to match Freedman's valuation – £15 million per year, a figure that was unheard of in those days.

I must say that we were tempted to go with Nike because of the potential of breaking into the American market, but they were a long way short of what we thought the deal was worth. If it had been closer we may have had a decision to make. Yet we had a sense of loyalty to Umbro. Unless something is substantially better, you're not going to walk away lightly. Umbro had done a good job over the past few years, so that August we signed another kit deal with them.

That summer of 1996 United were again the subject of a possible takeover. VCI were a video, publishing and music company which, earlier that year, had bought the rights to Manchester United's book and video publishing interests for £6 million. Looking to expand its operation, their chief executive Steve Ayers came to see me at Old Trafford to present his proposal for a takeover, with VCI looking to pay about £2 a share, which valued the club at £270 million. I also received an official offer in writing from VCI's chairman, Michael Grade.

It was a reverse takeover really, because VCI were a smaller company than we were, so it was never an attractive proposition. We believed there was a lot further to go in the price, as was proven just two years later when BSkyB put in their bid. We had to consider it, as we would have to consider any serious takeover bid, but it was never viable if we wanted to recognize the true worth of United.

As we looked forward to the new season we said goodbye to some players and welcomed several new recruits to the team. Due to Gary Neville making the right back position his own, Paul Parker must have realized he wasn't going to get too many games in the future. He'd also begun to pick up some injuries, so it felt like the right time for him to move on. He joined Derby County.

That's pretty much the reasoning behind why we let Lee Sharpe go as well. There had always been stories about Lee's partying lifestyle, and Alex probably felt that United had had the best of him. With Giggs and Beckham on the wings, we could afford to take the money in order to strengthen other positions. Leeds United were very interested in Lee and their cheif exec Bill Fotherby came on the phone one day to ask what we wanted for him. I put a figure of £4.5 million on the player and Lee went to Leeds.

I know a lot of supporters were sad to see Steve Bruce leave the club that summer. Steve had been disappointed not to have been picked for the FA Cup final and came to see me in my office one afternoon. He'd had a very good offer from Birmingham – it was more than he was on with us – and he asked for my advice. 'To be absolutely honest with you, Steve,' I said, 'I wouldn't talk you out of it. You didn't play in the Cup final, you're now thirty-six years old so your games here will be numbered, and you've got a great offer that could be the start of a new future for you.' Even though we were offering him new terms to stay at United, my final advice to him was that he'd be mad to turn the Birmingham job down. I think he appreciated that: I wasn't just looking at it from a Manchester United point of view, I gave Steve honest advice as to what I thought he should do. He deserved that much, because he had been a terrific stalwart for the club over many years.

As for new recruits to the team, Les Kershaw, our chief scout, came to see me one day about this player at Bordeaux who was available for £4 million. 'We should really be looking at this guy,' Les said. 'He's played in the French national team with Cantona, and I think we should be interested in buying him.' The name of the player was Zinedine Zidane.

I mentioned Zidane to Alex, who told me that Les had already brought up the subject with him. 'I've also talked to Eric about him,' confirmed Alex, 'and Eric raves about him. He rates him really highly. But Zidane plays in Eric's position and I'm just a bit worried, having got Eric back after the ban and persuading him to come and play for us again, that if I bring Zidane in, I'm giving myself a problem. So I'm not sure we need him at this moment.' That was that. Of course, within one season Eric had left us and Zidane went to Juventus to become a world superstar.

I can perfectly understand Alex's argument at the time for not taking Zidane. Alex couldn't have known that Eric was going to retire in a year's time. These things happen in football. It was very similar to the Lineker situation in Ron Atkinson's time, when Ron felt he already had enough strikers and passed on him. But Zidane playing in the red of United is certainly one of the big what-might-have-beens during my tenure at the club.

Someone Alex was keen to bring to United was Alan Shearer. Alex had earlier missed out on Shearer when he moved from Southampton to Blackburn back in 1992, and over the years Alan had undoubtedly become the deadliest centre forward in the English game. This time we had competition for his signature from Newcastle. I put a call through to Freddy Shepherd, chairman at Newcastle, and told him, 'Freddy, this Shearer thing could go on for ever. Why don't we agree a sensible figure and let Shearer decide where he wants to go.' So we agreed that both clubs would offer £10 million and the player would make the final decision. As far as I was concerned, Shepherd was happy with that idea.

In July, after Shearer had emerged as the top scorer at Euro 96, we officially wrote to Blackburn with our offer of £10 million. At the time Shearer was represented by Tony Stephens, who was also Beckham's agent. We met with Stephens and then Alan went to Alex's house, where he expressed a desire to come to United. Indeed, I even agreed Alan's terms with Stephens. Then, out of the blue, Freddy Shepherd rang me to say that he had reneged on our agreement and put an offer in for Shearer that day of £15 million, which had been accepted by Blackburn.

I doubt whether Shearer would have ever become a Manchester United player even if both clubs had stuck to the original £10 million deal, because Blackburn's owner Jack Walker was determined that he was not going to Old Trafford. It was only afterwards that Shearer revealed to Alex that Jack Walker was in tears about him leaving and had said, 'I don't want you to go but I'll let you go to Newcastle for £15 million; only over my dead body, though, are you going to United.'

Instead of laying out £10 million on Shearer, we spent some of that money on four European players. Ole Gunnar Solskjær was a young striker scoring plenty of goals for Molde FK in his native Norway. Les Kershaw had come to see me about the player and was insistent that he would be a good buy for us. However, Les hadn't been able to persuade Alex, who thought it was too much of a gamble because the league Solskjær was playing in was inferior to our own and he wasn't sure Ole could make the step up.

Les remained convinced he was worth the risk, so I brought up the subject during a conversation with Alex. 'I don't know whether he'll be quite good enough for us,' reiterated Alex. I remember saying, 'He's only £1.4 million, Alex. Even if he doesn't make it, we'll get our money back.' Alex pondered that for a while. 'Well, if you don't mind taking a chance, chairman, I'm happy to go ahead.' So we went out and bought him and sure enough we never looked back. Apart from scoring the winner in the Champions League final, which helps, he was prolific for us, scoring nineteen goals in his debut season. And the fans loved him. He was an out-and-out goal scorer. They called him the baby-faced assassin. I don't know who coined that but it was a pretty accurate description. I'll always remember him coming off the bench against Nottingham Forest and scoring four goals in about fifteen minutes. Off the field he was a lovely lad. Very quiet. Always smiling. He was just a delight to have around and was very popular with the other players. He had a very easygoing personality, which makes integration into the squad so much easier. It helps if they're good, too!

We signed another Norwegian that summer, a strong central defender called Ronny Johnsen. He had come to my attention thanks to a German friend of mine called Rolf Russmann, who used to play for FC Schalke, and in the late 1970s played in defence with Franz Beckenbauer for West Germany. Every so often Rolf would bring up the name of a player he believed would be a good fit for United. Earlier that year I happened to be in Germany along with my commercial manager Danny McGregor, looking for giant screens for Old Trafford. Rolf asked me if I'd heard of Ronny Johnsen, who was currently playing in the Turkish league for Beşiktaş. 'I think he can play in the English league,' said Rolf. 'I think he'll be a good centre half for you.' On my return to Manchester I mentioned Ronny to Alex, who said that some of his scouts had already been looking at him. Shortly afterwards we put in a bid of £1.5 million to buy him. Whether my conversation triggered anything I don't know, but Ronny was a real stalwart in our defence, especially during our Treble-winning season and that memorable Champions League final victory.

Much was also expected of our other two recruits that summer, but neither really were able to establish themselves at United. Karel Poborský was a speedy right-winger who had excelled for the Czech Republic at

Euro 96 and came in for a fee of £3.5 million from Slavia Prague. Karel was a skilful player but due to the growing influence of Beckham in that position he only lasted one and a half seasons with us.

Jordi Cruyff arrived from Barcelona for £1.4 million and was a cultured player who popped up with the odd goal but, like Karel, it didn't really happen for him at United. He could play wide or up front, but coming from the Spanish league I think he found it difficult to adapt to the more physically demanding Premier League, and had to fight for a place among that golden generation. He was determined to carve out a career in football on his own terms, away from the shadow of his famous father Johan. It's the reason why at United he insisted that the name on the back of his shirt should read Jordi rather than Cruyff.

The 1996–97 season was another success story for United as we again won the league, and by a comfortable margin in the end. Not to sound too cocky, but by this stage we were getting used to winning; it was our fourth league title in five years. The team were showing tremendous spirit and togetherness thanks to the special and almost unique bonding of those six young players who were all home grown and United through and through, ably supported by some excellent and experienced players around them like Keane, Irwin, Cantona and Schmeichel. It was a great combination.

We were still falling short in Europe, though, having in the two previous seasons bowed out of the Champions League at the group stage and succumbed to a first-round exit in the UEFA Cup respectively. That year we managed to get to the semi-final of the Champions League where we faced ultimate winners Borussia Dortmund over two legs but lost by a single goal in both matches. It was bitterly disappointing because we had a great opportunity that year to get to the final. Here we were totally dominant in domestic football but we hadn't been European Cup champions since 1968. That was the next big target and each year we played in Europe we were gaining valuable experience.

No sooner had the celebrations died down after winning the league than we were hit by an almighty bombshell. At thirty-one years old, Eric Cantona was to retire from football altogether. It came as a complete surprise to everyone at the club and was revealed to me during a private meeting Eric had requested in my office on the afternoon of 15 May. He gave a number of reasons for his decision. First, he didn't believe that United were capable of winning the Champions League. He also said that having played football for thirteen years, which he said was a long time, he wanted to take his life in another direction and pursue other things. Added to that, it had always been his plan to retire at the top. Eric wanted it known that his four and a half years at Manchester United were the happiest of his football career, along with his relationship with the manager, coaching staff and players, and not least the fans. And he wished Manchester United even more success in the future. Finally, he asked me to release the statement about his retirement while he was on holiday, when the press would be unable to contact him. Obviously we didn't want Eric to leave and I tried my hardest to persuade him to stay, but if a player wants to retire you can't do anything about it. You have to let him go.

After that we didn't see very much of Eric at the club, although he came to the opening of the Alex Ferguson stand in 2011, which I thought was a nice gesture. There was a big meal laid on before the ceremony in one of the suites, and Eric arrived late, but he went round every single table shaking hands, saying hello to everybody and apologizing for not being on time. There's no doubt that Eric has a strong affection for United and Alex.

Eric was clearly different to the other players; a bit of an outsider, really. He had a different personality. Some people would say it was confidence, others might call it arrogance; whatever it was, it seemed to do the trick. I always got on very well with him. He was extremely respectful and I liked him as a person. To be honest, I was slightly in awe of him, and I wouldn't say that about many players. But he did have something special: there was an aura about him, a swagger, not only on the pitch but off it as well. And the fact that he spoke broken English probably added to the whole image. I suspect, though, that he spoke better English than he let on – it was all part of his mystique.

Whenever we showed up for an away match, the player most of the opposing fans wanted to see was Eric. I can remember playing at Coventry once and when Eric came out of the dressing room all the Coventry ball boys started whispering, 'Here he is', 'Look, it's him.' That Cantona aura and touch of star quality elevated him above any of the other players.

In the modern era a lot of supporters have their own favourite player; some would go for Giggs, others for Keane, Scholes or Robson, but you mention Eric to United supporters and they will tell you that he was magical. If Eric was in the team you looked forward to going to the game because you knew something was going to happen; he could do something that was out of the ordinary, because he *was* out of the ordinary.

24 A WARNING TO ALEX

After successfully overseeing the construction of the North Stand, Robin Launders had decided to leave us. Leeds United had offered him the post of chief executive and he wanted to take it, which was absolutely fine by me. I think it was the right time for Robin to move on. He'd done a good job, having been in charge of delivering both of our new stands and overseeing the City flotation. That left us, though, looking for a new finance director.

We received numerous applications and eventually the list was whittled down to four candidates. Basically I was looking for someone dynamic who could take the company forward. The interviews took place at Old Trafford and the panel consisted of me, Roland Smith and Maurice Watkins. In February 1997 we chose David Gill. David was young, ambitious and very well qualified, with an impressive CV including an honours degree from Birmingham University. He was also a big United supporter, having followed the club since the Charlton, Law and Best days, and knew all about our history. So it was a combination of David's knowledge of football, his keenness, his youth and his academic qualification that won the day. And I liked his personality.

As the new finance director, David was very supportive and practical in the day-to-day running of the business, sitting in on all the important internal meetings. At first Roland didn't want him to be on the football club board: he was worried that he might get too immersed and bogged down in the football side of things. David, on the other hand, wanted very much to be on the football board, and it did seem odd having a finance director who was on the catering, merchandising and plc boards, yet not on the football club board – we were a football club, after all. So we sorted that out.

In the end David worked very closely with Roland, because whenever Roland wanted to know any financial information, or things to do with the City, he could go straight to David and get it done rather than coming to me for it. I welcomed that, as it took a bit of pressure off me and I could devote more time to other matters.

Just a couple of days after David's appointment, I was to make another highly significant one. Peter Kenyon was passing through Manchester, called me and we arranged to have lunch at Old Trafford. I'd known and dealt with Peter in his role as chief executive at Umbro for years and under his stewardship the company had come on leaps and bounds in terms of turnover and growth. During our lunch Peter revealed that he had decided to leave Umbro after ten years in the job. I listened to this and asked him what he planned to do next. Peter said he was still evaluating his options.

For a while I had been thinking of stepping down as chief executive at Manchester United. Back in 1995 at a private meeting in the Isle of Man, where Roland Smith had a house, I revealed to both Roland and Maurice Watkins that I was thinking of leaving my role. I had my reasons. I'd been doing the job by then for fifteen years and maybe that was enough. It was hard work. United was a full-on commitment and I was conscious of the fact that I wasn't spending as much time at home as I should have been. I also didn't feel that I was particularly appreciated. I had taken a lot of stick. I'd brought Alex in and we'd had considerable success, so the club was in good shape, and I just thought, well maybe it's time to let somebody else have a go at it. It was really a combination of things.

Roland and Maurice were quite taken aback by what I said. 'You can't do that,' they both implored. 'You're only fifty!' We talked about it and they persuaded me to stay on. 'Okay,' I said. 'I'll give it another five years.' If I was going to commit, I had to make a proper commitment. Besides, I tended to work in five-year cycles anyway. I'd done fifteen years and if I did another five it would take me to twenty. I'm glad I did because the team won another Double in 1996 and of course the famous Treble. I would have missed all that.

Inevitably, though, I had to think about who would eventually succeed me and how I would show them the ropes. Peter Kenyon seemed the perfect candidate. I knew some of the executives over at Umbro and they spoke very highly of him. He was also a local man and a big United fan. So before we'd finished that lunch I asked Peter whether, now he was a free agent, would he consider joining us at United. 'I'm looking to get out of the day-to-day running of the business in the next few years,' I told him. 'But I want to retain a definite interest. So I'm looking for somebody to put in that position. Why don't you come in to spend some time as a deputy and then move up to chief executive?' Peter was both surprised and flattered by my offer and said he wanted some time to think it over.

The funny thing is, had this been a year down the road I might have thought, hang on, I don't need to groom anybody else; I might have the answer here already in David Gill. However, when the opportunity presented itself to hire Peter, David had only just arrived and hadn't yet proved himself. I didn't know David that well at the time but I knew Peter and I was delighted when he accepted my offer, and took over as deputy chief executive that May.

One of the consequences of hiring Peter as my deputy was that it caused a huge conflict with Edward Freedman. Obviously Peter had a lot of experience with merchandising, so that was something he could take a watching brief over. But Edward felt that Peter coming in undermined his position in the business and that he was there to replace him in some way, although that was never my intention. Edward perhaps also believed that Peter's arrival would stop him gaining promotion. Truthfully, I'd never really thought of Edward in terms of chief executive, although I think Edward himself possibly thought that one day he might assume that position. That was really the beginning of the end for Edward at Manchester United. Within just three months of Peter's arrival he had left.

Edward had done a fine job building up the merchandising side during his five years at the club. It was just one of those things. In organizations you have to bring in fresh blood and promote others and some people do get put out. Edward firmly believed that hiring Peter was the wrong decision, that it would affect him, that it would give him less responsibility. I'm not sure how much it affected him, but nevertheless Edward was a casualty of Peter coming in and felt he had to move on.

I was sitting in my office one evening when I got a phone call from Alan Sugar. Something like two years earlier, I'd had a conversation with Brian Kidd in which he said that if ever we got a chance to sign Teddy Sheringham we should seriously look at him. It was probably the time that Eric Cantona got suspended and Alex had gone over to France to persuade him to stay, because Brian had told me, 'If Eric does leave we can do worse than get Sheringham.' At the next league meeting after that, I made a point of going over to Alan Sugar and mentioned that if Tottenham ever thought of selling Teddy Sheringham we'd be interested and would he give me first option. 'Fine,' he said. 'I'll let you know.'

So there I was sitting in my office when the phone rang. 'Martin, Alan Sugar here.'

'Hello,' I said. 'How are you? What can I do for you?'

'Do you remember a conversation we had a couple of years ago about Sheringham?'

'Yes, I do,' I said, my interest piqued.

'Well, we've decided to get rid of him and I'll give you first refusal.' I think they'd had a row or something had gone on but Alan was anxious to get rid of Sheringham and Teddy was keen to get away. Certainly Teddy was never complimentary about Alan Sugar. 'So, would you be interested?'

'We might well be, Alan. Will you leave it with me and I'll come back to you in the next half-hour.' I was just about to put the receiver down when I said. 'Oh by the way, what do you want for him?'

'Three and a half million pounds,' said Sugar.

'Right.' I hung up and immediately rang Alex at his home. 'Alex, how do you fancy Sheringham?'

'Yes, he'd do all right as a replacement for Eric.'

'I think we can get him,' I said. 'Alan Sugar's just been on the phone and given us first option on him.' With Alex enthused by the idea I rang Sugar back. 'Yes, we are interested but three and a half million is a bit steep. After all, he is thirty-one.'

'F***ing hell!' Sugar blasted down the line. 'I thought I was doing you a favour. If you don't want him, fine; I'm sure there will be plenty out there prepared to pay three and a half million for him.'

'Okay,' I said. 'We'll pay it.' And actually, that wasn't such a ridiculous fee. Although Sheringham was thirty-one, we managed to get four years out of him. And I must say I got on very well with him; he was a good pro, worked hard and just got on with things.

Besides Teddy, our only other signing that summer was Henning Berg, a classy Norwegian defender who we bought from Blackburn Rovers for a fee of £5.5 million. Henning played over sixty times for United and was always dependable, but earlier that year we had the chance to capture the signing of one of Europe's most combative defenders, Marcel Desailly. The French international had announced his intention to leave AC Milan and in February 1997 he not only agreed personal terms with us but signed a pre-contract agreement, subject to a medical and us agreeing a fee with Milan that would have seen him stay at Old Trafford until 2001. In the end it didn't work out and he decided to go to Chelsea instead. It's all hypothetical of course, but had Desailly signed with us Alex might not have felt the need later on to go after Jaap Stam. Although what a defensive partnership those two would have made.

Sadly the 1997–98 season ended in bitter disappointment. Although we had lost one of our key players to injury, Roy Keane, quite early in the campaign, it didn't seem to affect us, and on the last day of February United had the chance to open up an eleven-point lead at the top of the table if we beat Chelsea at Stamford Bridge. We managed just that with a rare goal from Phil Neville, and I remember returning to Old Trafford on the team coach thinking, we're not going to lose the league now. Yet we did exactly what Newcastle did the season before in allowing a huge lead to slip. Arsenal came from behind to pip us at the post, winning ten straight games, including a significant win at Old Trafford where they simply outplayed us. Not only that but Arsenal did the Double that year by claiming the FA Cup under their new manager, the astute Arsène Wenger.

We seemed to lose our way that year, being unceremoniously dumped out of the Cup by Barnsley and losing to Monaco in the quarter-finals of the Champions League, all of which added to a general feeling of despondency. A memorable 3–2 victory over Juventus in the Champions League group stages, however, at least proved that our team did possess the talent and mental strength to compete with the best in Europe.

Once the season was over and I'd enjoyed a much-needed holiday I returned to Old Trafford to evaluate what had gone wrong, because my feelings were that we shouldn't have lost the league that year. I went to see Roland Smith and he concurred with my assessment of where things had unravelled and which matters needed to be addressed. He was worried that United's golden run might be coming to an end and that Arsenal had the potential to match United, both in the way it was run, but also in the capability of the manager.

At the time Alex was on holiday with his family in France but we deemed the situation so important that we asked him to attend a meeting in London to talk things through. I don't think Alex was particularly happy about leaving his family but he agreed to fly back.

This meeting took place on 24 June 1998. Although we were candid in the way we talked of our dissatisfaction with Alex's recent performance, in no way did Roland or I wish to denigrate any of his accomplishments at the club. We just felt that he hadn't been as focused on his job as he had once been. In our view, outside forces, such as his celebrity status and his recent interest as a racehorse owner, had impinged too much on his time, to the detriment of his duties as manager of Manchester United.

About a week after this meeting Alex instructed his accountant, Alan Baines, to start negotiations over a new contract. My first reaction was surprise: *hang on a minute*, I thought, *there's a few things we need to iron out before we even start considering a new contract. For one, he needs to get back on track.* After that London meeting, Roland suggested I write down all the points that we had raised. This I did. I now decided to put these down formally in a letter to Alex. This was delivered to him internally at Old Trafford on the morning of 7 July.

The letter reiterated the concern both the board and I felt at the failure to win any silverware that season. The overriding objective was to win the Champions League, but it was imperative that the pursuit of the Premier League and the FA Cup did not suffer as a result. The agenda of the board was to challenge for all three competitions and not produce a team based solely for one competition to the detriment of the other two.

At that meeting in London with Alex, Roland and I had discussed the need for a proactive transfer policy, balancing the need to develop homegrown players in conjunction with thorough scouting methods and exhaustive player appraisal, which we now underlined. There was also reference to the need for careful consideration of the additional difficulties of purchasing overseas players.

We commended Alex for his youth policy, eradication of pockets of deadwood in the playing squad, improved fitness and skill training and, in particular, his ever-present hands-on policy in all team matters.

Alex's profile was expanding, as was his sphere of interests. There was always the risk that these outside interests could impair the quality of his performance in the myriad of detail involved in managing the club.

The board fully supported Alex, not wanting any distractions interfering with the club's burgeoning success. These distractions were inevitable but would be addressed when necessary.

One such issue was occasional media criticism of the plc board's perceived lack of support on player acquisition. We reassured Alex that he would always have appropriate support from the board but that there was a need to be cautious when commenting to the media.

We expressed our gratitude to Alex for the strength of his stewardship from the time of his arrival at the club. There was a compelling need to prevent any distractions from his unique hands-on and personal management style, which was bringing him and the club success. We did not wish to see any damage inflicted by outside influences.

At three o'clock that afternoon my secretary told me that Alex wanted to see me. This is going to be interesting, I thought. I could tell as soon as Alex came through the door that he wasn't happy. The letter, he said, had upset him greatly and if that was what we thought of him after all he'd achieved for the club, then he had no option but to resign. The language Alex used was a little bit more fruity, but that was the basic gist of it.

'Well,' I said. 'If that's the way you feel, Alex, we'll have to accept it.' Of course I didn't want him to go; in a sense I was calling his bluff, but having said that, we did have genuine views about where things could be improved. One of my duties as chief executive was to point out what I considered to be deficiencies. So while I didn't want Alex to resign I did want him to take on board the concerns I had expressed in the letter.

As I was preparing to leave the office that evening to head off home, Alex came on the phone. He said he wanted to withdraw his resignation. I was happy to accept. I'd had a feeling that he would eventually come round, although I am in no doubt that my letter must have hurt his professional pride. Having everything discussed and dissected out in the open is one thing but then to actually see it all on paper in stark black and white is quite another. But that letter was only ever meant to be constructive. All I wanted him to do was to take in what we were suggesting and to regain his focus, because there was no one better than a focused Alex Ferguson. That was proved by how he bounced back the following season by winning the treble. And contrary to media rumours this was the only major altercation I had in my working relationship with Alex Ferguson over a seventeen year period in which we won 17 major trophies.

25 MURDOCH AND UNITED

Two months before the start of what would prove to be the most momentous season in the club's history, in late June 1998, a call came through to my office from Mark Booth, chief executive of BSkyB. Booth wanted to know if I could come down to London to talk about pay-per-view television. Sky had recently proposed screening some of their live matches on a pay-per-view basis but the Premier League were not at all impressed with the notion, nor were quite a few of the clubs. We, on the other hand, along with a few others like Aston Villa, were fairly open to the idea.

On 1 July Maurice Watkins and I took the train down for a meeting at Sky's Isleworth headquarters. Lunch had been arranged and, as we began to tuck into our smoked salmon starter, Booth suddenly made a confession. 'Look, Martin,' he said. 'I have got you here under false pretences. When I rang to invite you for this lunch I said I wanted to talk about pay-per-view, but I have a bigger agenda, which I didn't want to say over the phone.'

Intrigued, I looked over and saw that Maurice was just as bemused as I was. Booth carried on. 'What I really wanted to talk about is Sky buying Manchester United. We have looked at it and we would like to make an offer to buy your company.'

To say that what Booth was proposing came as a complete surprise would be an understatement. We genuinely didn't have a clue that anything like this was on the agenda. Both Maurice and I tried to retain a calm exterior, but inside my brain was whirring with what this could mean for the club, my own position, the jobs of my fellow directors and our shareholders.

Booth obviously could see that his words had come as a shock and tried to reassure us that the only way he wanted the bid to proceed was on a friendly basis. 'The great attraction of this deal is the management you have built up at Old Trafford, Martin. It is superb. You have an extraordinary sports franchise and an extraordinary business. That is a key part of what we are proposing. The only way we want to do it is if you are equally enthusiastic, so I would ask you to think about it.'

Far from jumping at the offer straightaway, Maurice and I listened carefully and took in what was being said to us. Booth implied that there wouldn't be wholesale changes. They were interested in buying Manchester United because it was successful, so why change a winning team? He made all the right noises. He did not reveal how much Sky were prepared to pay, and I didn't ask for a figure; I just thanked him and said we would go away and carefully consider what he'd said.

You didn't have to be a genius to realize what made Manchester United so attractive to an organization like Sky. Owning the biggest club in British football gave them a huge say in future media rights and won them a seat on the negotiating table. They may also have been banking on the prospect of clubs one day having the freedom to negotiate their own television deals, and as owners of Manchester United that would put them in a very privileged position.

Once our meeting was over at Sky, Maurice and I travelled into the City of London and popped into Roland Smith's office. Roland was extremely positive about the news when I told him. After our recent poor season, and with Arsenal coming up on the rails as potential rivals, things weren't going to be quite as easy for us in the future, so the financial muscle of Sky couldn't have come at a better time.

After the shock had died down, my own personal view tallied with Roland's. Sky had a much bigger capitalization than Manchester United did at the time, and their backing could only make us stronger. But there were a lot of other things to think about first such as, what are they going to do with the whole business? Were they actually going to make wholesale changes, contrary to what Booth had suggested? Were they going to change the culture of the place? Only when I had considered these points did I begin to feel that the combined might of United and Sky was stronger than United staying on its own.

But would such a merger, unique in the English game, be allowed to go through? Sky had wanted to buy a football club for quite a while, but the previous chief executive had always rejected the idea because of his belief that it would run foul of competition laws. Booth saw things differently; as an American he was used to media companies owning sports clubs and franchises. After all, Murdoch himself had only just recently bought the LA Dodgers. Booth had also sought his own legal advice, which informed him that no action was likely to be taken if Sky went ahead with their purchase of Manchester United. We received much the same advice from our own lawyers: that any potential merger would be the subject of a lot of hype and considerable opposition, but that it couldn't be blocked.

I met Booth again in early July in London and then Maurice met with Sky's chief finance officer Martin Stewart later that month. It was at this meeting that the subject of price was discussed for the first time. Stewart wanted to know how much United expected Sky to pay for the club. Maurice scribbled some calculations on a piece of paper and handed it over. Stewart's mouth dropped open when he saw the figure of 290p per share, which valued the club at nearly £750 million. It was quite a bold opening gambit on Maurice's part. No club on earth had a price tag like that. But at least it got the ball rolling.

On 4 August Maurice and I met with Booth again and representatives of Sky in London. I remember that we were all so paranoid about our discussions leaking to the press that when the waiter came in with our coffee everyone froze and looked at him in stony silence. Unnerved, the poor man left the tray on a side table and beat a hasty retreat.

At the meeting Booth argued that Maurice's price of 290p was totally unrealistic and suggested that something like 190p was more reasonable. We were far from happy with that and there followed several hours of intense negotiation. By the end of the evening we had reached an agreement on 217.5p, which was a price I was happy to recommend to our board.

A couple of days later, and just over a week away from the first game of the brand new season, the United plc board met. It was Roland who stood up to announce that Sky had put in a bid for the club and there were quite a few startled faces around the table. I took over and explained that we had negotiated a satisfactory price and that I was recommending we go ahead.

Out of all the board members the one who voiced the greatest reservation was Greg Dyke, who had only recently become a director. We had asked Greg on to the board for practical reasons. Roland was always extremely conscious of the fact that the plc board should have strong, independent professional people on it for the City to retain confidence in us. He also felt, as everyone on the board did, that television was becoming more and more important going forward, so we wanted somebody who could give us an idea on values of TV rights. Who better to advise us on all this than the man who really acted as the catalyst for the Premier League when he was with ITV, coming forward with the deal that finally broke the cartel with the BBC. Greg was also a strong Manchester United fan, so he seemed an obvious choice.

Greg's main gripe was that he thought the price we were asking was too low, so the board decided to bring in HSBC to prepare its own valuation. They agreed that 217.5p was more than an acceptable price. However, this view ran contrary to the club's very own brokers, Merrill Lynch, who believed that the price ought to be in the region of 230p or even 240p. That really put the cat among the pigeons because by this stage there were voices in the boardroom broadly in agreement for the deal to go ahead, and others that were much more sceptical, in some cases because they were concerned about their own positions – a lot of people involved in this negotiation as it went along had different agendas. David Gill, for example, was wondering whether or not he was going to be in a job next year. Maurice was worried if he would be retained as the club's lawyer. Although I supported the bid, I did want to be involved in the initial stages of the takeover, to guide the club through it.

As the Sky negotiations continued I knew that my first priority as the director of a public company was to look after the shareholders and get a good price for their shares. Our share price was currently something like 157p, so once HSBC had recommended 217.5p, which was 60p above the current price, I was satisfied that we were not selling the shareholders short. Any improvement on that figure was fine by me: I wasn't going to argue about it; it was the icing on the cake. As far as I was concerned, the deal was either right for Manchester United or it wasn't. And if I thought the deal was right at 217.5p, it was certainly right at 240p. My only worry at this stage was that Sky might walk away if the price went up too far.

Matters were complicated further when on the morning of 6 September the story of Sky's bid for Manchester United was all over the Sunday papers. Somebody had leaked it. Perhaps the bigger shock was that we had been able to keep the media off the scent for so long, for just two days later in London we finally thrashed out a deal. It was tough going and the arguments lasted well into the night and had to be adjourned until the following morning. From a starting bid of 217.5p, Sky had upped their offer to 226p and then finally 230, which valued Manchester United at an astonishing £600 million. Even so, Greg Dyke remained of the opinion that we were selling off United too cheaply, especially when no one could foresee how valuable the club's television rights were going to be in the future. It was stalemate.

I put a call through to Booth, who was in the middle of a board meeting at Sky's headquarters. He came on the phone. 'I am sorry, Mark, but I can't do it,' I said. 'I can't deliver. It's Greg Dyke. Would you be prepared to do it without the full board, because everybody else has recommended it.' Booth said he wasn't. 'Well, if you want the entire board then I can only get them if you are prepared to go to 240p.'

There was silence at the other end of the line. 'I'll have to think about it,' said Booth.

That figure of 240p caused a certain amount of consternation over in Isleworth. It now meant that Sky were paying £623 million for Manchester United. As the tension ratcheted up it was Murdoch who intervened, telling Booth that whatever decision he made both he and the board would support him. Booth bit the bullet and agreed. The deal was done. Or so we thought.

The following morning, on the 9th, we held a press conference in London to officially announce the deal, then made our way back to Manchester to hold another one at Old Trafford. No sooner had the deal gone public than we got slaughtered in the papers by the anti-Murdoch brigade. One thing I did find strange was that the media people who opposed it so vehemently in their newspaper columns or editorials were privately saying to Sky what a fantastic deal they thought it was. I guess they had to sell papers, didn't they.

Many of our fellow Premier League teams were also hostile towards Sky's takeover, fearing that it would make us all-powerful. Other dissenting voices included Manchester City Council and both Labour and Conservative MPs, including the Minister for Sport.

As for the fans, the 'silent majority' were on our side. At our annual general meeting we took a vote on the issue and carried the day. Most fans don't really care who owns their clubs as long as they're successful and winning trophies. Are Manchester City fans anti-Abu Dhabi? Are they hell. There was, however, a vociferous and extremely vocal minority of supporters who wanted to stop it. Banners were unfurled at games and sections of supporters would shout, 'There's only one greedy bastard' in my general direction. For a long time I had been the subject of hostility and grief from sections of the home crowd, but this particular period I have to say was probably the worst.

For the most part, the fans' protest was an anti-Murdoch one. And that played out in the wider arena, too. Generally the detractors attacked the deal on the basis that it was Murdoch, not Sky. People perceived it and classified it as a Murdoch bid. The irony was that it wasn't as big a Murdoch bid as people made out. Obviously he was the majority shareholder in the company but I don't think Murdoch woke up one day and said to his minions, buy Manchester United. It was Mark Booth who wanted to do it and was pushing it, and Murdoch was there supporting him. During the whole process I never even met Murdoch. I still haven't.

I do think that it was this anti-Murdoch feeling, along with all the bad publicity and vocal opposition, that resulted in the deal being referred to the Monopolies and Mergers Commission by Peter Mandelson at the Office of Fair Trading. We had expected a referral, in truth, but, as I have already mentioned, both Sky and United had been advised by their lawyers that the Commission could not stop the bid.

However, we had an inkling of where things were going during our two meetings with the Monopolies and Mergers Commission. Their panel were extremely hostile towards us, both in their general manner and in their questioning. If anything, they were even more hostile in their dealings towards Sky. So we knew that they looked upon this deal in a very negative light. But we still didn't feel there were sufficient grounds to stop it.

Months passed, during which time Peter Mandelson was forced to quit his job with the government after details emerged of a secret loan he took from a ministerial colleague. His replacement at the Office of Fair Trading was Stephen Byers. In March 1999 Byers received the Monopolies and Mergers Commission's report on the Sky bid; it was 254 pages long and couldn't have been any more damaging. In its view there were not only public interest grounds but also competition grounds for stopping the takeover. In April Byers announced that the bid would not be allowed to go ahead. 'Under almost all scenarios considered by the MMC, the merger would increase the market power which BSkyB already has as a provider of sports premium channels,' went the argument. Byers also accepted the Commission's conclusions that the merger 'would damage the quality of British football by reinforcing the trend towards growing inequalities between the larger richer clubs and the smaller, poorer ones'. In other words they were worried that it was going to make United more powerful than we already were.

The bid was also ruled out for being anti-competitive. The fear was that, as owners of Manchester United, Sky would have an unfair advantage in television negotiations, and that they would have access to information about bids from rival broadcasters that their competitors were not privy to. Sky understood those concerns only too well and were prepared to withdraw from any TV contracts talks, but obviously their guarantees were not believed.

When news broke that the deal had collapsed, everyone thought I would be devastated, but I wasn't. I had taken a lot of the flack, of course, been called a greedy bastard, but price was never my main consideration. My overriding concern was: is the combined might of United and Sky stronger than United on its own? My belief right from the start was – yes, it was. It wasn't to do with money, greed or anything else, but with whether it was the right thing for Manchester United. And if the deal got blocked, which eventually it did, so be it. I didn't lose any sleep over it. I'd done my duty by the shareholders in trying to deliver it, because I believed it was the best thing for them, the club and its future. Once it gets kicked out, you move on.

26 THE YEAR OF THE TREBLE

After the disappointments of the previous season we showed our intent that summer of 1998 with two marquee signings. Jaap Stam was PSV Eindhoven's commanding centre back and had been on Alex's radar for quite some time. Both Alex and I met with Stam's agent to discuss buying the player as early as February 1998. Then on 8 April I flew to Amsterdam, and was picked up the next morning by Stam's agent, who drove me to Eindhoven where we met the chairman of PSV. It was quite a tricky negotiation because they wanted a lot more money than I was prepared to offer. In the end we got him for £10.8 million, still a record fee for a defender, and officially announced his signature on 5 May.

And what a debut season he had with us: to arrive in Manchester and straightaway do the Treble. What's more, he played most of the games that season. He was a very tough character, possessing great physical strength and stamina along with excellent technique. And he certainly looked the part.

Stam's arrival, along with the defenders we already had in place, Ronny Johnsen and Henning Berg, meant that it was time for Gary Pallister, at thirty-three, to move on. Gary had been a great servant to the club and

I was delighted that we managed to arrange for him to be transferred to his hometown club of Middlesbrough for, from our perspective, quite an attractive fee of £2.5 million.

Alex was also looking to add more firepower to United's attack. The gifted young Dutch striker at AC Milan, Patrick Kluivert, was an option but when we showed an interest he never even responded to our overtures, so we didn't ever get to the negotiating table and he went off to join Barcelona.

Instead we turned our attentions to a striker that I know Alex wanted badly, Aston Villa's Dwight Yorke. I think we started off by offering £10 million, but Villa's chairman Doug Ellis wanted £15 million. I'd known Doug ever since I first went on the board at United and had always got on well with him, but he was very reluctant to let Dwight go and wouldn't budge on the price. Even when we increased our offer to £12 million Doug remained intransigent.

Doug was very close to Dwight, having brought him over to England at the age of seventeen. It was during a tour of the West Indies that he and his manager Graham Taylor saw Dwight play and recognized his obvious talents. I think Doug treated Dwight a bit like a son; there was a special bond there, so you can understand his reluctance to let him go. But Dwight was very anxious to make the move happen and knew that we'd offered £12 million, which he felt was a fair price for him.

With time running out we put our final offer of £12 million in writing the day before the transfer window closed. I wrote to Doug giving him my mobile phone number and urging him to call me that evening. The following morning Dwight went to see Doug at his house almost in tears, explaining that he wanted to go to Manchester United and that he was being held back. And that probably tipped the whole thing in our favour, because Doug finally agreed to let him come to us for £12 million.

Dwight was a great signing. That first season with us was unbelievable. He and Cole had an instant understanding and overall they scored fifty-three goals between them, of which Dwight scored twenty-nine. Just incredible. They were pals off the pitch as well, which helped, and their play perfectly suited each other's. It was just the personal chemistry between them. And it worked so well for three seasons.

He was great in the dressing room, too: he made people laugh. He could be daft as a brush sometimes, but in a nice way. Dwight was a real character. And still is. I see him regularly and I always enjoy his company. He's always got a smile on his face and that Caribbean sunny disposition; a simple love for life.

Before the season got underway we made one more purchase, the Swedish winger Jesper Blomqvist from Parma for £4.4 million. At the same time we almost lost one of our players. Alex had given Ole Gunner Solskjær permission to talk to Tottenham Hotspur. Ole was now being used quite sparingly, coming on largely as a substitute, and I think he wanted more first-team football. These kinds of decisions were nothing to do with me. I never instructed Alex about which players he should be letting go; it was always up to him.

Spurs did indeed come back with a bid of £5.5 million and I agreed to the sale on the basis that Ole had agreed terms with the London club. The next thing I heard he had changed his mind and turned them down. Ole went to see Alex and had a private conversation that I wasn't privy to, but the upshot of it was that Ole stayed with United. Alan Sugar was not best pleased, especially after we'd done the Sheringham deal. I think he felt that I owed him a favour. But I can't force a player to leave if he doesn't want to. And as circumstances turned out, Ole's staying ended up being a pretty good decision.

The traditional season curtain raiser, the FA Charity Shield, ended disappointingly for us when Arsenal won 3–0. Much worse was a defeat at Highbury by the same scoreline that September. We'd also faltered by drawing our opening two games of the campaign. To compensate there were comprehensive wins against Charlton and our old foes Liverpool.

Off the pitch in September we launched MUTV, the club's very own television channel. Back in 1994 we had started up our own radio station, which had proved extremely popular. It went on the air on match days only, giving out traffic warnings as fans drove to the stadium, and team news – that kind of thing. We had a small studio in the ground quite near the directors' box in the South Stand and I would go and do the odd interview there. Now, because of the enormous success of football on television, it seemed like a logical step to start our own TV station. Everywhere you looked media companies were trying to get involved in football clubs; we were nearly bought by one of them. You also had Granada taking a stake in Liverpool and Leeds United. MUTV was the first of its kind in the country, probably in the world. Today it seems like every top club has their own TV channel.

For me the most important consideration was content. Obviously we couldn't show our own games live, which remains the case, but there was certainly enough other material such as magazine programmes, interviews with the players and staff, and archive clips. The channel could also be used as an advertising tool. But its main function was to nourish the supporter base.

The idea of MUTV came about in 1996 and was met with a lot of positive feedback from media outlets desperate to get involved. In the end we joined forces with Sky and Granada, who both put up the bulk of the initial funding. In those early years MUTV wasn't profitable, but everyone knew that it was a useful service to have and there was the hope that it would get to show some live games eventually, even if it was just friendlies, academy games or pre-season tours. Having grown substantially over the years, MUTV is still going strong today, and is more popular than ever.

A good example of the increasing power and influence of television on football was demonstrated that summer when there was talk of some of Europe's top clubs breaking away and forming their own super league. In May 1998 Peter Kenyon and Maurice Watkins were in Brazil attending a conference set up by Pelé to look at the restructuring of Brazilian football. While he was out there, Peter was approached by a company called Media Partners, which had been working on an alternative midweek knockout competition for the top European clubs. In essence, they wanted to take over from UEFA.

UEFA's relationship with clubs wasn't great at that time. They tended to be a bit aloof and wouldn't talk to you on an individual basis. If you wanted to enter into a dialogue with them you could only do it through your national association. So everything we wanted to say to UEFA had to be conducted through the FA. UEFA were also very dictatorial in terms of how they ran their competitions and we didn't think they were transparent enough. I think it's fair to say there was quite a bit of animosity between them and us. Media Partners came in and said that not only were they going to be a lot more transparent in the way they ran things, but there was going to be a lot more dialogue and liaison, and the prize money would be substantially increased. That all sounded very attractive.

The idea was for a competition of thirty-two clubs that would be selected on the basis of recent and historical success. It had always been the practice that every year different clubs could qualify and challenge for European glory, but Media Partners wanted to guarantee that the super clubs always retained a place in their competition. So one of their ideas was to include a group of founder members that would enjoy permanent membership.

Only a handful of clubs were interested at the beginning, but as more and more meetings took place, some of the other European big guns started to get involved. From Italy there were the two Milan clubs along with Juventus. There was Ajax from the Netherlands and Marseille and Paris Saint-Germain from France. Bayern Munich and Borussia Dortmund were to represent Germany. And from England, besides us, Arsenal and Liverpool. All of these great clubs were in discussions with Media Partners, all of which took place in secret and without the say-so or involvement of our national associations. Naturally when the press learnt of what was happening all hell broke loose and there were all sorts of threats from the Premier League about expelling those clubs that had been involved in the talks.

From the sidelines UEFA had watched all this unfold. They knew that if Media Partners took over, it could spell the end for them. Ultimately what happened was a thawing in their relationship with the clubs: they started to talk to us and enter into face-to-face meetings. They promised to look at prize money and at revamping their competitions. And that's exactly what took place – the clubs stayed within UEFA and Media Partners were marginalized and actually got nothing out of it in the end. But they were definitely the catalyst for UEFA moving in the right direction and making big changes. The biggest of which was a rule change that resulted in the top five European countries having more teams eligible for qualification in the Champions League. There would also be a much bigger share-out of TV and sponsorship monies. Consequently, many of the things that Media Partners were promising actually came to fruition.

I tried not to get too involved while all this was going on, as you get these kinds of proposals happening in football all the time. I was more than happy for Peter Kenyon and David Gill to handle the negotiations, because I could see an overall benefit at the end, even if all it did was shake up UEFA, which is exactly what it did. Things largely panned out the way I thought they would. I never truly believed that any of the clubs would walk away from UEFA – it was too risky a move.

Back on the pitch the team enjoyed a fruitful winter, including big wins away to Everton and Southampton and a 5–1 crushing of Wimbledon. But the year ended on a sour note when Brian Kidd decided to leave. Over the past couple of years Brian had received a lot of interest from other clubs and had nearly left us before for Everton and Manchester City. This time the interested club was Blackburn Rovers, who had just sacked their manager Roy Hodgson after a poor start to the season had left them languishing in the relegation zone. They wanted Brian to take over and were offering a million pounds per year, considerably more than we were paying him.

Brian informed us about the approach and I arranged a meeting with Roland Smith and Peter Kenyon to discuss the situation on 2 December, just before United faced Tottenham in the quarter-finals of the League Cup. Brian told us that he wanted to give management a try. On the two previous occasions he'd been tempted away we had improved his contract to the point where I think Brian was the highest-paid number two in the league. This time, however, it was too much for us; we weren't prepared to match what Blackburn were offering and agreed to let him go. Alex looked very closely at two candidates to bring in as a replacement: Steve McClaren at Derby and Preston's David Moyes. In the end McClaren was appointed.

I was disappointed to see Brian leave because he had done a good job. I'm not sure if he was ever manager material – he was a very good number two – but I respected the fact that he wanted to have a go and I wished him well. Sadly it didn't work out for him.

As the team entered 1999 we began to take charge of the league with some scintillating performances and crucial wins, but in the Champions League we had been presented with a tough draw. The expression 'group of death' is often overused, but here it proved an understatement as United found themselves up against both Barcelona and Bayern Munich. The sacrificial lambs were Schmeichel's old team Brøndby. The Bavarians ended up winning the group thanks to home and away wins over Barça, while we managed to successfully navigate any pitfalls to emerge undefeated as runners-up, our finest hour being an impressive 3–3 tie at the Nou Camp.

Back home in the FA Cup we faced a difficult fourth-round home tie against Liverpool. Things couldn't have got off to a worse start when Michael Owen headed the visitors into the lead in the third minute. Chasing the game we were energetic and purposeful but seemed to lack the required cutting edge until the eighty-eighth minute when Yorke tapped home the equalizer. Just when it looked to be heading for a replay at Anfield, Solskjær latched on to a pass from Scholes and tucked the ball into the net. It was high drama but, as it turned out, just a foretaste of what was in store for the club and our supporters.

Looking back on it now I don't think there was any talk of us winning the Treble until around the time of the now classic FA Cup semi-final replay against Arsenal at Villa Park. We should have won the first game really, because we had a perfectly good goal disallowed for offside. Feeling robbed by the referee we went into the replay more than a little aggrieved, but rose to the occasion and ought to have been more than 1–0 up before a deflected shot by Dennis Bergkamp put the Gunners on level terms.

Everything then seemed to go wrong. Keane was sent off for a foul on Marc Overmars and then, in stoppage time at the end of the game, Phil Neville's clumsy tackle on Ray Parlour earned Arsenal a penalty. The brilliant Bergkamp stepped up to take it and you thought, if he scores now we're out and all talk of the Treble is gone. A potentially deflating moment awaited. But Peter Schmeichel, so often a hero, made a terrific save, guessing the correct way and diving to his left to push the ball away. After that, of course, came the moment that lives in the heart of every United fan, one of the greatest goals the club has witnessed. In extra time Ryan Giggs picked the ball up in his own half after a tired Patrick Vieira pass and just ran with it, sailing past the likes of Lee Dixon and Martin Keown before smashing it into the roof of the net past David Seaman. It was just incredible and undoubtedly Ryan's greatest moment in a United shirt. What a way to win an FA Cup semi-final, especially when the side were down to ten men, with everything on the line and against your main rivals that year.

I must confess here, however, that I missed the goal. I'd seen a few scares in my time as chairman but the tension of this match really got to me and I left the directors' box to go for a walk. I was wandering around the car park when I heard the roar and rushed back to watch the final few minutes.

After you win a match under those kinds of circumstances you start to believe that this could really be your year, that something quite special might happen. But there was still a long way to go and tensions were rising to almost unprecedented heights.

We played Liverpool away on 5 May, just three weeks before the end of the season. With us leading 2–0, thanks to goals from Yorke and Irwin, referee David Elleray granted Liverpool a highly debatable penalty, which was duly dispatched, and then brandished a second yellow card at Denis Irwin for kicking the ball away when a free kick had been given. It wasn't as if Denis hoofed the ball into row Z – he just flicked it away – but as a result Denis, a great professional and as far from a dirty player as you could imagine, was going to miss the Cup final. I just felt that common sense could have prevailed there.

To cap it all off, Paul Ince, now at Liverpool after his stay at Inter Milan, struck an eighty-ninth-minute equalizer that looked to have delivered a serious blow to our title hopes, as it kept us three points behind Arsenal in second. With a game in hand, and three games left to play, it was far from a terminal blow, but there was a sense that our challenge had been derailed.

After the match I was livid and made some less than complimentary remarks about David Elleray in the press: 'If Arsenal or Chelsea win the Premiership this season by either one or two points, I trust they will strike a special commemorative medal for Mr Elleray because he will have done it for them.' A couple of days later I received a letter from the FA asking for clarification over my comments, which they believed had brought the game into disrepute. However, after an enquiry I escaped any censure.

Normally I never commented about controversial incidents in matches. As chairman you have to be careful what you say and during my years at Old Trafford this incident stands out above any other. The tension probably got the better of me: we were going for the Treble and this was a vital match. Obviously it was quite a hostile atmosphere at Anfield and I just felt that Elleray hadn't had his best game. Instead of the three points we should have had we ended up with just the one, which could have really cost us, and we had lost a key player for the Cup final too, so in the heat of the moment I said a lot more than I would normally have.

As a consequence of all this, Elleray got some death threats and some suggested he blamed me for this. Of course that was the last thing I wanted to happen and on reflection I had a lot of sympathy for him. In fact we made up afterwards. I saw him later and we shook hands.

Despite our slip-up at Anfield, coming into the final league fixture of the season it was between us and Arsenal for the title. Tasked with beating Tottenham to be sure of regaining the championship, we gave ourselves a huge problem by allowing in a sloppy goal from their striker, Les Ferdinand. After that we bombarded the Spurs goal and just before half time Beckham struck a thunderbolt and we were back on level terms.

Coming out in the second half we knew we still had to win and Alex made what turned out to be a key substitution, replacing Sheringham with Cole, who within minutes of coming on brilliantly controlled a long pass and deftly lifted the ball over their sprawling keeper. Then it was a case of sweating out the next forty-odd minutes, especially when news reached us that Arsenal were winning their game. Finally, referee Graham Poll blew his whistle and the Premier League title was once again heading to Old Trafford. That was the first leg of three complete.

On 22 May we made our way to Wembley for the FA Cup final. Our opponents were Newcastle and we dispatched them quite easily with goals from Sheringham and Scholes in a 2–0 victory. We'd done the Double, the third in six years, which was an incredible achievement in itself, but we still had the possibility of turning that Double into a Treble, which no English club had ever done before.

The road to the Champions League final had been hard fought and hard won. Defeating Inter Milan over two legs in the quarter-final had set up a semi-final confrontation with Juventus. And where Giggs was our saviour against Arsenal, it was to be Keane's finest hour that rescued us in Turin.

We'd only managed a draw at Old Trafford and after eleven minutes found ourselves 2–0 down in the second leg. We knew before the game started that we would have to score at least once to get through. Now we needed two goals to have any chance.

In the twenty-fourth minute Beckham flighted in one of his customarily accurate corners and Keane climbed highest to deliver a perfectly weighted glancing header into the net. Then, just ten minutes later, he was predictably booked for a late tackle on Zidane. Knowing that he was now suspended for the final, Keane did not allow emotion to rule his performance; instead he drove the team forward with sheer force of will and, thanks to goals from Yorke and Cole, United were through.

In the dressing room after the match, the feeling was euphoric at reaching the final, but we were going for the Treble: there was still a long way to go, so you don't celebrate for too long. It's back to business pretty quickly.

The whole team were magnificent that night, and that performance stands as one of our best ever in Europe, but Keane in particular was enormous. He got that vital first goal, which gave us belief and reignited us. Unfortunately Scholes also picked up a yellow card, which meant that both of our key midfield players would be missing from the final. I felt so sorry for the pair of them because they had been so influential that season and were now going to miss the potential crowning glory. Because of that I felt we were the underdogs against Bayern Munich. And that's the way the game panned out.

The final took place at the Nou Camp, just four days after our exertions on the Wembley pitch in the Cup final. Even though it was a neutral venue it seemed like we had the greater number of supporters in the stands, so it was a wonderful atmosphere. With Keane and Scholes absent, Alex played Butt and Beckham in central midfield with Blomqvist and Giggs on the wings. But we found ourselves a goal behind early on and I have to say Bayern looked the more likely to score again. In the second half they had three golden chances to put the game beyond us but they didn't take them, largely through a combination of bad luck, hitting the woodwork twice, and a fine save by Schmeichel.

When I saw that board go up with three minutes on it and we were still losing, I thought, well, it's not been our night. And then we produced those two magical goals. It was hard to believe what you were watching. Sheringham, who had come on for Yorke, managed to scramble the ball home from close range after Giggs sliced the ball into the box. All I was thinking at that stage was, thank God we've got back into the game. When you've been behind for almost the whole match and suddenly you score in injury time you're just glad to be still in with a chance; that you've got another thirty minutes to try to prove yourself. I was still coming down from that high when the second goal went in from Solskjær. I struggled to believe it. It was a testament to the great spirit we had in that team.

The Treble really was an unbelievable achievement, fairy tale stuff. The strange thing was, it all happened so quickly – within a period of ten days. We didn't win the league until the last game on the Sunday, the FA Cup final was the following Saturday and then in midweek came the Champions League final. It was almost a case of us not being able to relax and enjoy each triumph because we were always looking ahead to the next one.

After the final whistle I made my way into the dressing room to congratulate the players and the staff. The atmosphere was one of pure euphoria. Back at the hotel later that night we held a huge banquet and everybody was there. We had asked UEFA for three extra medals to be made, which I presented that night to Scholes and Keane, and also to Henning Berg, who missed the final through injury, so that they wouldn't feel left out of all the celebrations.

Quite rightly, that Treble-winning side will go down as one of the greatest in the club's history. It's comparable to that great 1994 side that I highly rate as well. It would have been interesting to see how far that team would have gone if it hadn't been penalized by UEFA's foreign player ruling. This team didn't have those disadvantages, and what they went on to do was nothing less than phenomenal.

On a personal note, I had made a promise to myself that I would step down as chief executive in 2000. Now here we were in 1999; it was almost the end of the road for me. I'd spent nineteen years trying to reach the holy grail of winning the Champions League, and we'd finally done it. It did take a bit of time to sink in. It was only really later on that I began to appreciate and realize what we'd achieved, and was able to look back with a glowing feeling: bloody hell, what have we done? It's unbelievable to win all three.

It wasn't until 2008 that United were crowned kings of Europe again. Having won it so spectacularly in 1999 you would have thought the team might have kicked on and gained more European glory. But it wasn't to be. Domestically the team achieved probably more than we ever anticipated or dreamed of. As far as the Champions League was concerned, I think if there is any criticism at all – and it is only a minor one – it's probably that we should have won more European trophies.

As champions of Europe, United were invited to play in the Intercontinental Cup in Tokyo against the champions of South America, Palmeiras of Sao Paulo in Brazil. It was the two strongest footballing continents battling it out and by winning that match – 1–0, the goal coming from Roy Keane – we effectively became world club champions, the first English club ever to achieve such a feat.

United's profile had never been higher and by the end of that season we had become the world's richest football club, having broken through the £1 billion valuation mark, and the most valuable sporting franchise on the planet. We'd come a long way from the time I took over, when the total value of Manchester United was £2 million.

27 HANDING OVER POWER

Commentators never tire of accusing Manchester United of being more of a glorified money-making operation than a football club, claiming that we have lost sight of our roots. But ever since the early 1990s and the days of Edward Freedman, we'd been expanding. On the back of Sky television and their overseas television contract, the global opportunities opened up and with it the chance to expand our merchandising and to sell products abroad.

We'd already set up a separate merchandising division, which had its own structure and its own management. Now we had an international division as well, set up for overseas merchandising business. All we were doing was capitalizing on the brand, which is what we've been accused of for years. Our merchandising power set us apart from every other club in the country because we were more successful at it. All it was really was sensible business practice.

The same could be said of the acquisition of a property manager, George Johnson. By 1998 United were owners of significant tracts of land in Trafford Park. Indeed, we were one of the biggest owners of land in the whole area. We always needed land and were constantly looking to add to facilities on match days. There are huge match-day car-parking needs. When you have 6,000 executive customers, that might mean 4,000 cars, not to mention everybody else, a large majority of whom come by car and want easy access.

In addition to Old Trafford and the training ground, United's property portfolio included several houses. The last thing foreign players who came over here wanted to confront was the hassle of looking around for a suitable place for their family to live. So we needed a property portfolio to accommodate them.

Another thing we were criticized for was the decision in 1998 to remove the words 'Football Club' from the club crest. Again critics jumped on this as further proof that we had thrown away our football identity. Nothing of the sort. It was purely a marketing decision and an idea of Peter Kenyon's. Peter believed that Manchester United was now such a worldwide brand that you didn't necessarily need the word 'Football Club'; Manchester United on its own was big enough.

A lot of people felt that this was slightly arrogant of us and, yes, maybe it was, but Manchester United is a brand, whether they liked it or not. Everybody knows we are a football club, our whole makeup is that we're a football club, and a great football club, but it says something when your name alone is enough for everybody to know who and what you are and what you stand for. It was a marketing statement, really. A global statement. Take for example the Harlem Globetrotters; they don't have the words 'Basketball Team' after their name, because everybody knows who they are. Being the verifiable best and richest football club in the world, United were now in that league.

From the ecstatic high of winning the Treble we soon found ourselves embroiled in one of the most damaging and controversial episodes in the club's history when we announced that we would not be defending the FA Cup in 2000. The outcry from those who didn't like United was predictably hostile but the criticism we received was in my opinion totally unjustified.

As winners of the Champions League, United had been invited to represent Europe in the inaugural FIFA Club World Championships, a pet project of Sepp Blatter, president of FIFA. It was an eight-team tournament involving the champions from each continent and other invited teams, and was due to take place over two weeks in January 2000 in Brazil. Unfortunately this clashed with the FA Cup fourth round and led to a huge dilemma, because not only were the FA insistent that we went to Brazil but the then Sports Minister Tony Banks was pushing for us to go as well.

From the beginning I didn't want anything to do with this tournament and neither did Alex, but the pressure began to grow for us to reconsider our position. The FA's prime consideration was their bid to stage the 2006 World Cup and how our refusal to play in Brazil would irrevocably damage our chances. This point was made even more starkly when after a meeting between United officials and the FA, Tony Banks wrote to Roland Smith:

> A refusal could have serious ramifications for England's 2006 World Cup bid. I have been personally informed by three FIFA executive members, all of whom had previously committed themselves to England's cause, that they will not vote for us in the event of Manchester United's non-appearance. I can appreciate how unfair it is to put such a burden upon you but it is clearly in the national interest for your club to compete in the FIFA World Club championships.

It was a difficult decision to make but ultimately I was persuaded that the best option was that United should attend. It was our patriotic duty, no less. What we now wanted from the FA was some kind of help with the inevitable fixture congestion that would result. We got nothing, despite our protestations. 'Something's got to give,' we argued. 'We can't play in every single competition.' Our suggestion that maybe we could have a bye in the Cup and come in at a later round was curtly dismissed. So too was help with the league fixtures.

In the end the only way we could deal with the situation was by reluctantly withdrawing ourselves from the FA Cup. I was never comfortable with that decision and we paid a heavy price for it. The press laid into us. They said we were doing it purely for greed and for our worldwide marketing. It was absolute nonsense. The *Daily Mirror* were the most vociferous in their condemnation and even launched a 'save the FA Cup' campaign. The newspaper's editor Piers Morgan rang me and we arranged a meeting in London. I tried to explain to him exactly what had happened and the pressure the FA had placed the club under, hoping for some understanding. It made no difference whatsoever. *The Mirror* continued its onslaught against us regardless.

Football fans and media commentators also had a field day. We were arrogant, they said; we were tarnishing the traditions and romance of the FA Cup. One suggestion was that we played our youth team in the Cup round. That's all well and good, but what happens to the confidence of those young players if they end up on the wrong end of a hammering?

The truth of the matter was that Manchester United were placed in an impossible situation not of its own making. Then, when the abuse began to be hurled around from all sides, we had no backing whatsoever from those people who had lobbied us so hard.

For me the lesser of the two evils was to go to Brazil and pull out of the Cup. Was I happy about that? No, I wasn't. Do I believe it was the right thing to do? Yes, I do, because had we refused and England lost the World Cup bid you can just imagine the headlines: 'United scupper England's World Cup bid.' So we couldn't win, whatever we did.

The irony is that England never had the remotest chance of holding the 2006 World Cup and we ended up performing badly at the tournament, even with the golden generation of players we had at our disposal, going out to Portugal on penalties.

On the domestic front, United were going to have to contest the 1999–2000 season without one of our talismen. In March 1998 Peter Schmeichel had come to see me in my office to announce that he was going to leave at the end of the following season. Now thirty-six years old, Peter was coming to the end of his career and wanted to leave us at the top. Although he carried on playing for a few more years, first going to Sporting Lisbon and then back into the Premier League for short spells with Aston Villa and Manchester City, Peter felt he could no longer deliver his absolute best for Manchester United.

Needless to say I was disappointed to see Peter leave but he had graciously given us a season's notice. He had also presented us with a major headache. When you have a player like Schmeichel who is so dominant in one particular position, it's sometimes almost impossible to replace them. Alex, however, was quietly confident that the man he had identified as Peter's replacement was up for the challenge. Mark Bosnich had been on United's books as a teenager before returning to play in his native Australia. In the early 1990s he joined Aston Villa, where he carved out a good reputation and was a favourite with the Villa faithful.

We first approached Mark in August 1998 and he was keen to return to Old Trafford. Then, on the evening of 5 November, after a board meeting at which it was agreed that Bosnich was our choice, Alex and I jumped in a car and raced to Mark's home in the Midlands to conclude the deal. A few months later, Alex came to see me. He was now having second thoughts about Bosnich and wanted the Ajax keeper Edwin van der Sar. 'How do we get out of it?' he said. 'We can't get out of it,' I replied. 'We've both agreed a deal with him, Alex. We've shaken his hand.'

As it turned out, things didn't quite work out with Mark. While he was a good shot stopper capable of outstanding saves, his biggest problem was with the ball on the ground and his distribution. In the old days that didn't matter so much but ever since the back pass rule came into effect, goalkeepers have needed to be nimble on their feet. They've got to be almost as good with their feet as an outfield player.

Another factor with Bosnich were complaints from Alex about his weight and general fitness. When he pulled his hamstring early in the season, Alex hurriedly searched for a backup. I remember I was on holiday at the time when I got a call saying that Alex wanted to bring in Massimo Taibi from Venezia. The fee was £4.9 million. I was agreeable to this and told him to go ahead, and the deal was done extremely quickly. Poor Massimo only lasted four games before he returned to Italy. After some calamitous mistakes he was picked on by the press and I think his confidence was completely shot.

Alex again tried to reinforce the goalkeeping position by bringing in Fabien Barthez from Monaco in the summer of 2000 at a cost of £7 million. This was actually the last transfer that I handled before stepping down as chief executive. Fabien had fantastic feet and was terrific with the ball on the ground but I always thought he was a bit too short for a top-class goalkeeper. Yes, he was a World Cup winner with France but I never thought he was quite top drawer.

Although we did have goalkeeping issues, it didn't stop the team romping to another Premier League title. Ironically that controversial trip to Brazil probably helped us a bit. People were quick to complain that we had sought an unfair advantage by going off to the sunshine for two weeks. But we really did storm the league that year, winning it by eighteen points from Arsenal. It was total domination and another incredible achievement. And it was the same team that had won the Treble, with two additions, the South African Quinton Fortune, who arrived from Atlético Madrid for £1.5 million, and Mikaël Silvestre, who joined us from Inter Milan for £3.8 million and became a regular in the first team for many years.

The 1999–2000 season saw not only United dominating on the pitch but enormous and significant improvements off it, and not just to Old Trafford. The Cliff in Salford had been the main training ground for United since 1938. Understandably there was a lot of tradition attached to the old place, but by the mid-1990s it had really become too small for our needs. Covering just six acres, The Cliff had only the one full-size outdoor pitch and limited remedial and rehabilitation facilities. Alex had also regularly complained that it was too accessible to the press and the general public.

As a stopgap I had purchased twenty-one acres of land at Littleton Road, which was only a short distance from The Cliff. This comprised five full-size pitches but poor changing rooms and no rehabilitation facilities. It was critical to our continued success that we build a modern training complex. It had become common practice for our players to train at one site and then be bussed to the other site to continue their programme. Because neither The Cliff nor Littleton Road could be developed to create a totally integrated facility, we began a determined search for other available land.

After looking at a number of possibilities it was our chief scout Les Kershaw who pointed us in the direction of a business friend of his called John Tomlinson who knew of 100 acres of secluded land in Carrington, close to Old Trafford. I remember going down to view it in 1995 and immediately saw that it met all of our needs. The land was privately owned by Shell and after a lot of negotiations we purchased it for the sum of £720,000. There followed a long period during which we had to carry out various surveys and seek planning permission, as well as fend off some opposition from environmentalists and local farmers. At one point the famous eco-warrior known as Swampy threatened to join the fight against our development plans by burrowing underneath the proposed site. In the end, though, local councillors raised no objections and building work finally went ahead in 1999.

Funnily enough, John Gardiner of Tozer Gallagher, who was the quantity surveyor on the project, was a friend of mine who I used to play rugby against when he played for Sale. He had the keys and used to take me down to Carrington on a Sunday to see how the construction was coming along. So I closely followed its progress and was also involved in the planning, as were Alex and his training staff, whose requirements were vitally important, along with their input about the layout, how they wanted the pitches, the equipment they needed and so on.

When Carrington opened in the summer of 2000, at a cost of £14.3 million, I think it ranked as one of the best of its kind in the world. It had nine full-size grass pitches and other training pitches, a full-sized indoor AstroTurf pitch, a gym, a pool, a steam room, physiotherapy rooms, medical facilities, a press room and numerous offices. Over the years other buildings have been added, bringing the total cost of construction to over £60 million. As for The Cliff and Littleton Road, these were retained by the club and are used for academy matches and coaching and by footballing charities in the local community.

Old Trafford, too, needed something of a facelift, so we submitted plans to Trafford council for the redevelopment of the East stand. Our thinking behind this was to increase capacity by 12,000, achieved by the creation of a second tier of seating. Again, executive boxes and facilities were added so that in time the stands would start paying for themselves.

We also wanted to move the offices from where they were in the South Stand, because they were getting overcrowded. There were also offices on Sir Matt Busby Way and our plan was to bring them all into the East Stand. We called in the architects and requested they design a modern office block with a prestige frontage. The one we liked best was the large glass frontage that you see today. It was certainly befitting that the biggest club in the country should have a spectacular-looking entrance. We also put the megastore in there and moved Sir Matt's statue to just outside the main entrance. Then we completely pedestrianized the whole area so that people could congregate there at any time. Before that, all the directors, staff and VIPs used to park their cars in this area.

Work on the two stands finished ahead of schedule with a combined cost of £30 million. During construction, as seats became available, Old Trafford was setting new Premier League record attendances almost every week. When completed, capacity stood at 67,000. Old Trafford could now truly be called a stadium fit for champions.

I must say that the stadium redevelopments done in my time are one of my proudest legacies. Back in the mid-1980s, football went through a horrendous time with all those disasters – the Bradford fire, Heysel and then Hillsborough. The Taylor Report came along and clubs had to spend fortunes on their grounds. Of all the money we made from merchandising, TV, and all other commercial activities, yes some of it went in dividends, and we used to get criticized because of our dividend policy, but investors only put money into something if they know they are going to get a return. Paying dividends is part of business. It was never a huge amount anyway. No, the bulk of our money either went on the team or on stadium development, making Old Trafford safer as a consequence of the Taylor Report. At one point capacity was as low as 32,000, because we had to put all seating in. Then we settled down at 44,000-odd, then 55,000 and eventually 67,500. Today the capacity is over 75,000. We were building it up all the time; we were spending fortunes on our stadium. All through the years that we were successful on the pitch we were making Manchester United stronger by putting money into a stadium that was going to last for decades. Old Trafford doesn't need a lot of money spending on it now because the hard work was done in those years in the 1990s. That ground was built for the next century. It's definitely one of my proudest achievements.

By the time the refurbished East and West stands opened in the summer of 2000 I had recently stepped down as chief executive of Manchester United plc, although I stayed on as chairman of the football club board, and Peter Kenyon had taken over. Even though I had less responsibility now and could be as involved as little or as much as I wanted, I still found that I was going into Old Trafford every day and working full time. Roland, as chairman of the plc, was anxious that the link between me and the plc remained so that if he wanted to know something about the football club he could still feel free to ring me and I would know what was going on. I also continued to represent the club at Premier League meetings, along with Peter. I had twenty-odd years' experience of attending such meetings while Peter was new to it all, so Roland thought that it was important I carried on in that capacity. And as chairman of the football club I continued to preside over our monthly football club meetings. So I remained very much in the loop so far as the day-to-day running of United was concerned.

However, there were certain decisions being made that I wasn't fully in agreement with. I remember being very disappointed when we bought Juan Sebastián Verón in 2001. We had just won the league again, we had Nicky Butt in the reserves who couldn't get in the team every week, and I just felt, why do we now need to go out and spend £28 million on one player who was going to cost £5 million per year in wages? We were breaking the wage structure I'd put in place on a player that I didn't think was necessary at that time.

So strong were my reservations that the night before the plc board was due to approve the transfer I had a long conversation with Roland. My main fear was that as soon as the other top players in the team found out what Verón was earning there would be repercussions. Roland listened to what I had to say and was sympathetic, but he told me, 'Martin, in all your years as chief exec I supported you. This is Peter's first year, I've got to support him.' That was his reasoning.

Sure enough Verón arrived from Lazio as the most expensive player in British football history and within three years we were lucky to get £15 million back from Chelsea for him. With that huge fee and wages we ended up paying a lot of money for a player who I didn't think improved us. I think he had trouble adapting to the faster pace of the Premiership and was not allowed the same time and space on the ball that he had enjoyed in Italy, so he wasn't a success at United. And as I'd suspected, the players, but more especially their agents, did get to hear what Verón was earning and all that did was inflate our wage bill unnecessarily.

When I stepped down as chief executive it was agreed that Peter Kenyon would take over, but I also persuaded the board that David Gill ought to move from finance director to deputy chief executive. David had been with us for three years and was well versed in the running of the club, and I believed he would be a very useful deputy to Peter, especially when it came to any financial decision that needed to be made. I felt the combination of those two would be a good succession.

Looking back today, I still feel that 2000 was the right time for me to step down as chief executive and I have no regrets. I was fifty-five and had been running the club for twenty years but had begun to feel that the emphasis was changing. The plc, which I had brought about and which had been good for United over the years, as it had created the money and the facilities needed to do all the successful things we'd done, was for me becoming too onerous.

Back in my time, the non-executives I'd brought in were people like Maurice Watkins, Sir Roland Smith, Al Midani and Greg Dyke. Now Midani had gone, Maurice was no longer considered independent because he'd been on the board for ten years, and Dyke had stepped down as a result of becoming Director General of the BBC. Roland himself was close to retiring and in wanting to secure his successor had brought in a number of high-ranking figures from the world of banking and business in January 2000: Roy Gardner, Ian Much and Philip Yea. And as soon as they came in the dynamics of the board changed. They wanted more reportage, so suddenly I was being asked to produce a regular report to the board. To me it was a backward step. I had taken Manchester United from a successful football club to the number one in the world; I didn't want to spend my time producing endless reports for non-executive directors.

Board meetings had also become a bit cumbersome and interrogatory: How do we justify this? How do we justify that? These new non-exec directors were only doing their job, I suppose, but I got the feeling that they wanted more control over the running of United than non-execs had in the past, or when I was in charge. Even though we'd been a public company for nine years and I'd been chief exec I hadn't had non-exec directors on the board questioning my every move. It just wasn't an environment that I was particularly going to enjoy. No criticism of them, but I felt, *This is not for me, I've had my era, and if they think they can do better, fine.*

I had begun to lose the control that I had previously enjoyed partly because I'd sold off a lot of my shares over the last few years, really ever since we floated, so by the time I stepped down as chief executive I wasn't a significant shareholder any more. I knew I was stepping down, so it made sense to begin reducing my shareholding. I just didn't feel the need any longer to have a large stock of shares. It was a Scottish millionaire businessman called Harry Dobson who ended up buying almost all of the remaining shares that I held with United. The deal was done through my broker, so I never met Mr Dobson personally, even though as a consequence of the deal he became the third-highest shareholder at United, after Sky and the racehorse owners and breeders John Magnier and J. P. McManus. Although I was happy to relinquish the shares, it wasn't lost on me that for the first time since my father took over United an Edwards was no longer among the club's main shareholders. Times were changing.

28 SAYING GOODBYE

Before stepping down as chief executive at the end of July 2000, I was involved with the groundwork for a record-breaking £303 million merchandising deal with US sports gear giant Nike. The deal dwarfed previous Nike football partnerships, such as the one with the Brazilian national team, and was at the time thought to be the biggest of its kind ever signed.

Back in 1996 Nike had missed out on becoming our kit supplier when we decided to stick with Umbro, but circumstances had changed dramatically since then. With United winning the Treble and the worldwide coverage the club enjoyed through Sky, Nike decided they wanted to make a big name for themselves in the English game and we were the obvious choice.

With his experience in the field of marketing, Peter Kenyon also played a significant role in the deal and on 15 August he and I, along with David Gill and Steve Richards, who was our managing director of merchandise, flew out to the States for three days of meetings at Nike's headquarters in Beaverton. The Nike deal was huge because it changed the whole basis of our merchandising operation. Effectively it outsourced control of Manchester United's global replica-kit and merchandising business to the sportswear giant. The club had two years to run on its current kit deal with Umbro, so the Nike deal came into effect in August 2002 and covered a thirteen-year period. It was described as a 'strategic alliance between two global brands'.

Earlier that year, in February, I had announced at a press conference another record-breaking deal when the logo of the mobile phone company Vodafone replaced that of long-term sponsors Sharp on all United shirts. They had given us notice that they no longer wanted to continue as our sponsor. Sharp had been with us since 1982; that's a partnership of eighteen years, which must be the longest sponsorship by any company of a football club. The press speculated who our new potential sponsors would be when Sharp stepped down and companies as diverse as British Airways, Emirates and internet firms Yahoo! and Amazon.com were all linked with us.

In the end Vodafone were anxious to come on board. At the time they were the largest telecoms company and doing a lot of sponsoring in the sport arena, not least their association with the English cricket team. It just seemed like a natural fit at the time and we agreed a £30 million four-year deal with them. Another significant development that year was the launch of the club's official website, which was our first foray into the online world and could help us reach a much broader audience.

On the field United continued its dominance, winning the league title in 2001 for a third season in a row, becoming only the fourth side in history to do so. The achievement was overshadowed by the announcement that Alex intended to retire at the end of the following season.

I have to say that his decision came as both a surprise and a shock to all of us. Once we realized that he was very serious about it and that his mind was made up, there were lots of discussions at board level about a possible replacement. Our first choice was Arsène Wenger. Since joining Arsenal in 1996 Wenger had been pretty successful, especially in his first full season in charge when he won the Double. And while it's true to say that he has suffered hard times since, at the time we all thought he was the best candidate to replace Alex. Certainly he was my number-one choice.

So we made our approach and Wenger did show a little bit of interest, enough to want to meet with both Peter Kenyon and me at his house in London to listen to what we had to say. In fact, we had a couple of meetings with him and for a while we thought there was a possibility of him joining us. But I think Wenger felt a loyalty towards David Dein. He was very close to David, and that was the reason he gave us in the end for turning down United. He felt that he had started something with Arsenal and that his attachment to the club was too great, he didn't want to break that bond.

With Wenger out of the running the next man in the frame was Sven-Göran Eriksson, then the current England manager. Peter was particularly anxious to get Eriksson and the board were fully supportive of the idea. I wasn't really involved in those negotiations because, to be truthful, I wasn't 100 per cent sure he was the right man for the job. Yes, he'd had a bit of success and had a good track record, but he'd spent a lot of money in achieving that success. He'd been quite a big spender. Also, he was unproven in English club football. So I had my reservations.

The negotiations with Eriksson went well: he agreed terms and everything looked set for him to be named as the next manager of Manchester United when Alex suddenly changed his mind about retiring. That meant we had to go back to Eriksson to tell him that even though we had agreed terms, nothing had as yet been signed and Alex was now staying on, a decision made public in February 2002, which I assume was a huge let-down for him.

Alex has always said it was his family that changed his attitude about retirement and made him think again about it. They were anxious about what he was going to do. His whole life had revolved around football and his wife Cathy had said something along the lines of, 'I don't want you under my feet all the time', and his boys must have said, 'What are you going to do, Dad, you'll be bored to bloody death.'

Alex has also admitted that his decision to retire was probably the biggest mistake he made as Manchester United manager. It had a hugely detrimental effect on the team and we ended up having the most disappointing season for years, finishing third. We'd won the league in

1999, 2000 and 2001, and won it fairly comfortably, and in 2002 we were nowhere. Alex stayed and in 2003 we won the league again. He remained with us for another ten years, and although he had to contend with the further rise of Arsenal and the arrival of Roman Abramovich at Chelsea, there were many more good times still to come.

The summer of Alex's surprise announcement that he planned to retire, the club had spent heavily on the Dutch striker Ruud van Nistelrooy. It was the culmination of a long and fraught transfer saga.

Back in April 2000, when I was still chief executive, Alex had wanted to bring in another striker and had earmarked van Nistelrooy, who had been prolific playing in the Dutch league for PSV Eindhoven, as his man. It wasn't a particularly easy negotiation because Alex had made all sorts of noises about it and I think the top brass at Eindhoven felt we were tapping the player up. After speaking with Ruud's agent and the club, we finally agreed a deal in the region of £16 million.

Everyone was excited when Ruud arrived at Old Trafford for his medical. That excitement quickly evaporated when the medical staff got in touch with me. The prognosis was not good. Ruud had a serious problem with a cruciate ligament and the belief was that he could break down at any moment. With much regret we had to let Ruud go back to Eindhoven and obviously he was very upset.

In spite of this, Alex stayed in contact and when Ruud did eventually get the injury, after breaking down in training, and had an operation, we followed his progress closely. After proving that he had overcome the injury and was still effective, we went back in again for him and he arrived in July 2001 for a fee of £19 million.

Ruud was an instant hit with the supporters and his goal tally was remarkable, a staggering return of 150 goals in 219 appearances – many of those in the biggest matches. He ranks as one of United's all-time great forwards, and I was just happy to have played my part in bringing another great player to the club.

My final two years at United were characterized by a couple of high-profile departures. Jaap Stam leaving the club in the summer of 2001 came as a big surprise. I think Alex's decision to let him go surprised the player, too. As it turned out, everyone jumped to the wrong conclusion, that Alex had sold Stam because of the player's recently published autobiography in which he accused United of tapping him up while he was still at PSV Eindhoven. Stam's book was never discussed at board level as the reason for the player leaving. It was Alex's belief that after an Achilles operation Stam, who had turned thirty, was never quite the same player, and when Lazio came in with a staggering offer of £16.5 million he felt it was the best deal. I think Alex genuinely believed that we'd had the best out of him.

Stam's replacement was Laurent Blanc, who came to us on a free. I never felt that transfer worked. Blanc had been an excellent centre half, one of the best in Europe, but he was past his prime and I don't think he improved the team, while at the same time we had let one of the best defenders in world football leave. It was a terrible mistake and Alex has since admitted that it was a misjudgement on his part.

Our fans were dealt another blow in the summer of 2003 with the departure of David Beckham to Real Madrid. The writing was on the wall a long time before that infamous incident in the dressing room, though. That came after an FA Cup tie at Old Trafford against Arsenal that February, which we lost 2–0. Alex was angry that David had failed to track back to prevent Arsenal's second goal, and during a heated exchange after the match Alex kicked a football boot lying on the floor, which flew into the air, catching David in the face, just above the eye. Of course it was all over the newspapers the next day and David appeared in public with a highly visible plaster covering the wound. Although much was made of this incident, it was just a freak accident and the repercussions were never discussed at any board meeting.

While that dressing-room incident may have played a part in David eventually leaving the club, there were other contributory factors. Alex felt that David's celebrity image was getting in the way of his football and that his form was dipping. He didn't feel that David was as committed to the team as he had once been; he had another agenda now, and his wife Victoria had a say in that agenda and was having more and more of an influence on him. The club comes first and Alex probably felt that David had slipped in that respect. If you've got one player who thinks he's a star and can get away with things that the other players can't, that's no good for discipline. Alex had to make a judgement as to how everyone fits in, what the mix is and what the chemistry is within a team. If he believed that somebody was not pulling their full weight then he'd rather move them on and bring somebody else in who was going to toe the line.

Over the years United has had its fair share of star players. We had George Best, Ryan Giggs, Cantona, Beckham, and then Ronaldo. They were all stars in their own right, they all sold shirts, but ultimately Manchester United is what sells, not individuals. The most important thing is success on the field. Our success was not reliant on the marketing of individuals, and should never be.

Within just a few weeks of Beckham leaving, his replacement Cristiano Ronaldo arrived, who turned out to be quite a player. I had already stepped down by the time Ronaldo arrived, but during my last couple of years at the club we had tried to bring in other marquee names. Back in June 2001 we had approached Arsenal with a view to prising away Patrick Vieira, but were firmly rebuffed. Vieira would have been a great addition to the side. It's true to say that over the years he and Roy Keane had enjoyed a heated rivalry, most notably their infamous spat in the tunnel before a game at Highbury that was caught on camera, but what a formidable midfield pairing they would have made together.

In January 2002 Diego Forlán arrived from Argentine club Independiente for £7 million and became a cult hero when he scored a double at Anfield. But our big summer signing that year was Rio Ferdinand, who was first brought to my attention by our scout Les Kershaw. At the time Rio was playing in the youth team at West Ham and Les was convinced about his potential. I remember calling up West Ham's manager Harry Redknapp to talk to him about the possibility of bringing Rio to United, but I was told there was absolutely no chance of getting him. Then the next thing I heard he'd gone to Leeds United for £18 million, which was a huge blow. As it transpired Rio only stayed with Leeds for two seasons but it took around £30 million, a record fee for a defender, to lever him away from the Yorkshire club. For me that was money well spent: Rio became a rock in our defence and was one of the most cultured centre backs to grace the modern game in this country.

When Manchester United were crowned Premier League champions at the end of the 2002–03 season, for the eighth time in eleven years, it seemed the most opportune time to step down as chairman of the football club. I had made the decision back in December and given the board notice of my intentions. A little over a week later, on 28 May, Old Trafford played host to the Champions League final between Juventus and Inter Milan. It was the first time the club had hosted a major European final and was a lovely way to see out my reign.

The decision had been an easy one to reach. In March 2002 Roland had stepped down as chairman of the plc and been replaced by Roy Gardner, who was then chief executive of the energy and services company Centrica. I had always had a very close relationship with Roland, and was very sorry when he died not long after retiring, having suffered from cancer for some months. Roy Gardner was very different to Roland. I don't think he particularly liked the football club board. He felt that having a chairman of the football club took something away from his role as chairman of the plc. That never bothered Roland. I also got a feeling that the plc didn't really like the idea of the alternative football club board. In their mind the plc board was the controlling board and the most important board within the club. They probably thought the football club board got too much recognition.

As a result, my influence began to lessen. Roy never really used to come to me for information in the way that Roland used to do. He seemed to want more direct contact with Peter Kenyon than with me and this led to a feeling that I was being marginalized and that my role within the club was becoming less important, even though I was still representing Manchester United at Premier League meetings in London. Over the three years that I had stayed on as chairman after stepping down as chief executive, the influence that I had once held was slowly diminishing and I didn't want to stay on just for the sake of it.

When Roy Gardner took over from Roland, both men decided that when I eventually stepped down as chairman of the football club I would become its president. Throughout its entire history Manchester United had only bestowed that title upon two people: one was John Henry Davies, who saved the club from going bust in 1902, and the other, of course, was Sir Matt. For me to take on the role of president was a huge honour after being involved with the club for thirty-three years as a director, as chief executive and chairman, and it's a position I proudly hold to this day. When you include my father's time as well, between us the Edwards family can claim fifty-five years of service to Manchester United, including thirty-eight as chairmen.

In the end, then, I thought it was the easier option to just step down as chairman and take on the mantle of president. It was an easy decision to make. Manchester United had been part of my life for so long, but I felt that the time was right.

The club threw a wonderful leaving dinner for me on 3 June, where I was able to say goodbye to all the staff, some of whom had worked for me from my very first day in charge back in 1980; people like Ken Merrett and Ken Ramsden, also Cath on the switchboard and my secretary Pauline. It was very emotional. But I didn't quite leave Old Trafford behind when I finally stepped down at the end of June, because I retained my office there.

In 2001 I was appointed chairman of the Premier League Audit and Remuneration Committee, which oversees the monitoring of the League's internal financial controls, accounting policies and fixing salaries of the senior executives. I chaired the meetings until I stepped down in 2011. In need of an office I decided to use my old one at Old Trafford and paid rental on it, coming in nearly every day because I had other things to do there as well. I did this for two years until the Glazers took over the club and wanted it back. Today I have a seat in the directors' box and try never to miss a home game. I am still as passionate as ever about seeing my beloved team play.

How do I begin to sum up my years at Manchester United? Really I can only judge it from when I took over in 1980 to what it has now become. When I succeeded my father as chairman, the shareholding value of Manchester United was £2 million. Our turnover for that year, 1980, was £2.15 million and our net profit before tax was £210,000. Jump ahead to just after we won the Treble in 1999. We had become the number-one sporting franchise in the world with a net worth of over a billion pounds. We also employed over 500 full-time staff and 1,275 temporary match-day staff, a huge increase in staffing numbers from when I first took over. Indeed, the year I stepped down as chairman in 2003, our turnover had grown to £173 million and we made a profit of £39.3 million and paid dividends of £10.4 million. In the twelve years since flotation in 1991 we made profits of £243 million and paid over £54 million in dividends. We made a profit every year, even after spending over £164 million on thirty players and continually increasing the dividend. Those figures really do tell a story of how far Manchester United have come as well as how much football has changed in the modern era.

But that's only the financial side of things. Just look at what the team achieved on the pitch, with all those trophies and league titles. It was a long time in coming. Alex arrived in November 1986 and we had to be patient for his first trophy, which came in 1990. It was a full seven years before we won the league but after that it was pretty much constant success: there was the Double in 1994, the Double in 1996, the Treble in 1999 and all the other trophies along the way. It was an amazing achievement by Alex and the team, and the most successful period in the club's history.

Then there is Old Trafford itself. Over the time I was in charge we completely renovated the stadium. From the flotation in 1991 we rebuilt the Stretford End, the North Stand and then the East Stand, major developments all of them. Indeed, during the 1990s we spent a total of £112 million on ground improvements. And then there's the training facility at Carrington, which cost 14.3 million. When I stepped down I knew that I had set something up for the future. Very little has been spent on the ground since because all the hard work was done in the 1990s and early 2000s. These are all achievements that I remain immensely proud of.

During my time at Manchester United my prudent stewardship of the club probably didn't find favour with a lot of fans, but I had to balance all the different aspects of the business. We had shareholders and we had to pay a dividend; that was a discipline we had to contend with. We had to develop the stadium, which we managed to do out of club profits – no one came in with a load of cash. We had to do it ourselves and we did it out of genuine business profits. There was also the spending on the acquisition of players and wages. In other words, supporting the manager and the team. I had to balance all of those things, so prudence had to come into it.

One of my greatest strengths as chairman and chief executive, I believe, was being a good delegator. Most of my staff would say that I supported them and let them get on with their job. People have different styles of management. Some are very hands on and want to know every single thing that's going on, while others say, 'right he can do that job, I don't need to be on his back the whole time'. I always worked on the principle that if any of my staff needed help they would come to me. Let them get on with what they have to do, but in the knowledge that I'm always available. That was my management style. I appointed people who I thought were right for the job and then let them get on with it and didn't interfere.

The best example of this was Alex Ferguson. I tried as much as I could to give him the tools to get the job done. Alex was football through and through: he ate, slept and drank football, so he knew what he was doing. Yes, he was a bad loser. But then you find that a lot of winners are bad losers; just look at someone like John McEnroe. In the early days Alex and I had a very close relationship. After the club floated on the stock market in 1991 I had a lot more responsibilities and had to devote more time to the business of the club, so I was pulled away and wasn't as close to Alex as I had been in the early years. That didn't actually affect the running of the club, because most of the time Alex got what he wanted. I was always supportive of what he was trying to do, particularly with the youth and team building, buying players and paying the higher wages that we had to accept eventually. The point is that although I was in greater demand now that United was a plc, I knew Alex could get on with things and he knew he could always come to me if he needed something. I believe the way I supported Alex shows in the results and the trophies we amassed over the years.

I don't begrudge Alex any of the plaudits he received during his years as manager of Manchester United: he deserved every single one of them. Yet, however important his role as manager was at United, Alex was part of a clearly defined system that helped enable his success. The two different sides to United – the plc board on the one hand and the subsidiary boards including the football club board on the other – operated separately, and the club board listened totally to Alex when he told them what he wanted to do. Yet he took no part in the running of the plc board or any of their subsidiary boards.

Alex's role as manager was quite distinct from the rest of the business. He was not the old-fashioned type of manager; his role was quite sharply defined. He would report directly to me as chief executive. We went to considerable lengths to separate Alex's role as the man who handles the team from the rest of the business. For example, unlike many other Premier League managers Alex didn't have an office at Old Trafford. His office was over at the training ground. That was his domain and where he prepared the team for matches.

Alex benefited from a well-run company that was supportive and that created the revenue that allowed him to buy the best players. Back in 1998 when the team won nothing I don't believe any other club at the time would have gone out and bought Stam and Yorke for a combined sum of £23 million. When things got tough and our ascendency in the domestic game looked like it was slipping, we had the means and the resources to sort it out. Had we not done that we would never have won the Treble the following season, no matter how good the manager was.

One of my great sources of pride is that I built a massive business at Manchester United that was capable of carrying on into the future and that could look to a time when Alex was no longer the manager. The fact is that businesses have to carry on, and United was structured in a way that its legacy would always last and hopefully grow even stronger. Our loyal supporters expect and deserve nothing less.

AFTERWORD: MY ALL-TIME GREATEST UNITED TEAM

People are always asking me to name my favourite players from the time I was in charge at Manchester United, or asking who in my opinion were the greatest ever to wear a United shirt. The only way to answer that question once and for all is to compile my ultimate Manchester United eleven, not just from my tenure at Old Trafford, but of all time.

Let's start with the team during my time at United. My thinking here is to stick to the twenty years I was in charge, in other words from 1980 to 2000. That means players like Rio Ferdinand and Ruud van Nistelrooy, who were only at the club for a short while during my time, were not considered, since this would be unfair to the ones who played for so many years during my tenure. The same goes for players who were already at the club when I took over, the likes of Steve Coppell who left soon after and also Martin Buchan, who was there during my time but didn't play many games, so I've not included them either. I've gone for a 4-4-2 formation, which is really the classic United way.

Starting with the goalkeeper, it's difficult to see beyond Peter Schmeichel. Of all the other keepers during my time, I've picked Gary Bailey as my No. 2 to sit on the bench. But Schmeichel is the obvious choice. There's no contest, really; he was in a league of his own.

With regards to full backs, I've gone for Gary Neville, who was captain of that famous United youth team and went on to establish himself as a very capable and steady right back, forming a terrific partnership on the right with Beckham, and then Denis Irwin as left back. Honourable mentions go to Phil Neville, who won six championship league medals, and Arthur Albiston, who played in the team for many years and was a good strong left back. Then you had the likes of John Gidman, Paul Parker and Viv Anderson, all of whom played for England. But in the end Gary Neville and Irwin stand out.

At centre half I've gone for Jaap Stam, who was instrumental in us doing the Treble, and although he was only at United for three seasons we won the league every year he was there. That says a lot about his prowess. Partnering Stam in the centre of defence I've picked Gary Pallister, who was also a very cultured centre half. He played for England, won championship medals and had a tremendous partnership with Steve Bruce over many years. I have to say this was a difficult choice because often in picking central defenders it's all about them forming great partnerships, as Rio did with Vidić. Pallister and Bruce were indeed great together, but Stam's dominance makes him simply too difficult to leave out.

My two wide players are Beckham on the right and Giggs on the left. Both of them could track back and both worked hard for the team. Andrei Kanchelskis came in for consideration because he was part of that terrific front line, along with Cantona, Hughes and Giggs, that won us the league in 1994. In the end, though, Beckham shades it because he had a fantastic delivery on crosses – so good that I don't think we've seen the like since – and was such a good free-kick taker. Giggs, I think, is automatic. He has to be in the team.

As for my two central midfielders, this was another extremely difficult decision because I've had to leave Scholes out and also Paul Ince. But if I'm going for 4-4-2 the formation dictates just two midfielders and I just found it impossible to look beyond Keane and Robson. Bryan Robson was a more prolific goal scorer than Keane. On the other hand Keane was such a dominant presence. Both were outstanding leaders on the pitch and both were captains in their day, although I've gone with Robson as my captain here. He really was captain marvel and there was nobody better to lift a team and drag them across the line to victory.

Up front was arguably the toughest choice. United really were blessed with so many outstanding strikers during my time, from Andy Cole to Ole Gunnar Solskjær, Teddy Sheringham to Dwight Yorke. But in the end I've gone for Mark Hughes with Eric Cantona playing off him. Hughes was a scorer of great goals and had wonderful technical ability, while Cantona was just a magical player. When you think of Eric's five seasons at United, we won the league four times and would have won the fifth too if he hadn't been suspended. His huge influence on the team's fortunes earned him his place.

That's my team. On the substitutes bench I've got Bailey as my back-up keeper and I've brought Brucie in as my only defensive substitute because I've got Ince in the side, who could cover for left back if needs be. Robson could also play full back. My other midfield sub is Scholes and I've put Kanchelskis in as back-up for either wing. The substitutes up front are Cole and Solskjær. Cole because he is still the third-highest scorer in Premier League history, and Solskjær because he was so good at coming off the bench and making an impact.

I've had to leave some great players out, but I think it's a formidable line-up and a testament to the strength of the sides we had and that Alex kept on rebuilding.

Schmeichel

G. Neville	Stam	Pallister	Irwin
Beckham	Keane	Robson	Giggs

Cantona

Hughes

SUBS: BAILEY, BRUCE, INCE, SCHOLES, KANCHELSKIS, COLE, SOLSKJÆR

Moving on to my all-time United eleven. My criteria here was to only include players from the time I started following United. So this is really post the Munich air crash. I started going to Old Trafford on a regular basis from March 1958 and the crash happened in February, so I haven't considered players like Duncan Edwards, Tommy Taylor or Roger Byrne, because I never saw them play.

We start again with the goalkeeping position, and the best goalkeeper I've seen at Old Trafford since I've been watching football there was still Peter Schmeichel. We've had some good goalkeepers over the years, like Bailey and Alex Stepney. I thought Edwin van der Sar was a magnificent keeper and he gets a position on my bench over someone like David de Gea, who is an outstanding young goalkeeper but hasn't been around long enough to warrant a place. I think there is more to come from de Gea and maybe in five years my thinking might change. Picking my team today, though, all you have to do is look at van der Sar's stats and the number of clean sheets he kept to understand why he edges out the Spaniard. But Peter Schmeichel will always be my number one.

Moving to the defence, at left back I've gone for Tony Dunne, who was in the 1968 European Cup-winning side and was a fantastic left back. I did seriously consider Patrice Evra, who played in three Champions League finals for United and was a very reliable left back and a real fan-favourite, but in the end I went for Tony Dunne.

In central defence I've gone with Stam again. I don't think there has been a better centre half at United. As Stam's partner I've picked Rio Ferdinand. Rio wasn't considered for my other team because he arrived during my last year, but for my overall team he and Stam would form a great partnership.

Again, my formation is 4-4-2, and my wingers I think pick themselves: I've gone for Cristiano Ronaldo and George Best, both European footballers of the year, and both legends of the game. Now, in midfield, this is very difficult because over the years there have been some great midfield players plying their trade at Old Trafford, but I still come back to Keane and Robson, who were absolutely dominant and rock solid and had creative ability as well. Robson was up and down the pitch all the time and scored ninety-nine goals for us, often in important matches, and Keane got the odd useful one, too. I've had to leave people like Pat Crerand out, who was very instrumental in us winning the European Cup in 1968, and Scholes, although a superlative player, just fell short.

Up front, it has to be Bobby Charlton and Denis Law, with Bobby playing off the front and Denis up top. Again, they were two European footballers of the year, so their credentials are self-evident. Indeed, that entire attacking front four were all European footballers of the year, so it's very difficult to leave any of them out.

That means you've got a hell of a bench. Van der Sar is my reserve keeper, and I've picked Martin Buchan and Nemanja Vidić as my reserve defenders. I've picked Scholes again in midfield, because he was just magical. Giggs is my reserve winger, since he could play left or right. And I've gone with Cantona as reserve for Charlton and van Nistelrooy as my reserve striker. That means there's no room for Wayne Rooney. The club's record goal scorer was on my list but I had to choose between him and van Nistelrooy, and I feel that Ruud is more of a natural replacement for Law as a predatory finisher.

Schmeichel

Irwin	Stam	Ferdinand	Dunne
Ronaldo	Keane	Robson	Best

Charlton

Law

SUBS: VAN DER SAR, BUCHAN, VIDIĆ, SCHOLES, GIGGS, CANTONA, VAN NISTELROOY

Those are my two teams, both from my period in charge and of all time. I have lots of memories of watching them grace the Old Trafford turf. All of them have left their mark on the history of this great club. I hope that in my own way I did, too.

APPENDIX 1
MANCHESTER UNITED LEAGUE POSITIONS 1980–2003

1980–81 First Division

Position	Club	P	W	D	L	F	A	GD	Pts
1	Aston Villa	42	26	8	8	72	40	+32	60
2	Ipswich Town	42	23	10	9	77	43	+34	56
3	Arsenal	42	19	15	8	61	45	+16	53
4	West Bromwich Albion	42	20	12	10	60	42	+18	52
5	Liverpool	42	17	17	8	62	42	+20	51
6	Southampton	42	20	10	12	76	56	+20	50
7	Nottingham Forest	42	19	12	11	62	44	+18	50
8	**Manchester United**	**42**	**15**	**18**	**9**	**51**	**36**	**+15**	**48**
9	Leeds United	42	17	10	15	39	47	-8	44
10	Tottenham Hotspur	42	14	15	13	70	68	+2	43
11	Stoke City	42	12	18	12	51	60	-9	42
12	Manchester City	42	14	11	17	56	59	-3	39
13	Birmingham City	42	13	12	17	50	61	-11	38
14	Middlesbrough	42	16	5	21	53	61	-8	37
15	Everton	42	13	10	19	55	58	-3	36
16	Coventry City	42	13	10	19	48	68	-20	36
17	Sunderland	42	14	7	21	52	53	-1	35
18	Wolves	42	13	9	20	43	55	-12	35
19	Brighton & Hove Albion	42	14	7	21	54	67	-13	35
20	Norwich City (R)	42	13	7	22	49	73	-24	33
21	Leicester City (R)	42	13	6	23	40	67	-27	32
22	Crystal Palace (R)	42	6	7	29	47	83	-36	19

1981–82 First Division

Position	Club	P	W	D	L	F	A	GD	Pts
1	Liverpool	42	26	9	7	80	32	+48	87
2	Ipswich Town	42	26	5	11	75	53	+22	83
3	**Manchester United**	**42**	**22**	**12**	**8**	**59**	**29**	**+30**	**78**
4	Tottenham Hotspur	42	20	11	11	67	48	+19	71
5	Arsenal	42	20	11	11	48	37	+11	71
6	Swansea City	42	21	6	15	58	51	+7	69
7	Southampton	42	19	9	14	72	67	+5	66
8	Everton	42	17	13	12	56	50	+6	64
9	West Ham United	42	14	16	12	66	57	+9	58
10	Manchester City	42	15	13	14	49	50	−1	58
11	Aston Villa	42	15	12	15	55	53	+2	57
12	Nottingham Forest	42	15	12	15	42	48	−6	57
13	Brighton & Hove Albion	42	13	13	16	43	52	−9	52
14	Coventry City	42	13	11	18	56	62	−6	50
15	Notts County	42	13	8	21	61	69	−8	47
16	Birmingham City	42	10	14	18	53	61	−8	44
17	West Bromwich Albion	42	11	11	20	46	57	−11	44
18	Stoke City	42	12	8	22	44	63	−19	44
19	Sunderland	42	11	11	20	38	58	−20	44
20	Leeds United (R)	42	10	12	20	39	61	−22	42
21	Wolves (R)	42	10	10	22	32	63	−31	40
22	Middlesbrough (R)	42	8	15	19	34	52	−18	39

1982-83 First Division

Position	Club	P	W	D	L	F	A	GD	Pts
1	Liverpool	42	24	10	8	87	37	+50	82
2	Watford	42	22	5	15	74	57	+17	71
3	**Manchester United**	**42**	**19**	**13**	**10**	**56**	**38**	**+18**	**70**
4	Tottenham Hotspur	42	20	9	13	65	50	+15	69
5	Nottingham Forest	42	20	9	13	62	50	+12	69
6	Aston Villa	42	21	5	16	62	50	+12	68
7	Everton	42	18	10	14	66	48	+18	64
8	West Ham United	42	20	4	18	68	62	+6	64
9	Ipswich Town	42	15	13	14	64	50	+14	58
10	Arsenal	42	16	10	16	58	56	+2	58
11	West Bromwich Albion	42	15	12	15	51	49	+2	57
12	Southampton	42	15	12	15	54	58	-4	57
13	Stoke City	42	16	9	17	53	64	-11	57
14	Norwich City	42	14	12	16	52	58	-6	54
15	Notts County	42	15	7	20	55	71	-16	52
16	Sunderland	42	12	14	16	48	61	-13	50
17	Birmingham City	42	12	14	16	40	55	-15	50
18	Luton Town	42	12	13	17	65	84	-19	49
19	Coventry City	42	13	9	20	48	59	-11	48
20	Manchester City (R)	42	13	8	21	47	70	-23	47
21	Swansea City (R)	42	10	11	21	51	69	-18	41
22	Brighton & Hove Albion (R)	42	9	13	20	38	68	-30	40

1983–84 First Division

Position	Club	P	W	D	L	F	A	GD	Pts
1	Liverpool	42	22	14	6	73	32	+41	80
2	Southampton	42	22	11	9	66	38	+28	77
3	Nottingham Forest	42	22	8	12	76	45	+31	74
4	**Manchester United**	**42**	**20**	**14**	**8**	**71**	**41**	**+30**	**74**
5	Queens Park Rangers	42	22	7	13	67	37	+30	73
6	Arsenal	42	18	9	15	74	60	+14	63
7	Everton	42	16	14	12	44	42	+2	62
8	Tottenham Hotspur	42	17	10	15	64	65	−1	61
9	West Ham United	42	17	9	16	60	55	+5	60
10	Aston Villa	42	17	9	16	59	61	−2	60
11	Watford	42	16	9	17	68	77	−9	57
12	Ipswich Town	42	15	8	19	55	57	−2	53
13	Sunderland	42	13	13	16	42	53	−11	52
14	Norwich City	42	12	15	15	48	49	−1	51
15	Leicester City	42	13	12	17	65	68	−3	51
16	Luton Town	42	14	9	19	53	66	−13	51
17	West Bromwich Albion	42	14	9	19	48	62	−14	51
18	Stoke City	42	13	11	18	44	63	−19	50
19	Coventry City	42	13	11	18	57	77	−20	50
20	Birmingham City (R)	42	12	12	18	39	50	−11	48
21	Notts County (R)	42	10	11	21	50	72	−22	41
22	Wolves (R)	42	6	11	25	27	80	−53	29

1984–85 First Division

Position	Club	P	W	D	L	F	A	GD	Pts
1	Everton	42	28	6	8	88	43	+45	90
2	Liverpool	42	22	11	9	68	35	+33	77
3	Tottenham Hotspur	42	23	8	11	78	51	+27	77
4	**Manchester United**	**42**	**22**	**10**	**10**	**77**	**47**	**+30**	**76**
5	Southampton	42	19	11	12	56	47	+9	68
6	Chelsea	42	18	12	12	63	48	+15	66
7	Arsenal	42	19	9	14	61	49	+12	66
8	Sheffield Wednesday	42	17	14	11	58	45	+13	65
9	Nottingham Forest	42	19	7	16	56	48	+8	64
10	Aston Villa	42	15	11	16	60	60	+0	56
11	Watford	42	14	13	15	81	71	+10	55
12	West Bromwich Albion	42	16	7	19	58	62	−4	55
13	Luton Town	42	15	9	18	57	61	−4	54
14	Newcastle United	42	13	13	16	55	70	−15	52
15	Leicester City	42	15	6	21	65	73	−8	51
16	West Ham United	42	13	12	17	51	68	−17	51
17	Ipswich Town	42	13	11	18	46	57	−11	50
18	Coventry City	42	15	5	22	47	64	−17	50
19	Queens Park Rangers	42	13	11	18	53	72	−19	50
20	Norwich City (R)	42	13	10	19	46	64	−18	49
21	Sunderland (R)	42	10	10	22	40	62	−22	40
22	Stoke City (R)	42	3	8	31	24	91	−67	17

1985–86 First Division

Position	Club	P	W	D	L	F	A	GD	Pts
1	Liverpool	42	16	4	1	58	14	+52	88
2	Everton	42	16	3	2	54	18	+46	86
3	West Ham United	42	17	2	2	48	16	+34	84
4	**Manchester United**	**42**	**12**	**5**	**4**	**35**	**12**	**+34**	**76**
5	Sheffield Wednesday	42	13	6	2	36	23	+9	73
6	Chelsea	42	12	4	5	32	27	+1	71
7	Arsenal	42	13	5	3	29	15	+2	69
8	Nottingham Forest	42	11	5	5	38	25	+16	68
9	Luton Town	42	12	6	3	37	15	+17	66
10	Tottenham Hotspur	42	12	2	7	47	25	+22	65
11	Newcastle United	42	12	5	4	46	31	−5	63
12	Watford	42	11	6	4	40	22	+7	59
13	Queens Park Rangers	42	12	3	6	33	20	−11	52
14	Southampton	42	10	6	5	32	18	−11	46
15	Manchester City	42	7	7	7	25	26	−14	45
16	Aston Villa	42	7	6	8	27	28	−16	44
17	Coventry City	42	6	5	10	31	35	−23	43
18	Oxford United	42	7	7	7	34	27	−18	42
19	Leicester City	42	7	8	6	35	35	−22	42
20	Ipswich Town (R)	42	8	5	8	20	24	−23	41
21	Birmingham City (R)	42	5	2	14	13	25	−43	29
22	West Bromwich Albion (R)	42	3	8	10	21	36	−54	24

1986–87 First Division

Position	Club	P	W	D	L	F	A	GD	Pts
1	Everton	42	26	8	8	76	31	+45	86
2	Liverpool	42	23	8	11	72	42	+30	77
3	Tottenham Hotspur	42	21	8	13	68	43	+25	71
4	Arsenal	42	20	10	12	58	35	+23	70
5	Norwich City	42	17	17	8	53	51	+2	68
6	Wimbledon	42	19	9	14	57	50	+7	66
7	Luton Town	42	18	12	12	47	45	+2	66
8	Nottingham Forest	42	18	11	13	64	51	+13	65
9	Watford	42	18	9	15	67	54	+13	63
10	Coventry City	42	17	12	13	50	45	+5	63
11	**Manchester United**	**42**	**14**	**14**	**14**	**52**	**45**	**+7**	**56**
12	Southampton	42	14	10	18	69	68	+1	52
13	Sheffield Wednesday	42	13	13	16	58	59	−1	52
14	Chelsea	42	13	13	16	53	64	−11	52
15	West Ham United	42	14	10	18	52	67	−15	52
16	Queens Park Rangers	42	13	11	18	48	64	−16	50
17	Newcastle United	42	12	11	19	47	65	−18	47
18	Oxford United	42	11	13	18	44	69	−25	46
19	Charlton Athletic	42	11	11	20	45	55	−10	44
20	Leicester City (R)	42	11	9	22	54	76	−22	42
21	Manchester City (R)	42	8	15	19	36	57	−21	39
22	Aston Villa (R)	42	8	12	22	45	79	−34	36

1987–88 First Division

Position	Club	P	W	D	L	F	A	GD	Pts
1	Liverpool	40	26	12	2	87	24	+63	90
2	**Manchester United**	**40**	**23**	**12**	**5**	**71**	**38**	**+33**	**81**
3	Nottingham Forest	40	20	13	7	67	39	+28	73
4	Everton	40	19	13	8	53	27	+26	70
5	Queens Park Rangers	40	19	10	11	48	38	+10	67
6	Arsenal	40	18	12	10	58	39	+19	66
7	Wimbledon	40	14	15	11	58	47	+11	57
8	Newcastle United	40	14	14	12	55	53	+2	56
9	Luton Town	40	14	11	15	57	58	−1	53
10	Coventry City	40	13	14	13	46	53	−7	53
11	Sheffield Wednesday	40	15	8	17	52	66	−14	53
12	Southampton	40	12	14	14	49	53	−4	50
13	Tottenham Hotspur	40	12	11	17	38	48	−10	47
14	Norwich City	40	12	9	19	40	52	−12	45
15	Derby County	40	10	13	17	35	45	−10	43
16	West Ham United	40	9	15	16	40	52	−12	42
17	Charlton Athletic	40	9	15	16	38	52	−14	42
18	Chelsea (R)	40	9	15	16	50	68	−18	42
19	Portsmouth (R)	40	7	14	19	36	66	−30	35
20	Watford (R)	40	7	11	22	27	51	−24	32
21	Oxford United (R)	40	6	13	21	44	80	−36	31

1988–89 First Division

Position	Club	P	W	D	L	F	A	GD	Pts
1	Arsenal	38	22	10	6	73	36	+37	76
2	Liverpool	38	22	10	6	65	28	+37	76
3	Nottingham Forest	38	17	13	8	64	43	+21	64
4	Norwich City	38	17	11	10	48	45	+3	62
5	Derby County	38	17	7	14	40	38	+2	58
6	Tottenham Hotspur	38	15	12	11	60	46	+14	57
7	Coventry City	38	14	13	11	47	42	+5	55
8	Everton	38	14	12	12	50	45	+5	54
9	Queens Park Rangers	38	14	11	13	43	37	+6	53
10	Millwall	38	14	11	13	47	52	−5	53
11	**Manchester United**	**38**	**13**	**12**	**13**	**45**	**35**	**+10**	**51**
12	Wimbledon	38	14	9	15	50	46	+4	51
13	Southampton	38	10	15	13	52	66	−14	45
14	Charlton Athletic	38	10	12	16	44	58	−14	42
15	Sheffield Wednesday	38	10	12	16	34	51	−17	42
16	Luton Town	38	10	11	17	42	52	−10	41
17	Aston Villa	38	9	13	16	45	56	−11	40
18	Middlesbrough (R)	38	9	12	17	44	61	−17	39
19	West Ham United (R)	38	10	8	20	37	62	−25	38
20	Newcastle United (R)	38	7	10	21	32	63	−31	31

1989–90 First Division

Position	Club	P	W	D	L	F	A	GD	Pts
1	Liverpool	38	23	10	5	78	37	+41	79
2	Aston Villa	38	21	7	10	57	38	+19	70
3	Tottenham Hotspur	38	19	6	13	59	47	+12	63
4	Arsenal	38	18	8	12	54	38	+16	62
5	Chelsea	38	16	12	10	58	50	+8	60
6	Everton	38	17	8	13	57	46	+11	59
7	Southampton	38	15	10	13	71	63	+8	55
8	Wimbledon	38	13	16	9	47	40	+7	55
9	Nottingham Forest	38	15	9	14	55	47	+8	54
10	Norwich City	38	13	14	11	44	42	+2	53
11	Queens Park Rangers	38	13	11	14	45	44	+1	50
12	Coventry City	38	14	7	17	39	59	−20	49
13	**Manchester United**	**38**	**13**	**9**	**16**	**46**	**47**	**−1**	**48**
14	Manchester City	38	12	12	14	43	52	−9	48
15	Crystal Palace	38	13	9	16	42	66	−24	48
16	Derby County	38	13	7	18	43	40	+3	46
17	Luton Town	38	10	13	15	43	57	−14	43
18	Sheffield Wednesday (R)	38	11	10	17	35	51	−16	43
19	Charlton Athletic (R)	38	7	9	22	31	57	−26	30
20	Millwall (R)	38	5	11	22	39	65	−26	25

1990–91 First Division

Position	Club	P	W	D	L	F	A	GD	Pts
1	Arsenal	38	24	13	1	74	18	+56	83
2	Liverpool	38	23	7	8	77	40	+37	76
3	Crystal Palace	38	20	9	9	50	41	+9	69
4	Leeds United	38	19	7	12	65	47	+18	64
5	Manchester City	38	17	11	10	64	53	+11	62
6	**Manchester United**	**38**	**16**	**12**	**10**	**58**	**45**	**+13**	**59**
7	Wimbledon	38	14	14	10	53	46	+7	56
8	Nottingham Forest	38	14	12	12	65	50	+15	54
9	Everton	38	13	12	13	50	46	+4	51
10	Tottenham Hotspur	38	11	16	11	51	50	+1	49
11	Chelsea	38	13	10	15	58	69	−11	46
12	Queens Park Rangers	38	12	10	16	44	53	−9	46
13	Sheffield United	38	13	7	18	36	55	−19	46
14	Southampton	38	12	9	17	58	69	−11	45
15	Norwich City	38	13	6	19	41	64	−21	45
16	Coventry City	38	11	11	16	42	49	−7	44
17	Aston Villa	38	9	14	15	46	58	−12	41
18	Luton Town	38	10	7	21	42	61	−19	37
19	Sunderland (R)	38	8	10	20	38	60	−22	34
20	Derby County (R)	38	5	9	24	37	75	−38	24

1991–92 First Division

Position	Club	P	W	D	L	F	A	GD	Pts
1	Leeds United	42	22	16	4	74	37	+37	82
2	**Manchester United**	**42**	**21**	**15**	**6**	**63**	**33**	**+30**	**78**
3	Sheffield Wednesday	42	21	12	9	62	49	+13	75
4	Arsenal	42	19	15	8	81	47	+34	72
5	Manchester City	42	20	10	12	61	48	+13	70
6	Liverpool	42	16	16	10	47	40	+7	64
7	Aston Villa	42	17	9	16	48	34	+14	60
8	Nottingham Forest	42	16	11	15	60	58	+2	59
9	Sheffield United	42	16	9	17	65	63	+2	57
10	Crystal Palace	42	14	15	13	53	61	−7	57
11	Queens Park Rangers	42	12	18	12	48	47	+1	54
12	Everton	42	13	14	15	52	51	+1	53
13	Wimbledon	42	13	14	15	53	53	0	53
14	Chelsea	42	13	14	15	50	60	−10	53
15	Tottenham Hotspur	42	15	7	20	58	63	−5	52
16	Southampton	42	14	10	18	39	55	−16	52
17	Oldham Athletic	42	14	9	19	63	67	−4	51
18	Norwich City	42	11	12	19	47	63	−16	45
19	Coventry City	42	11	11	20	35	44	−9	44
20	Luton Town (R)	42	10	12	20	39	71	−32	42
21	Notts County (R)	42	10	10	22	40	62	−22	40
22	West Ham United (R)	42	9	11	22	37	59	−22	38

1992–93 Premier League

Position	Club	P	W	D	L	F	A	GD	Pts
1	**Manchester United**	42	24	12	6	67	31	+36	84
2	Aston Villa	42	21	11	10	57	40	+17	74
3	Norwich City	42	21	9	12	61	65	−4	72
4	Blackburn Rovers	42	20	11	11	68	46	+22	71
5	Queens Park Rangers	42	17	12	13	63	55	+8	63
6	Liverpool	42	16	11	15	62	55	+7	59
7	Sheffield Wednesday	42	15	14	13	55	51	+4	59
8	Tottenham Hotspur	42	16	11	15	60	66	−6	59
9	Manchester City	42	15	12	15	56	51	+5	57
10	Arsenal	42	15	11	16	40	38	+2	56
11	Chelsea	42	14	14	14	51	54	−3	56
12	Wimbledon	42	14	12	16	56	55	+1	54
13	Everton	42	15	8	19	53	55	−2	53
14	Sheffield United	42	14	10	18	54	53	+1	52
15	Coventry City	42	13	13	16	52	57	−5	52
16	Ipswich Town	42	12	16	14	50	55	−5	52
17	Leeds United	42	12	15	15	57	62	−5	51
18	Southampton	42	13	11	18	54	61	−7	50
19	Oldham Athletic	42	13	10	19	63	74	−11	49
20	Crystal Palace (R)	42	11	16	15	48	61	−13	49
21	Middlesbrough (R)	42	11	11	20	54	75	−21	44
22	Nottingham Forest (R)	42	10	10	22	41	62	−21	40

1993–94 Premier League

Position	Club	P	W	D	L	F	A	GD	Pts
1	**Manchester United**	42	27	11	4	80	38	+42	92
2	Blackburn Rovers	42	25	9	8	63	36	+27	84
3	Newcastle United	42	23	8	11	82	41	+41	77
4	Arsenal	42	18	17	7	53	28	+25	71
5	Leeds United	42	18	16	8	65	39	+26	70
6	Wimbledon	42	18	11	13	56	53	+3	65
7	Sheffield Wednesday	42	16	16	10	76	54	+22	64
8	Liverpool	42	17	9	16	59	55	+4	60
9	Queens Park Rangers	42	16	12	14	62	61	+1	60
10	Aston Villa	42	15	12	15	46	50	−4	57
11	Coventry City	42	14	14	14	43	45	−2	56
12	Norwich City	42	12	17	13	65	61	+4	53
13	West Ham United	42	13	13	16	47	58	−11	52
14	Chelsea	42	13	12	17	49	53	−4	51
15	Tottenham Hotspur	42	11	12	19	54	59	−5	45
16	Manchester City	42	9	18	15	38	49	−11	45
17	Everton	42	12	8	22	42	63	−21	44
18	Southampton	42	12	7	23	49	66	−17	43
19	Ipswich Town	42	9	16	17	35	58	−23	43
20	Sheffield United (R)	42	8	18	16	42	60	−18	42
21	Oldham Athletic (R)	42	9	13	20	42	68	−26	40
22	Swindon Town (R)	42	5	15	22	47	100	−53	30

1994–95 Premier League

Position	Club	P	W	D	L	F	A	GD	Pts
1	Blackburn Rovers	42	27	8	7	80	39	+41	89
2	**Manchester United**	**42**	**26**	**10**	**6**	**77**	**28**	**+49**	**88**
3	Nottingham Forest	42	22	11	9	72	43	+29	77
4	Liverpool	42	21	11	10	65	37	+28	74
5	Leeds United	42	20	13	9	59	38	+21	73
6	Newcastle United	42	20	12	10	67	47	+20	72
7	Tottenham Hotspur	42	16	14	12	66	58	+8	62
8	Queens Park Rangers	42	17	9	16	61	59	+2	60
9	Wimbledon	42	15	11	16	48	65	−17	56
10	Southampton	42	12	18	12	61	63	−2	54
11	Chelsea	42	13	15	14	50	55	−5	54
12	Arsenal	42	13	12	17	52	49	+3	51
13	Sheffield Wednesday	42	13	12	17	49	57	−8	51
14	West Ham United	42	13	11	18	44	48	−4	50
15	Everton	42	11	17	14	44	51	−7	50
16	Coventry City	42	12	14	16	44	62	−18	50
17	Manchester City	42	12	13	17	53	64	−11	49
18	Aston Villa	42	11	15	16	51	56	−5	48
19	Crystal Palace (R)	42	11	12	19	34	49	−15	45
20	Norwich City (R)	42	10	13	19	37	54	−17	43
21	Leicester City (R)	42	6	11	25	45	80	−35	29
22	Ipswich Town (R)	42	7	6	29	36	93	−57	27

1995–96 Premier League

Position	Club	P	W	D	L	F	A	GD	Pts
1	**Manchester United**	**38**	**25**	**7**	**6**	**73**	**35**	**+38**	**82**
2	Newcastle United	38	24	6	8	66	37	+29	78
3	Liverpool	38	20	11	7	70	34	+36	71
4	Aston Villa	38	18	9	11	52	35	+17	63
5	Arsenal	38	17	12	9	49	32	+17	63
6	Everton	38	17	10	11	64	44	+20	61
7	Blackburn Rovers	38	18	7	13	61	47	+14	61
8	Tottenham Hotspur	38	16	13	9	50	38	+12	61
9	Nottingham Forest	38	15	13	10	50	54	−4	58
10	West Ham United	38	14	9	15	43	52	−9	51
11	Chelsea	38	12	14	12	46	44	+2	50
12	Middlesbrough	38	11	10	17	35	50	−15	43
13	Leeds United	38	12	7	19	40	57	−17	43
14	Wimbledon	38	10	11	17	55	70	−15	41
15	Sheffield Wednesday	38	10	10	18	48	61	−13	40
16	Coventry City	38	8	14	16	42	60	−18	38
17	Southampton	38	9	11	18	34	52	−18	38
18	Manchester City (R)	38	9	11	18	33	58	−25	38
19	Queens Park Rangers (R)	38	9	6	23	38	57	−19	33
20	Bolton Wanderers (R)	38	8	5	25	39	71	−32	29

1996–97 Premier League

Position	Club	P	W	D	L	F	A	GD	Pts
1	**Manchester United**	38	21	12	5	76	44	+32	75
2	Newcastle United	38	19	11	8	73	40	+33	68
3	Arsenal	38	19	11	8	62	32	+30	68
4	Liverpool	38	19	11	8	62	37	+25	68
5	Aston Villa	38	17	10	11	47	34	+13	61
6	Chelsea	38	16	11	11	58	55	+3	59
7	Sheffield Wednesday	38	14	15	9	50	51	−1	57
8	Wimbledon	38	15	11	12	49	46	+3	56
9	Leicester City	38	12	11	15	46	54	−8	47
10	Tottenham Hotspur	38	13	7	18	44	51	−7	46
11	Leeds United	38	11	13	14	28	38	−10	46
12	Derby County	38	11	13	14	45	58	−13	46
13	Blackburn Rovers	38	9	15	14	42	43	−1	42
14	West Ham United	38	10	12	16	39	48	−9	42
15	Everton	38	10	12	16	44	57	−13	42
16	Southampton	38	10	11	17	50	56	−6	41
17	Coventry City	38	9	14	15	38	54	−16	41
18	Sunderland (R)	38	10	10	18	35	53	−18	40
19	Middlesbrough (R)	38	10	12	16	51	60	−9	39
20	Nottingham Forest (R)	38	6	16	16	31	59	−28	34

1997–98 Premier League

Position	Club	P	W	D	L	F	A	GD	Pts
1	Arsenal	38	23	9	6	68	33	+35	78
2	**Manchester United**	**38**	**23**	**8**	**7**	**73**	**26**	**+47**	**77**
3	Liverpool	38	18	11	9	68	42	+26	65
4	Chelsea	38	20	3	15	71	43	+28	63
5	Leeds United	38	17	8	13	57	46	+11	59
6	Blackburn Rovers	38	16	10	12	57	52	+5	58
7	Aston Villa	38	17	6	15	49	48	+1	57
8	West Ham United	38	16	8	14	56	57	−1	56
9	Derby County	38	16	7	15	52	49	+3	55
10	Leicester City	38	13	14	11	51	41	+10	53
11	Coventry City	38	12	16	10	46	44	+2	52
12	Southampton	38	14	6	18	50	55	−5	48
13	Newcastle United	38	11	11	16	35	44	−9	44
14	Tottenham Hotspur	38	11	11	16	44	56	−12	44
15	Wimbledon	38	10	14	14	34	46	−12	44
16	Sheffield Wednesday	38	12	8	18	52	67	−15	44
17	Everton	38	9	13	16	41	56	−15	40
18	Bolton Wanderers (R)	38	9	13	16	41	61	−20	40
19	Barnsley (R)	38	10	5	23	37	82	−45	35
20	Crystal Palace (R)	38	8	9	21	37	71	−34	33

1998–99 Premier League

Position	Club	P	W	D	L	F	A	GD	Pts
1	**Manchester United**	38	22	13	3	80	37	+43	79
2	Arsenal	38	22	12	4	59	17	+42	78
3	Chelsea	38	20	15	3	57	30	+27	75
4	Leeds United	38	18	13	7	62	34	+28	67
5	West Ham United	38	16	9	13	46	53	−7	57
6	Aston Villa	38	15	10	13	51	46	+5	55
7	Liverpool	38	15	9	14	68	49	+19	54
8	Derby County	38	13	13	12	40	45	−5	52
9	Middlesbrough	38	12	15	11	48	54	−6	51
10	Leicester City	38	12	13	13	40	46	−6	49
11	Tottenham Hotspur	38	11	14	13	47	50	−3	47
12	Sheffield Wednesday	38	13	7	18	41	42	−1	46
13	Newcastle United	38	11	13	14	48	54	−6	46
14	Everton	38	11	10	17	42	47	−5	43
15	Coventry City	38	11	9	18	39	51	−12	42
16	Wimbledon	38	10	12	16	40	63	−23	42
17	Southampton	38	11	8	19	37	64	−27	41
18	Charlton Athletic (R)	38	8	12	18	41	56	−15	36
19	Blackburn Rovers (R)	38	7	14	17	38	52	−14	35
20	Nottingham Forest (R)	38	7	9	22	35	69	−34	30

1999–2000 Premier League

Position	Club	P	W	D	L	F	A	GD	Pts
1	**Manchester United**	38	28	7	3	97	45	+52	91
2	Arsenal	38	22	7	9	73	43	+30	73
3	Leeds United	38	21	6	11	58	43	+15	69
4	Liverpool	38	19	10	9	51	30	+21	67
5	Chelsea	38	18	11	9	53	34	+19	65
6	Aston Villa	38	15	13	10	46	35	+11	58
7	Sunderland	38	16	10	12	57	56	+1	58
8	Leicester City	38	16	7	15	55	55	0	55
9	West Ham United	38	15	10	13	52	53	−1	55
10	Tottenham Hotspur	38	15	8	15	57	49	+8	53
11	Newcastle United	38	14	10	14	63	54	+9	52
12	Middlesbrough	38	14	10	14	46	52	−6	52
13	Everton	38	12	14	12	59	49	+10	50
14	Coventry City	38	12	8	18	47	54	−7	44
15	Southampton	38	12	8	18	45	62	−17	44
16	Derby County	38	9	11	18	44	57	−13	38
17	Bradford City	38	9	9	20	38	68	−30	36
18	Wimbledon (R)	38	7	12	19	46	74	−28	33
19	Sheffield Wednesday (R)	38	8	7	23	38	70	−32	31
20	Watford (R)	38	6	6	26	35	77	−42	24

2000–01 Premier League

Position	Club	P	W	D	L	F	A	GD	Pts
I	**Manchester United**	**38**	**24**	**8**	**6**	**79**	**31**	**+48**	**80**
2	Arsenal	38	20	10	8	63	38	+25	70
3	Liverpool	38	20	9	9	71	39	+32	69
4	Leeds United	38	20	8	10	64	43	+21	68
5	Ipswich Town	38	20	6	12	57	42	+15	66
6	Chelsea	38	17	10	11	68	45	+23	61
7	Sunderland	38	15	12	11	46	41	+5	57
8	Aston Villa	38	13	15	10	46	43	+3	54
9	Charlton Athletic	38	14	10	14	50	57	−7	52
10	Southampton	38	14	10	14	40	48	−8	52
11	Newcastle United	38	14	9	15	44	50	−6	51
12	Tottenham Hotspur	38	13	10	15	47	54	−7	49
13	Leicester City	38	14	6	18	39	51	−12	48
14	Middlesbrough	38	9	15	14	44	44	0	42
15	West Ham United	38	10	12	16	45	50	−5	42
16	Everton	38	11	9	18	45	59	−14	42
17	Derby County	38	10	12	16	37	59	−22	42
18	Manchester City (R)	38	8	10	20	41	65	−24	34
19	Coventry City (R)	38	8	10	20	36	63	−27	34
20	Bradford City (R)	38	5	11	22	30	70	−40	26

2001–02 Premier League

Position	Club	P	W	D	L	F	A	GD	Pts
1	Arsenal	38	26	9	3	79	36	+43	87
2	Liverpool	38	24	8	6	67	30	+37	80
3	**Manchester United**	**38**	**24**	**5**	**9**	**87**	**45**	**+42**	**77**
4	Newcastle United	38	21	8	9	74	52	+22	71
5	Leeds United	38	18	12	8	53	37	+16	66
6	Chelsea	38	17	13	8	66	38	+28	64
7	West Ham United	38	15	8	15	48	57	−9	53
8	Aston Villa	38	12	14	12	46	47	−1	50
9	Tottenham Hotspur	38	14	8	16	49	53	−4	50
10	Blackburn Rovers	38	12	10	16	55	51	+4	46
11	Southampton	38	12	9	17	46	54	−8	45
12	Middlesbrough	38	12	9	17	35	47	−12	45
13	Fulham	38	10	14	14	36	44	−8	44
14	Charlton Athletic	38	10	14	14	38	49	−11	44
15	Everton	38	11	10	17	45	57	−12	43
16	Bolton Wanderers	38	9	13	16	44	62	−18	40
17	Sunderland	38	10	10	18	29	51	−22	40
18	Ipswich Town (R)	38	9	9	20	41	64	−23	36
19	Derby County (R)	38	8	6	24	33	63	−30	30
20	Leicester City (R)	38	5	13	20	30	64	−34	28

2002–03 Premier League

Position	Club	P	W	D	L	F	A	GD	Pts
I	**Manchester United**	38	25	8	5	74	34	+40	83
2	Arsenal	38	23	9	6	85	42	+43	78
3	Newcastle United	38	21	6	II	63	48	+15	69
4	Chelsea	38	19	10	9	68	38	+30	67
5	Liverpool	38	18	10	10	61	41	+20	64
6	Blackburn Rovers	38	16	12	10	52	43	+9	60
7	Everton	38	17	8	13	48	49	−1	59
8	Southampton	38	13	13	12	43	46	−3	52
9	Manchester City	38	15	6	17	47	54	−7	51
10	Tottenham Hotspur	38	14	8	16	51	62	−11	50
II	Middlesbrough	38	13	10	15	48	44	+4	49
12	Charlton Athletic	38	14	7	17	45	56	−11	49
13	Birmingham City	38	13	9	16	41	49	−8	48
14	Fulham	38	13	9	16	41	50	−9	48
15	Leeds United	38	14	5	19	58	57	+1	47
16	Aston Villa	38	12	9	17	42	47	−5	45
17	Bolton Wanderers	38	10	14	14	41	51	−10	44
18	West Ham United (R)	38	10	12	16	42	59	−17	42
19	West Bromwich Albion (R)	38	6	8	24	29	65	−36	26
20	Sunderland (R)	38	4	7	27	21	65	−44	19

APPENDIX 2
PROFIT AND TURNOVER AT MANCHESTER UNITED 1980-2003

YEAR	INCOME (in 000s)	NET PROFIT (AFTER TRANSFERS, in 000s)	DIVIDEND (in 000s)
1980	2,149	210	50
1981	2,408	(352)	50
1982	2,648	(2,282)	–
1983	3,929	636	–
1984	5,226	1,731	151
1985	6,788	280	101
1986	6,677	824	–
1987	6,718	810	101
1988	7,585	(1,296)	–
1989	9,556	1,767	–
1990	11,292	(3,071)	–
1991	17,816	5,375	–
1992	20,145	5,056	2,189
1993	25,177	4,202	2,372
1994	43,815	10,776	2,554
1995	60,622	20,014	2,737
1996	53,316	15,399	3,221
1997	87,939	27,577	4,026
1998	87,875	27,839	4,416
1999	110,674	22,411	4,676
2000	116,005	16,788	4,936
2001	129,569	21,778	5,195
2002	146,062	32,347	8,053
2003	173,001	39,345	10,391

N.B. Figures in brackets denote losses.

APPENDIX 3
MAJOR HONOURS AT MANCHESTER UNITED 1980–2003

PREMIER LEAGUE: 1993, 1994, 1996, 1997, 1999, 2000, 2001, 2003

FA CUP: 1983, 1985, 1990, 1994, 1996, 1999

FOOTBALL LEAGUE CUP: 1992

EUROPEAN CHAMPIONS LEAGUE: 1999

EUROPEAN CUP WINNERS' CUP: 1991

UEFA SUPER CUP: 1991

INTERCONTINENTAL CUP: 1999

PICTURE CREDITS

All photos in the picture section courtesy and copyright of Martin Edwards, with the exception of the below.

Page 7 (top): Colorsport/REX/Shutterstock

Page 7 (top): Dan Smith/Getty Images

Page 7 (bottom): Reuters/Alamy

Page 8 (top): Past Pix/SSPL/Getty Images

Page 8 (bottom): SSPL/Getty Images

Page 9 (top): Trinity Mirror/Mirrorpix/Alamy

Page 9 (bottom): Ted Blackbrow/REX/Shutterstock

Page 10 (top): Popperfoto/Getty Images

Page 10 (middle): Trinity Mirror/Mirrorpix/Alamy

Page 10 (bottom): Popperfoto/Getty Images

Page 11 (top): Jim Hutchison/Associated Newspapers/REX/Shutterstock

Page 11 (middle): Colorsport/REX/Shutterstock

Page 15: Jamie Wiseman/Daily Mail/REX/Shutterstock

Page 16 (top): David Kendall/PA Images

Page 16 (bottom): John Peters/Man Utd via Getty Images